# CULTURAL ATTRACTIONS AND EUROPEAN TOURISM

This book is dedicated to the memory of
Violet and Roger Wrightson

# Cultural Attractions and European Tourism

*Edited by*

## Greg Richards
*Department of Leisure Studies*
*Tilburg University*
*Tilburg*
*The Netherlands*

CABI *Publishing*

CABI *Publishing* is a division of CAB *International*

CABI Publishing
CAB International
Wallingford
Oxon OX10 8DE
UK

CABI Publishing
10 E 40th Street
Suite 3203
New York, NY 10016
USA

Tel: +44 (0)1491 832111
Fax: +44 (0)1491 833508
Email: cabi@cabi.org
Web site: http://www.cabi.org

Tel: +1 212 481 7018
Fax: +1 212 686 7993
Email: cabi-nao@cabi.org

A catalogue record for this book is available from the British Library, London, UK.

**Library of Congress Cataloging-in-Publication Data**
Richards, Greg
    Cultural attractions and European tourism / edited by G. Richards.
        p.   cm.
    Includes bibliographical references.
    ISBN 0-85199-440-7 (alk. paper)
        1. Heritage tourism--Europe.   I. Title.

G156.5.H47 R53 2001
338.4'7914--dc21                                                    00-063019

ISBN 0 85199 440 7

Typeset by AMA DataSet Ltd, UK.
Printed and bound in the UK by Biddles Ltd, Guildford and King's Lynn.

# Contents

**Contributors**                                                                                    vii

**Preface**                                                                                         ix

**Part I  Development of Cultural Tourism and Cultural Attractions**    1

  1  The Development of Cultural Tourism in Europe                      3
     *Greg Richards*

  2  The Market for Cultural Attractions                                     31
     *Greg Richards*

  3  The Experience Industry and the Creation of Attractions      55
     *Greg Richards*

  4  The Cultural Attraction Distribution System                          71
     *Greg Richards, Saskia Goedhart and Carla Herrijgers*

**Part II  Case Studies of European Cultural Attractions**              91

  5  The Bonnefanten Museum, Maastricht                                  93
     *Wil Munsters*

6 Urban Regeneration and Glasgow's Galleries with Particular
  Reference to the Burrell Collection                                111
  *David Leslie*

7 Clonmacnoise: a Monastic Site, Burial Ground and Tourist
  Attraction                                                         135
  *Frances McGettigan and Kevin Burns*

8 Cultural Heritage Sites and Their Visitors: Too Many for
  Too Few?                                                           159
  *Sue Berry and Graham Shephard*

9 Urban Heritage Tourism: Globalization and Localization             173
  *Michael Green*

10 The Budapest Spring Festival: a Festival for Hungarians?          199
   *László Puczkó and Tamara Rátz*

11 The Consumption of Cultural Tourism in Poland                     215
   *Barbara Marciszewska*

12 Creative Industries as Milieux of Innovation: the
   Westergasfabriek, Amsterdam                                       227
   *Caro Bonink and Erik Hitters*

13 European Cultural Attractions: Trends and Prospects               241
   *Greg Richards*

**Index**                                                           255

# Contributors

**Sue Berry,** School of Service Management, Faculty of Business, University of Brighton, Eastbourne, BN20 7UR, UK. Present address: 4 Juggs Close, Lewes, BN7 1QP, UK

**Caro Bonink,** Caro Consulting, Haarlemmerstraat 104, 1013 EW Amsterdam, The Netherlands

**Kevin Burns,** Dundalk Institute of Technology, Dundalk, Co. Louth, Ireland

**Saskia Goedhart,** LA Group, Leisure and Arts Consulting, Saphatistraat 708, 1018 AV Amsterdam, The Netherlands

**Michael Green,** Department of Physical Education, Sports Science and Recreation Management, Loughborough University, Leicestershire, LE11 3TU, UK

**Carla Herrijgers,** Pelikaan Reizen, Stationstraat 12, 4761 BS Zevenbergen, The Netherlands

**Erik Hitters,** Department of Arts and Cultural Studies, Erasmus University Rotterdam, PO Box 1738, 3000 DR Rotterdam, The Netherlands

**David Leslie,** Department of Hospitality, Tourism and Leisure, Glasgow Caledonian University, 1 Park Drive, Glasgow, G3 6LP, UK

**Barbara Marciszewska,** Department of Tourism and Recreation, University School of Physical Education, Wiejska 1, 80-336 Gdañsk, Poland

**Francis McGettigan,** Athlone Institute of Technology, Dublin Road, Athlone, Co. Westmeath, Ireland

**Wil Munsters,** Hoge Hotelschool Maastricht, PO Box 3900, 6202 NX Maastricht, The Netherlands

**László Puczkó,** Tourism Research Centre, H-1093 Budapest, Fovám tér 8, Hungary

**Tamara Rátz,** Tourism Research Centre, H-1093 Budapest, Fovám tér 8, Hungary

**Greg Richards,** Tilburg University, Department of Leisure Studies, PO Box 90153, 5000 LE Tilburg, The Netherlands

**Graham Shephard,** School of Service Management, Faculty of Business, University of Brighton, Eastbourne, BN20 7UR, UK

# Preface

This volume represents the latest collection of research findings from the European Cultural Tourism Research Project, which has been running since 1991. The project is managed by the European Association for Tourism and Leisure Education (ATLAS), an international network of higher education institutions which undertakes research and curriculum development in the tourism and leisure subject areas.

The research programme was originally funded by DGXXIII (now the Enterprise Directorate) of the European Commission, to provide some basic information on the scale and nature of cultural tourism in the European Union (EU). The first research phase was completed in 1993, and the results published in 1996 in a volume entitled *Cultural Tourism in Europe*. Since then, not only has the EU expanded, but the work of ATLAS has also grown to encompass Central and Eastern Europe. These developments necessitated an expansion of the research programme as well. This volume presents the findings of the field research undertaken in 1997. The 1997 research built on and expanded the 1992 surveys, particularly in the area of cultural tourism motivations. Responding to comments made about *Cultural Tourism in Europe*, it was also decided to adopt a different approach to the organization and analysis of the research findings. Whereas *Cultural Tourism in Europe* presented a national perspective with reviews of cultural tourism in each of the (then) 12 EU Member States, the current volume looks at the relationship between tourists and specific cultural attractions.

Over the years the project has been supported by a wide range of organizations and individuals, and it would be impossible to acknowledge or thank them all individually. However, there are a number of people who have made specific contributions that should be mentioned. In particular, the research would not have been possible without the researchers who organized the surveys in the various attractions. A number of those people have contributed chapters to the current volume, and they need to be doubly thanked for the surveys and for their writing. In addition, however, a number of individuals also helped to undertake surveys, even though they are not present in this book, including Ahmed Ojuolape, Lars Aronsson, Carlos Fernandes, Peter Roth, Brian O'Connor, Seppo Aho, Alan Kildare, David Hind, Fred Coalter, Satu Miettinen and Katerina Tzanakaki. Our thanks also go to all the cultural attractions that collaborated in the research programme in 1997.

The research has also been helped by a number of students at Tilburg University who undertook specific studies of cultural tourism. Saskia Goedhart, Michael Green and Carla Herrijgers have contributed to the current volume, but in addition Ellen Roetman, Suzanne van 't Riet and Teresa Velázquez all made contributions to the research. The data analysis would not have been possible without the efforts of innumerable students undertaking the data entry, or without the coordination of Leontine Onderwater. My thanks also go to the Department of Leisure Studies at Tilburg University for allowing me the time to work on this project.

Thanks are also due to Professor Tej Vir Singh, for permission to reproduce Fig. 3.1 from *Tourism Recreation Research*.

Greg Richards
Tilburg
July 2000

# Development of Cultural Tourism and Cultural Attractions

**I**

# The Development of Cultural Tourism in Europe

## Greg Richards

*Tilburg University, Department of Leisure Studies, Tilburg, The Netherlands*

---

In the future, it will be a relief to find a place without culture.
Talking Heads, *Stop Making Sense* sleeve notes.

In the past, only hardened cultural tourists seemed to suffer from 'monument fatigue' or could overdose on museums. This condition now seems to be spreading. 'That's enough culture' screamed a newspaper headline recently (Glancey, 1999), describing the surge of museum development which saw over €600 million being invested in new attractions in the UK in the year 2000. In Spain, the number of museums has doubled during the post-Franco era (Herrijgers, 1998). According to the European Commission, there are now approximately 200,000 protected monuments in the European Union (EU), and 2.5 million buildings of historical interest (European Commission, 1998).

These developments underline the increasing centrality of culture and cultural attractions in modern societies. As MacCannell (1976, p. 154) commented: 'the construction, exchange and movement of attractions is a perfect index of modernisation'. As the development of tourism proceeds, so 'entire cities and regions, decades and cultures have become aware of themselves as attractions' (1976, p. 16).

Cultural attractions have become particularly important in this modern form of pilgrimage called tourism. Not only do cultural attractions such as museums and monuments constitute the largest sector of the European attractions market, but they are also increasingly being placed at the centre of urban and rural development strategies and image enhancement programmes.

This book examines the reasons why culture has become such an important element of the attractiveness of places, and examines the development, management and marketing of cultural attractions.

## The Growing Attractiveness of Culture

Culture has always been a major object of travel, as the development of the Grand Tour from the 16th century onwards attests (Towner, 1985). In the 20th century, however, culture has ceased to be the objective of tourism: tourism is culture (Urry, 1990).

The basic markers of the tourist culture are arguably the major cultural attractions. Sites such as the Louvre in Paris, the British Museum in London and the Metropolitan Museum in New York attract millions of visitors to their displays of culture. Some attractions, such as the Eiffel Tower, Big Ben, the Pyramids or the Coliseum, come to represent entire cultures. These attractions are held in awe not just by those who travel from afar to gaze upon them, but they also become important elements of national or even international consciousness and identity. Threatened monuments, such as the Atomium, the Leaning Tower of Pisa and the City of Venice must be saved at all cost. In fact these attractions have become so important that they have to be saved from the tourists themselves, as Bennetton's recent campaign to rid Venice of day trippers demonstrates (*Colors*, 1999).

The dilemma of Venice illustrates a major problem for cultural attractions. Culture is considered essential to attracting tourists to many locations, and yet 'cultural' consumption may account for a very small proportion of total activity. In Venice, for example, even those tourists who do stay overnight spend only 2% of their money on culture – the bulk goes on accommodation (45%) and shopping (21%) (*Colors*, 1999). But how many of the staying tourists would come to Venice without its cultural attractions, not to speak of the millions of day visitors?

The problem with trying to stem the tide of attraction-driven tourism is that cultural attractions have become 'must-see sights' (MacCannell, 1976). The lemming-like intensity of this consumption has prompted one psychologist to label it 'musterbation' (Ad Vingerhoets, personal communication, 1999). It is this apparent compulsion that gives attractions a central role in tourism. Although Leiper (1990) has argued that attractions do not literally 'attract' visitors, they certainly do provide a focus for much tourist activity, and are an essential weapon in the arsenal of tourism destinations engaged in a competitive struggle for tourist business (Richards, 2000).

Cultural attractions play an important role in tourism at all levels, from the global highlights of world culture to attractions that underpin local identities. At a global level cultural attractions are often seen as icons of important streams of global culture. This idea is enshrined in the designation of World Heritage Sites, or in the support from the EU to the restoration of buildings such as the Parthenon or the designation of the Cultural Capital of Europe each year (see Chapter 3, this volume).

Cultural attractions have also played a leading role in cultural policy and in efforts to promote cultural development. For example, the UNESCO *World Decade for Cultural Development* (1988–1997) emphasized the importance of conserving cultural heritage as a means not only of stimulating economic development but also promoting identity and cultural diversity. The report draws parallels between cultural heritage and nature conservation. Particularly elements of the immaterial heritage, such as languages, are in danger of extinction. Historic monuments are often seen as an endangered species, and yet the recent trend towards designating large numbers of historic structures as monuments indicates that this is one endangered species that is thriving.

At the EU level, culture is viewed as an essential resource that not only provides work but which can also develop cultural harmony within the EU. Cultural tourism was always a difficult area for the European Commission in the past, because neither culture nor tourism was specifically named in the Treaty of Rome as an area of competence for the EU. This has changed since the Treaty of Maastricht in 1991, which incorporated Article 128, emphasizing the importance of culture as an area for policy development. Since then, the EU has adopted what it calls 'a new approach to culture'. In the light of this new approach, the EU has resolved that culture should be considered in all policy areas, much in the same way as sustainable development has been viewed as a generic policy consideration. This underlines the growing importance of culture in European policy. Cultural tourism and cultural attractions have also become central to much of the regional economic development activity financed by the European Commission (Richards, 1999).

The Council of Europe has also been actively developing cultural tourism as a means of supporting culture. In particular the Council of Europe has been active in creating a number of European cultural Itineraries, including the famous Camiño de Santiago (Murray and Graham, 1997). The motive for the Council of Europe in promoting cultural tourism is to ensure the spread of European culture, and to provide resources for the preservation and conservation of the cultural artefacts visited by tourists.

In addition to the economic importance of culture, its role in establishing and reinforcing identity has also played a big part in the growing interest in various aspects of heritage. In particular, as modernity has swept away many traditions and traditional cultural practices, there has been a rush to preserve cultural heritage before it disappears. This process started with the development of open-air museums in Scandinavia in the late 19th century, and extended to many other areas as a result of the mechanization of the countryside, particularly after the Second World War (Forni, 1999). These ethnographic museums were initially focused on the preservation of rural heritage in the face of urbanization, but during the 20th century the disappearance of extractive and manufacturing industries and their associated working cultures has led to a new round of conservation of 'industrial heritage'. Today France has some 400 ecomuseums, and Italy has about 500 ethnological collections.

More recently the nostalgia industry has contributed a wide range of new attractions to the cultural scene. The increasing pace of life and the feeling of disorientation and loss associated with modernity have ensured that the preservation of the past has become big business (Hewison, 1987). Membership of organizations dedicated to heritage preservation has grown considerably in recent decades. For example, membership of the National Trust in the UK grew from 278,000 in 1971 to 2,189,000 in 1993 (Advertising Association, 1996) and English Heritage membership rose from 270,000 in 1992/93 to 374,000 in 1996/97 (Hanna, 1998). It seems that the combination of nostalgia for the past, the need to reassert national and local identities and the perceived economic benefits of cultural development have had a dramatic effect on the supply of cultural attractions.

Some observers, in common with Hewison, have decried the growth of the 'heritage industry' and the attendant growth of heritage centres and themed 'experiences' (Wright, 1985), although other authors have found Hewison's analysis exaggerated (Samuel, 1996). These differing reactions reflect a strong division of opinion about the preservation of heritage. Not everybody agrees about what kind of culture should be presented or preserved, or how it should be presented, or for whom. Conflicts have often arisen over the development and interpretation of cultural attractions (Tunbridge and Ashworth, 1996), such as the plans to develop Stonehenge (Bender and Edmonds, 1992), or the conservation of the Voortrekker Monument in South Africa (Grobler, 1998).

What this book seeks to examine is why the consumption of cultural attractions has become such an important aspect of our daily lives. The thematic chapters and attraction case studies that follow provide a range of different viewpoints on this question, based on an analysis of a range of different cultural attractions, from 'high' to 'popular' culture. The rest of this chapter looks at some of the basic questions surrounding the concept of culture and its use as a basis for visitor attractions – what aspects of culture attract tourists? Is interest in culture growing? Why is the supply of cultural attractions growing?

## What is Culture?

A basic question which needs to be addressed before we can go much further is – what is culture? Given the fact that 'culture' was identified by Raymond Williams (1983) as one of the most complicated words in the English language, it is not surprising that cultural tourism is extremely difficult to define. This problem has been accentuated in recent years by the additional meanings and functions attributed to 'culture' as a result of the democratization of culture and the increasing convergence of culture and everyday life. As Rásky (1998, p. 76) points out, 'culture' has taken on a growing range of responsibilities, or to put it another way 'culture has to a certain extent made itself unrecognisable because as an inflationary and inflated concept it has assumed immeasurable dimensions'.

The same trend of inflated meanings can be identified in the usage of the word 'culture' in relation to tourism. Cultural tourism, heritage tourism, arts tourism, ethnic tourism and a host of other terms seem to be almost interchangeable in their usage, but it is rarely clear whether people are talking about the same thing.

According to the conceptual definition of cultural tourism proposed by Richards (see Chapter 2 this volume), the distinction between cultural tourism and other forms of tourism is basically to be found in the learning function. Cultural tourists can learn about the culture of a destination and gain new experiences related to that culture in a number of ways, depending on the forms of culture they consume. Littrell (1997) argues that culture can be viewed as comprising what people think (attitudes, beliefs, ideas and values), what people do (normative behaviour patterns, or way of life) and what people make (artworks, artefacts, cultural products). Culture is therefore composed of processes (the ideas and way of life of people) and the products of those processes (buildings, artefacts, art, customs, 'atmosphere'). Looking at culture in this way, cultural tourism is not just about visiting sites and monuments, which has tended to be the 'traditional' view of cultural tourism, but it also involves consuming the way of life of the areas visited. Both of these activities involve the collection of new knowledge and experiences. Cultural tourism therefore covers not just the consumption of the cultural products of the past, but also of contemporary culture or the 'way of life' of a people or region. Cultural tourism can therefore be seen as covering both 'heritage tourism' (related to artefacts of the past) and 'arts tourism' (related to contemporary cultural production).

In this volume, therefore, both heritage attractions and arts attractions will be analysed as 'cultural attractions'. The case studies presented in Part II of this volume also deal with attractions based on products (such as museums displaying material culture) and attractions based on culture as process (as in the case of cultural events and festivals).

## A Growing Interest in Culture?

It is clear that there is a growing range of phenomena that can be classified as 'cultural'. Richards (1996) has argued that this may at least partly explain the apparent growth in cultural tourism. With more tourism attractions being seen as 'cultural', it is almost inevitable that there will be more cultural tourists. To what extent is the growth of cultural tourism an artefact of the growing definition of culture, and to what extent are specific aspects of culture becoming more popular with consumers?

Culture is consistently argued to be a major determinant of the growth of tourism and leisure consumption. The World Tourism Organization, for example, asserted that cultural tourism accounted for 37% of global tourism, and forecast that it would grow at a rate of 15% per year. Such figures are often bandied around (e.g. Janarius, 1992; Bywater, 1993), but are rarely backed up with empirical research.

The basic assumption of many authors seems to be that a growing number of people are 'interested in culture', and that this leads to more demand for cultural tourism (Urry, 1990). But is there actually hard evidence for a growing interest in culture? Most of the studies that report a growth in cultural interest are not based on empirical evidence, but rather broad assertions.

Looking at some of the available data, we can identify a growth in the popularity of specific types of cultural attractions.

According to the European Heritage Group, attendance at museums, historical monuments and archaeological sites has doubled between 1977 and 1997 (European Commission, 1998).

Other estimates indicate that between 1982 and 1995, the attendance at museums and monuments across Europe grew by about 25% (Richards, 1996). Even the higher growth rate in cultural attendance is about the same as the growth in international tourism in Europe, which has expanded at 4.5% a year over the past 20 years. Growth in cultural attendances has also not been particularly steady, tending to dip in periods of recession, and individual countries also showing localized declines periodically. In Greece, for example, museum and archaeological site visits dropped significantly in 1990, largely thanks to a decrease in foreign tourism. Although visits have since started to grow again, they have still not recovered to pre-1990 levels.

Growing attendance at cultural attractions does not in itself constitute evidence that people are becoming more interested in culture. It may be that more people are travelling or taking day trips, which may lead to more people visiting cultural attractions simply because there are more visitors present at a particular location. In The Netherlands there is evidence that cultural tourism is stimulated by the growth of tourism as a whole (de Haan, 1997). In other words, there is little direct evidence that people are becoming more interested in culture, as measured by visits to attractions – cultural attractions are being visited more because there are more tourism and leisure visits in total.

One way of gauging if there is an increasing interest in cultural attractions is to see if there is any evidence of a shift in the balance of attraction visits towards cultural attractions. If culture is becoming more popular, one would expect to see cultural attractions gaining a larger share of the attraction market.

Recent data indicate that cultural attractions have not increased as a proportion of all visits to tourist attractions. Figures on attraction attendance in the UK, for example, show an average growth in attraction visits of 15% between 1989 and 1997, compared with a 9% increase for historic properties and 14% for museums and galleries (Table 1.1). As a proportion of total visits, museums and galleries slipped from 23.1% in 1991 to 19% in 1997, and historic properties grew slightly from 19.1% to 20% over the same period. Longer term trends for England indicate a slower growth rate for cultural attractions between 1976 and 1991, with historic properties (+24%) and museums and galleries (+23%) lagging behind the growth for all attractions (+35%).

Surveys on the degree of cultural motivation among tourists also offer little support for growing interest in culture. In Germany, for example, the proportion of tourists indicating culture as their motivation for travel remained almost constant at around 8–9% between 1981 and 1994 (Richards, 1996). In the UK, studies of domestic tourism indicated that the proportion of visitors motivated by culture actually fell from 14% of visitors in 1989 to 4% in 1997, while the proportion participating in cultural activities fell from 37% to 31% over the same period (Table 1.2). Looking at inbound tourism to the UK, more overseas visitors visited cultural attractions in 1996 than in 1990 (Table 1.3). There was, however, a slight fall in the proportion of 'culturally motivated' visitors to Britain over the same period. This tends to indicate that the trend towards general, rather than specific cultural tourism noted in Richards (1996) is continuing.

This trend is also visible in some countries as far as the amount of time spent on cultural activities is concerned. In The Netherlands, for example, the amount of time spent on passive cultural consumption (museum and theatre visits, cinema) declined between 1985 and 1995. These forms of cultural consumption now account for less than 1% of leisure time in The Netherlands (de Haan, 1997).

**Table 1.1.** Visitor trends at UK attractions 1989 to 1997 (per cent change).

| Attraction type | Constant sample | Total market |
| --- | --- | --- |
| Farms | +65 | +71 |
| Visitor centres | +17 | +55 |
| Gardens | +26 | +28 |
| Country parks | +22 | +23 |
| Workplaces | +15 | +15 |
| Museums and galleries | +11 | +14 |
| Leisure parks | +6 | +12 |
| Historic properties | +8 | +9 |
| Steam railways | +7 | +9 |
| Wildlife attractions | −8 | −1 |
| Total | +11 | +15 |

**Table 1.2.** Cultural motivation and participation for UK domestic tourists, 1989–1997.

| Cultural activity | 1989 | 1990 | 1991 | 1992 | 1993 | 1994 | 1995 | 1996 | 1997 |
|---|---|---|---|---|---|---|---|---|---|
| UK domestic tourists – culture as main motivation to travel (per cent of all tourists) | | | | | | | | | |
| Watching performing arts | 2 | 2 | 1 | 2 | 1 | 1 | – | 1 | 1 |
| Visiting heritage sites | 8 | 4 | 4 | 5 | 3 | 3 | 2 | 1 | 2 |
| Visiting heritage exhibitions | 4 | 2 | 2 | 3 | 2 | 2 | 1 | 1 | 1 |
| UK domestic tourists – all participating in cultural activities (per cent of all tourists) | | | | | | | | | |
| Watching performing arts | 5 | 5 | 5 | 7 | 14 | 1 | 2 | 4 | 7 |
| Visiting heritage sites | 22 | 14 | 17 | 21 | 17 | 19 | 17 | 14 | 17 |
| Visiting heritage exhibitions | 10 | 7 | 8 | 12 | 8 | 10 | 7 | 7 | 7 |

**Table 1.3.** Attendance of overseas visitors to the UK at cultural attractions, 1996. (From British Tourist Authority, 1997, Overseas Leisure Visitor Survey, 1996.)

| | 1990 All visitors | | 1996 Leisure visitors | |
|---|---|---|---|---|
| Cultural activity | Per cent participating | Per cent important in decision to visit Britain | Per cent participating | Per cent important in decision to visit Britain |
| Visiting heritage sites | 51 | 37 | 63 | 37 |
| Visiting artistic/heritage exhibitions | 40 | 30 | 51 | 29 |
| Exploring historic towns/cities | | | 51 | 29 |
| Performing arts | | | 38 | 16 |
| Classic concert | 7 | 6 | 6 | 3 |
| Pop concert | 5 | 5 | 4 | 2 |

There seems to be little evidence for an increase in the proportion of attraction visits at cultural attractions, or that cultural motivations are becoming stronger. It is therefore difficult to support the argument that tourists are becoming more interested in culture on the basis of their stated motivations or behaviour. One possible explanation for the apparent divergence between assertions of growing interest in culture and levels of cultural attraction visits may simply be the widening definition of culture. More visits may be taking place at 'new' types of cultural attractions which are not always classified as such in the tourism statistics. In The Netherlands, for example, one of the greatest growth areas in attraction visits is the category 'diverse' attractions, which are basically all those new attractions which are difficult to fit into existing categories (Bonink and Richards, 1997). Another possible complication may be the fact that cultural consumers are becoming increasingly 'omnivorous', tending to visit many different forms of culture. The proportion of cultural consumers may therefore not grow as rapidly as the number of cultural visits.

## Growth in Cultural Supply

Richards (1996) argues that one of the major factors stimulating increased cultural visits is the fact that there are more cultural attractions to visit. There is, however, a strong chicken and egg flavour to the relationship between supply and demand in the cultural attractions market. One of the major reasons why there is a growth in the number of attractions may be because cultural consumption is perceived to be growing – even though the evidence presented above indicates that cultural attraction visits are difficult to explain in this way.

What does seem to be happening, however, is that expenditure on cultural attractions, both in terms of public funding and admission and other revenues, is increasing. Budgets for heritage preservation have grown significantly in many countries as the cultural, social and economic benefits of conservation have become more widely accepted. This has produced a growth in the number of designated monuments and the number of buildings open to the public (Richards, 1996).

A particular driving force behind the development of 'new' cultural attractions appears to be the competitive struggle between European cities to develop themselves as consumption spaces. As the European Commission (1998, p. 22) notes: 'The supply of culture is unevenly distributed within the Member States and from one Member State to another. It is concentrated in major conurbations and capital cities'.

Cultural attractions such as museums and monuments have become important means of attracting not only visitors but also inward investment to urban areas. As Green shows in Chapter 9 of this volume, cities such as Bilbao and Tilburg have used cultural attraction development as a way of making themselves more attractive as a place to live and work, as well as to attract tourists. Such strategies have become so widespread that there has been considerable discussion about the effectiveness of cultural development strategies in stimulating the economy and cultural life of urban areas in Europe (Bianchini and Parkinson, 1993; Roche, 1994; Gómez, 1998).

While this debate rages, however, the policy makers continue to invest in cultural attractions. This is often a matter of local pride and prestige. Every town and city feels that it is important enough to warrant its own theatre, concert hall, museum or heritage centre, regardless of the local demand for such facilities. In many cases, such developments can only be deemed feasible by invoking external demand – in other words tourism. Attracting tourists therefore becomes part of the task allotted to new cultural facilities, even if they are not always suitable for attracting large numbers of visitors.

The problems of growing cultural competition between cities has more recently led to a shift in emphasis from consumption-led to production-led strategies. In particular the 'creative industries' are now being promoted as a vital underpinning for the cultural development of urban areas. As Bonink and Hitters show in Chapter 12, the creative activities concentrated in major urban areas (including film, fashion, music, publishing, visual and performing arts and new media) can act as a catalyst not only for economic activity and jobs, but also to revitalize the cultural life of the city itself. Such strategies have led to what van Elderen (1997, p. 126) has termed the festivalization of towns and cities in Europe, or 'the (temporary) transformation of the town into a specific symbolic space in which the utilization of the public domain . . . is under the spell of a particular cultural consumption pattern'.

Culture is not only an important stimulus for the growth of attractions in urban areas. Rural areas are also being increasingly constituted as sites of cultural consumption. The meanings of landscapes draw on the cultural codes of the society for which they were made. Specific landscapes are the product of particular cultural practices. For example, the distinctive 'minifundia' landscape of the Alto Minho region of northern Portugal is closely related to a history of intensive land use with continual division of land holdings. This has produced a distinctive pattern of small plots surrounded by stone walls interspersed with vineyards. The distinctive agricultural products of the region are in turn the basis for a distinctive local cuisine and local handicrafts, such as small-scale textile production (Edwards *et al.*, 2000).

Rural landscapes therefore reflect the productive activities associated with agriculture combined with the cultural interpretations of the 'rural' which are associated with different cultures. Rural areas of Europe have become important sites of tourism and leisure consumption. The growth of rural tourism is a reflection of a middle class taste for 'authenticity' in consumption, related to the search for a lost rural past (Munt, 1994). This demand has in turn been met by a growth in 'real' country holidays (Swarbrooke, 1996), which are specifically designed to meet the needs of tourists in search of the authentic, 'off the beaten track' rural landscape. In its most extreme form, this can lead to the deliberate re-creation or staging of traditional rurality for tourists. Guidelines from Bord Failte, the Irish Tourist Board, give explicit instructions to farmers on how to create a 'rural' atmosphere and look to their farms, in which the realities of modern production methods intrude on the desires of the tourists as little as possible (Carroll, 1995). As Kneafsey (1994, p. 112) points out, 'the representation of Ireland and its people is predominantly rural . . .' and 'rural Ireland is given the character of something of an artefact, a curiosity, and the image of the slow old-fashioned lifestyle'. Such 'simulacra' abound in the 'rural' environments consumed by tourists. This cultural construction of the countryside determines the consumption even of those who wish to escape from such 'inauthentic' environments.

This commodification of the rural has been linked in the UK to processes of privatization and deregulation, which have provided more scope for the commercial sector to exploit rural areas (Cloke, 1993). In developing the concept of a 'rural idyll' for tourist consumption, such developments constitute an 'identity-giving spectacle', in which nature appears only as a theme. If nature is becoming a theme in rural environments, it is even having to give ground to artificial attractions in 'wilderness' areas. For example the recent construction of attractions such as Santa Claus World in Lapland was apparently prompted by the fact that 'the cultural and natural advantages of Lapland were insufficient in attracting tourists in their desired numbers' (Pretes, 1995, p. 8). It seems that traditional culture is not sufficient – popular culture must be added to the product mix.

Cultural attractions are therefore no longer confined to the centres of major cities, but are increasingly interwoven into the fabric of tourist environments everywhere. The supply of cultural attractions has been stimulated by a wide range of social, economic and cultural processes which have ensured an increased number and variety of cultural attractions in a wide range of different environments. What all of these features have in common is that they are designed to attract visitors. A major concern of theorists dealing with cultural attractions has therefore been to explain the 'attractiveness' of these features.

## The Field of Dreams

All too often, cultural attractions have been developed on the *Field of Dreams* principle. In the 1989 film *Field of Dreams* Kevin Costner plays an Iowa farmer who hears voices telling him 'build it and he will come'. On the advice of the voices he builds a baseball field on his isolated farm, which is subsequently occupied by Shoeless Joe and other dead baseball heroes who proceed to attract hoards of baseball fans. This dream scenario is now being repeated in real life, as thousands of baseball fans flock to the 'Field of Dreams Movie Site' created on the original set. In Hollywood movies having a dream is enough to create an attraction. In real life the process is somewhat more complex, but policy makers everywhere seem to be fatally attracted by the dream of having their own museum, theatre, opera house or monument.

In the past, the public have tended to come to the attractions that have been built. There has undoubtedly been a significant growth in the consumption of cultural attractions, particularly in the longer term. In The Netherlands, for example, the number of museum visitors rose from just over 2 million in 1946 to almost 23 million in 1993 (de Haan, 1997). This long-term bull market has tended to make cities blasé about the chances of success for new cultural attractions. In recent years, however, the Field of Dreams principle has let many people down. Disappointing visitor figures for newly opened museums, such as the Royal Armouries in Leeds or the Bonnefanten Museum in Maastricht (see Munsters, Chapter 5 this volume) have tended to dispel the myth that there is a natural audience for culture.

The growing maturity of the cultural attraction market and the attendant growth in competition between attractions means that more attention needs to be paid to question why people visit cultural attractions. As the tourism literature has developed, a number of theoretical perspectives on the development and consumption of attractions have emerged.

The American historian Daniel Boorstin (1964) opened up the debate about the relationship between the tourist and tourist attractions in his book *The Image: a Guide to Pseudo Events in America*. Boorstin saw tourism as a superficial pursuit of contrived experiences – a collection of 'psuedo events'. In his view, tourists sought to escape everyday reality through the consumption of shallow, inauthentic experiences. He contrasted the comfortable 'bubble' of the modern tourist with the hardened traveller of previous centuries. Travel was previously closely linked to adventure – a journey into the unknown, with 'real' risks and dangers. Travel was not necessarily a pleasure – which also meant that there were fewer fellow travellers to get in the way of having a 'real' experience.

Boorstin dates the change from travel to tourism to the middle of the 19th century. Travel changed from being an active experience to a passive one, from being dangerous to being relatively comfortable. Boorstin (1964, p. 79) describes this as marking the decline of the traveller and the rise of the tourist. 'The multiplication, improvement and cheapening of travel facilities have carried more people to distant places . . . the experience has become diluted, contrived, prefabricated. The modern American tourist now fills his experience with pseudo-events'.

For Boorstin the acme of the modern tourist experience is the tourist attraction. He dates the word 'attraction' used in the sense of a feature that draws people to it only from 1862. Boorstin argues that these are 'a new species: the most attenuated form of a nation's culture . . . of little signifi-cance for the inward life of a people, but wonderfully saleable as tourist commodity'. Tourist attractions, in other words, are prime examples of pseudo events, round which the tourist is guided by guide books with their star system for 'must see' sights. The tourist experience therefore consists of ticking off attractions – been there, seen it, done it.

In the view of Dean MacCannell (1976, p. 9), Boorstin's attack stemmed from the fact that 'it is intellectually chic nowadays to deride tourists'. MacCannell argues that Boorstin criticized tourists not for travelling, but for being satisfied with superficial experiences.

MacCannell tries to counter this perspective by analysing the roots of travel motivations in modern society. MacCannell (1976, p. 57) posits tour-ism as an attempt to overcome the discontinuities of modernity. As industrial production becomes increasingly useless as a source of meaning for individuals, leisure and tourism have become a way of creating new meanings. Cultural productions replace actual production as the focus of society. 'Work was once the locus of our most important social values and the exclusive anchor point connecting the individual and society. Now it is only one stop among many in tourists' itineraries'.

MacCannell sees a qualitative change from what he terms 'industrial society' to 'postindustrial' or 'modern society', represented by an internalization of differentiation. What he is describing is the emergence of postmodernity or late modernity – a process which is indexed most importantly by the growth of tourism.

MacCannell identifies tourist attractions as the ultimate symbols of modern consciousness, removed as they are from their original context, and re-situated in the new differentiations of modernity. Sightseeing is therefore a modern ritual – a feeling that certain sights must be seen, as an almost obligatory rite of passage. One cannot visit Egypt without seeing the Pyramids or Paris without visiting the Eiffel Tower.

MacCannell also made an important contribution to the study of attractions by exposing the process by which attractions are created. Using a semiotic approach to the study of attractions, he suggested that tourist attractions are signs. He identifies a homology between the theoretical role of signs, as something that represents something to the observer and the practical function of tourist attractions as 'an empirical relationship between a *tourist*, a *sight*, and a *marker* – a piece of information about a sight' (MacCannell 1976, p. 41). Using this relationship, he was also able to explain the process by which tourist attractions are created through 'sight sacralization'. For an attraction to be created, an object first has to be marked off from others as worth seeing or visiting. After this first naming phase, the object is then framed by placing an official boundary round the sight and it is then elevated above other potential sights as being worth visiting. The third stage is the enshrinement of the sight, in which a special setting is created for the veneration of the sight. Once the attraction becomes a sacred object to be visited, it is then subject to mechanical reproduction through the making of photographs, posters and models. 'It is the mechanical reproduction phase of sacralization that is most responsible for setting the tourist in motion on his [sic] journey to find the true object. And he is not disappointed. Alongside of the copies of it, it has to be The Real Thing' (MacCannell, 1976, p. 45). In the final stage, social reproduction, whole destinations begin to name themselves after famous attractions, such as 'Shakespeare Country' in the UK.

Through the process of differentiation, attractions are sacralized and set apart from other objects, and at the same time are linked to each other. The proliferation and reproduction of attractions means an increasing emphasis on seeing the original, the authentic sights of a region. Certain sights therefore become marked off as 'must see sights' without which the destination or its culture cannot be consumed. Cultural attractions in particular become the key to learning about the destination, as well as acting as markers of taste and distinction on the part of the tourist.

MacCannell therefore takes a very different view to Boorstin – he sees attractions as being created through a search for meaning on the part of the tourist. Subsequent research on specific attractions has tended to confirm MacCannell's basic model, even if the stages of sight sacralization do not always follow the sequence he envisaged (e.g. Jacobsen, 1997).

Neil Leiper (1990) has developed the ideas of MacCannell regarding the creation of tourist attractions into the notion of an 'attraction system', which relates the production of attractions to the motives of the tourists visiting them. 'A tourist attraction is a system comprising three elements: a tourist or human element, a nucleus or central element, and a marker or informative element. A tourist attraction comes into existence when the three elements are connected' (Leiper, 1990, p. 371).

According to Leiper, tourists are not magically 'attracted' by tourist attractions, but are 'pushed' towards them by their own motivations. In this sense Leiper also follows MacCannell's lead in seeing tourist attraction visitation as a purposeful behaviour, rather than the pure escapism envisaged by Boorstin.

Guy Debord (1995, p. 141) also shows that Boorstin's concern with the rise of the tourist attraction as a pseudo event misread the real significance of society's dependence on images:

> Boorstin cannot see that the proliferation of prefabricated 'pseudo events' – which he deplores – flows from the simple fact that, in face of the massive realities of present-day social existence, individuals do not actually experience events . . . pseudo-history has to be fabricated at every level of the consumption of life.

For Debord (1995, p. 12) 'The whole life of those societies in which modern conditions of production prevail presents itself as an immense accumulation of spectacles'. The rise of the spectacle in modern life was for him a logical consequence of the downgrading of being into having, and ultimately the shift from having to appearing. In a world dominated by signs or appearances, 'The only thing being generated, the only thing to be seen and reproduced, is the spectacle – albeit at higher-than-usual levels of intensity. And what has been passed off as authentic life turns out to be merely a life more *authentically spectacular*' (Debord, 1995, p. 112).

In the society of the spectacle, the contradictions of culture manifest themselves. Culture, in detaching itself from the rest of existence, 'embarked on an imperialistic career of self enrichment' as the sphere of generalization and representation of lived experience, but at the same time became a 'dead thing to be contemplated in the spectacle' (Debord, 1995, p. 132).

Debord's identification of tourist attractions as important commodity signs in consumer society has recently been extended by George Ritzer

(1999), who sees tourist attractions as modern 'cathedrals of consumption'. Ritzer argues that the centrality of the means of production in industrial societies is being replaced by a 'new means of consumption' in consumer societies. The new means of consumption comprise: 'The almost dizzying proliferation of settings that allow, encourage, and even compel us to consume so many of those goods and services' (Ritzer, 1999, p. 2).

These settings include, according to Ritzer, fast food restaurants, chain stores, shopping malls, cruise ships, casinos and museums. The urge to consume in these settings takes on the same kind of pilgrimage-like features as MacCannell identified earlier in modern tourism:

> The new means of consumption can be seen as 'cathedrals of consumption' – that is, they have an enchanted, sometimes even sacred, religious character for many people. In order to attract ever-larger numbers of consumers, such cathedrals of consumption need to offer, or at least appear to offer, increasingly magical, fantastic, and enchanted settings in which to consume.
>
> (Ritzer, 1999, p. 8)

The cathedrals of consumption are 'designed artistically and scientifically to lure people into consumption' (Ritzer, 1999, p. 38). A part of their attraction is the presence of large numbers of other people, which gives 'atmosphere' to the setting. In order to attract people, the cathedrals of consumption need to offer spectacle:

> The new means of consumption create spectacles not as ends in themselves but in order to bring in large numbers of people to buy more goods and services. A mall, a casino, or a theme park that is half empty . . . does not generate the same excitement as a full house.
>
> (Ritzer, 1999, p. 107)

Although commercial facilities such as theme parks and cinemas are far more advanced in the creation of spectacle, Ritzer (1999, p. 126) argues that other tourist attractions are not far behind:

> 'authentic' tourist destinations have been turned into simulations, at least in part. Examples include the colonial town of Williamsburg in Virginia and Windsor Castle in England, among many others. The motivation behind these transformations is that the 'real' sites are no longer spectacular enough to attract tourists and their money.

In the attraction inflation of the society of the spectacle, the tourist is presented with a constantly expanding universe of attractions. Ritzer (1999, p. 181–182) argues that cultural attractions are not immune from this process:

> What of the concert hall? Or the opera? Surely they are oases free of this pressure? But the fact is that major concert halls are increasingly characterized by shops and kiosks selling food and souvenirs of various types.

The proliferation of attractions can be viewed as the creation of symbolic value and meaning, but according to more recent research, the growth of attractions does not stop there. Attractions can also be interpreted and used by different groups of visitors in different ways, allowing different 'versions' of the same attraction to coexist in the same space. As Edensor (1998) demonstrates in his detailed study of tourist behaviour at the Taj Mahal, tourists become literally 'performers', creating experiences for themselves and their fellow visitors to consume. These performances take place in settings consumed by tourists and staged by the tourist industry or the host community. Edensor suggests that there are two basic types of stages on which tourist performances take place: enclavic spaces and heterogeneous spaces. Enclavic space is characterized by the hotels and attractions developed by the international tourist industry, which are carefully controlled in terms of dominant discourse and visitor behaviour. In contrast, heterogeneous spaces are unplanned, multifunctional areas where locals and tourists can mix and create their own dialogue. Tourists can use these different types of spaces to stage different performances, ranging from the 'disciplined rituals' characteristic of the guided tour to the improvised performances of the backpacker or the 'post-tourist'. The combination of different stages, different groups of actors and different modes of performance means that tourist attractions may be experienced in very different ways by individuals or groups of tourists, according to their viewpoint. The quantitative increase in the number of attractions is therefore magnified by the ability of tourists to produce and consume differing versions of the physical attraction setting.

The performances of tourists and their hosts become part of the culture of the attraction itself. The importance of the narratives surrounding cultural attractions is emphasized by postmodern theorists. In the case of many cultural attractions, such as museums and monuments, narratives of modernity (e.g. the nation-state telling stories about its origins through the construction of monuments) have been replaced by postmodern narratives in which multiple voices are being recognized. The creation of alternative narratives and histories has led to the establishment of a number of new museums, monuments and other cultural attractions. Such 'alternative' attractions are often created in peripheral spaces in major cities, occupying spaces which have fallen vacant as a result of the retreat of manufacturing industry. Shaw and Macleod (2000) describe how attractions such as the London Cultural Heritage Centre have been created in the fringe of the City of London to provide a different vision of the history of London to that provided by the Tower of London and other traditional heritage attractions.

Cultural attractions have therefore increased not just in number, but also in complexity and variety. The production of cultural attractions has been stimulated by a desire to propagate, display or sell culture to citizens and consumers, but that production has also benefited from the fragmentation of cultures and arguments about the interpretation of culture. The fact that these attractions have become so popular might also suggest they are meeting a basic human need. Whether this is a search for meaning (MacCannell, 1976), to satisfy curiosity or a form of escape from the drudgery of everyday life (Boorstin, 1964), people clearly consider them to be an essential element of tourism and leisure consumption. The popularity of cultural attractions in turn seems to provide a rationale for their provision, whether by the commercial sector or the public sector. But the real 'hook' seems to be the argument that cultural tourism is good for you, and it is also good for the areas you visit.

## The Growth of Cultural Tourism

At the same time as cultural attractions were coming to be conceived of as central to modern society, the notion of culture itself was changing in ways conducive to the production and consumption of cultural attractions. In the past, culture had been conceptualized as a process of cultivation of the individual, but over time new meanings developed. These centred largely on culture as a way of life of a particular people or period, or the products of such cultures. Our notions of 'culture' also expand through the processes that John Urry (1990) identifies as the 'culturisation of society' and the 'culturisation of tourist practices'. Through such culturization processes, and the aestheticization of everyday life, there is a growing convergence of 'high' and 'popular' culture, and a widening of the concept of culture itself.

The infusion of culture into all aspects of everyday life arguably coincided with the elevation of culture as a force for social good, for example in the UNESCO Decade for Cultural Development 1988–1997 (Pérez de Cuélla, 1996). The role of culture as a force for good in society was echoed in approaches to tourism between the 1960s and the 1980s. The rise of mass tourism in the 1960s came to be associated with encroaching modernization, particularly in the developing world. As people abandoned their traditional lifestyles and became caught up in the market economy and growing commercialization, it was feared that traditional cultural manifestations and practices would be lost forever. At the same time, most observers felt that the tide of modernization could not be stemmed, but should at least be harnessed to serve culture rather than destroy it. If the tourists came to a destination for the purposes of consuming culture, it was argued, this would not only restore the pride of local people in their culture, but lead them to actively conserve their culture, while at the same time tourist revenues would provide the finance necessary to achieve this.

The result was, Picard (1996, p. 108) argues, that international bodies such as the World Tourism Organization and UNESCO, postulated cultural tourism as a 'good' form of tourism which could help to counter the 'bad' forms of mass tourism:

> . . . good tourism, therefore, is *cultural tourism*, which is presented by the experts of the World Tourism Organization as conducive to a *cultural renaissance* in the host societies in that it stimulates in local populations a pride and interest in their traditions, threatened with obsolescence by modernization.

By creating cultural tourism as a force for good, tourism itself is purged of all ills, since the 'good' forms of tourism can drive out the 'bad'. There is nothing wrong with tourism itself, you just need to develop the right form of tourism. This idea lies at the heart of what Picard (1996, p. 180) calls 'the doctrine of cultural tourism' in Indonesia. 'In less than a decade, the doctrine of Cultural Tourism has come to blend the "fostering of culture" with the "development of tourism" to the extent of entrusting the fate of Balinese culture to the care of the tourism industry.'

The doctrine of cultural tourism works by resolving the fundamental opposition between 'outside' and 'inside' and cultural values and economic values. Qualifying tourism as cultural bestows it with the attributes of culture, negating the threat of destruction and legitimizing its development. But while tourism must become cultural to be acceptable to the Balinese, culture must become touristic in order to be marketable to tourists. 'In other words, it is not enough that tourism becomes "cultural"; Balinese culture must become to some extent "touristic"' (Picard, 1996, p. 180).

This is expressed in the Balinese discourse about cultural tourism by dividing their culture into what predates and is essentially untouched by tourism (heritage – *warisan*) and must be protected and the culture which has been transformed through tourism into 'capital' (*modal*) which can be exploited.

> It is precisely this play permitted by the evolution from a heritage value to a capital value that authorizes the discourse of Cultural Tourism to justify the priority given to the development of tourism – for it is tourism now that is supposed to ensure the vitality of the culture on which its development depends.
>
> (Picard, 1996, p. 182)

Cultural tourism is employed as a discourse to overcome the conflicts arising in society:

> this accounts for the imperative character of the discourse of Cultural Tourism, whose incantatory pronouncements multiply and which functions as a truly magic formula, a holy mantra, promising that social reality will be determined by its inscription into the discourse and will thus coincide with what one says about it.
>
> (Picard, 1996, p. 185)

Cultural tourism has therefore become a solution which names 'the situation in the hope of controlling it symbolically' (Picard, 1996, p. 185). Cultural Tourism also involves the touristification of society – a process that proceeds not from without (as most studies of the impact of tourism suppose) but from within, by changing the way its members see themselves.

> . . . the process of touristification operates by blurring the boundaries by which members of a society distinguish between 'us' and 'them', between that which belongs to the culture and that which pertains to tourism.
>
> (Picard, 1996, p. 198–199)

The Balinese have therefore made an art of integrating tourism into their culture, but similar attitudes to tourism as a force for good can be found in other contexts as well. In Catalonia, for example, Dodd (1999, p. 54) describes how the tourism planners saw cultural tourism as an effective antidote to the problems of mass tourism:

> They quickly established that tourists who visited cultural sights are more likely to be tourists with a high level of education and therefore hold a high professional position . . . Once the planners in Barcelona had identified their market sector they went about ruthlessly creating the conditions which would attract this type of tourism.

Culture is therefore seen in some quarters as the salvation of tourism. In view of the importance of tourism in the economy of so many countries, therefore, it is hardly surprising that cultural tourism has become one of the most popular forms of tourism with policy makers at the start of the 21st century. It is surpassed perhaps only by sustainable tourism, which has the twin virtues of moral impeccability and inherent vagueness (Mowforth and Munt, 1998).

The major difference between cultural and sustainable tourism is that cultural tourism is conceived of as a dichotomy between culture and tourism, but sustainable tourism is posited as a triad – tourist, community, environment (English Tourist Board, 1991). Whereas cultural processes can be seen as belonging to the community, the placing of environment as external to the community in sustainable tourism defuses the power of the community – the environment remains as capital outside the community which can be exploited by everyone. This underlines the potential impotence of the concept of sustainable tourism as well as its power (Bramwell *et al.*, 1998). In cultural tourism the culture–tourism dichotomy can add power, if the community can gain or retain control of the cultural resource that is desired by the tourist. This feature of cultural tourism perhaps explains the positive view of it adopted by many local groups. But in order to ensure that the local community benefits from cultural tourism without suffering the worst excesses of commodification and commercialization, careful distinction needs to be made between internal (largely 'way of life') aspects and external (often product-related) aspects of culture. The former must be viewed as inalienable elements of the culture itself, whereas the products of that culture can be represented, displayed and sold to tourists (Macdonald, 1997).

A wide range of social, political and economic forces have therefore combined to push culture to the forefront of the policy agenda. This in turn has led to a marked increase in cultural and cultural tourism policy making (Richards, 1999), and a growing use of cultural attractions in image formation, cultural development, cultural tourism and economic policy. The preoccupation of modern society with the creation of attractions has led to a profusion of cultural attractions of all types, forms, shapes and sizes. The sheer variety of cultural attractions makes it difficult to construct a simple typology or conceptual framework which can encompass their diversity and simultaneously capture the common threads that bind these elements together.

The following section considers the problem of developing attraction typologies in the area of culture.

## Attraction Typologies

The diversity of cultural attractions is reflected in the range of typologies constructed to describe them. Cultural attractions not only feature large in general tourist attraction typologies, but they have also generated a whole range of more specific typologies as well.

Polácek and Aroch (1984) produced a typology of tourist attractions with a view to identifying those cultural sights of potential interest to foreign tourists. Of the seven categories of attraction identified, three were primarily cultural: cultural and historical monuments, artistic and cultural manifestations and traditional events. The study conducted by the Irish Tourist Board (1988) provides a more detailed analysis of cultural attractions, including a wide range of art forms. The typology of cultural attractions in this study is based very clearly on 'high culture' and the arts. Architecture, sculpture and painting account for over three-quarters of the attractions listed (Table 1.4).

The typology drawn up by ECTARC (1989) as their contribution to the Charter for Cultural Tourism was similarly based on high cultural forms, such as architecture, art, music and drama (Box 1.1). Unlike the EU typology, however, there is more emphasis on cultural processes, rather than simply cultural products. This indicates the growing interest in popular

**Table 1.4.** Distribution of cultural attractions in the EU by type, 1988. (From Irish Tourist Board, 1988.)

| Type of attraction | Number of attractions listed |
| --- | --- |
| Music | 33 |
| Opera | 8 |
| Theatre | 28 |
| Dance | 6 |
| Painting | 565 |
| Sculpture | 428 |
| Architecture | 2145 |
| Language and literature | 70 |
| History | 771 |
| Religion | 72 |
| Total | 4126 |

---

**Box 1.1.**   ECTARC cultural attraction typology.

---

1. Archaeological sites and museums
2. Architecture
3. Art, sculpture, crafts, galleries, festivals, events
4. Music and dance
5. Drama
6. Language and literature study
7. Religious festivals, pilgrimages
8. Complete culture and sub-cultures

---

and folk culture in the development of cultural attractions, particularly in rural areas.

Munsters (1994) constructed a 'general typology of cultural tourism resources' based on the type of cultural resources being offered to tourists. These resources were split into static attractions (monuments, museums, routes and theme parks) and events (cultural–historic events and art events). Similarly, Hall and McArthur (1993) lists artefacts, buildings, sites, town-scapes and landscapes as heritage attractions.

A comparison of these different typologies makes it clear that they are largely based on cultural products, although there is an increasing tendency to emphasize the role of cultural events. These typologies are also predominantly descriptive in nature. Lew (1987) identified three types of attraction typology: ideographic (formal perspective), organizational perspective and the cognitive approach. Almost all the existing typologies relating to attractions in general and cultural and heritage attractions in particular are ideographic in nature – that is they are based on the attributes of the attraction. This is perhaps not surprising as the typologies tend to focus on cultural products, rather than considering their organization or their consumption by tourists.

The current descriptive typologies therefore give an impression of the range and type of cultural attractions. However, they do not provide an analytical framework that can identify the differences and similarities of cultural attractions in terms of form and function.

In attempting to construct an appropriate framework in which the attractions described in this volume can be situated, the starting point taken here is the type of resources which form the cultural basis of the attraction, and the purpose to which these cultural resources are put. The cultural basis of an attraction can vary from a presentation of the material products of a culture to the active transmission of elements of the living culture, or culture as way of life. This dimension represents the continuum of definitions of culture, from culture as product to culture as process (Richards, 1996). The second dimension represents the use or purpose to which the cultural resources are put in an attraction. This cultural purpose dimension ranges from educational uses of culture to culture as the basis of entertainment. This dimension also reflects the debate about authenticity – from 'serious' attractions designed to present an 'authentic' picture of the culture, to 'staged' entertainment designed to meet the needs of the audience (Velázquez, 1996).

These two trajectories can be related to create a field in which different types of cultural attractions can be positioned (Fig. 1.1).

Quadrant 1 contains the major 'traditional' cultural attractions based largely on heritage and other cultural products of the past – museums, monuments and galleries. Quadrant 2 features more contemporary types of attractions based on cultural processes, such as language courses and art exhibitions. On the right-hand side of the diagram are attractions focused more on providing entertainment, and therefore more orientated towards the needs of the cultural audience than preserving cultural resources. In the top left quadrant are grouped attractions related to entertainment – arts festivals and performances. Theme parks arguably fall across the boundary between quadrant 3 and quadrant 4, because they not only present contemporary entertainment but also exploit historical resources, such as historical themes and attractions. Quadrant 4 is bounded by a number of attraction types, including heritage centres and folklore festivals, where there is a mixture of educational and entertainment elements based on historical resources.

One of the problems with this and any other typology of cultural attractions is that the formerly distinct categories of attraction are increasingly disappearing. This is also evident from the analysis of different types of attractions contained in Part II of this volume. As Wil Munsters demonstrates

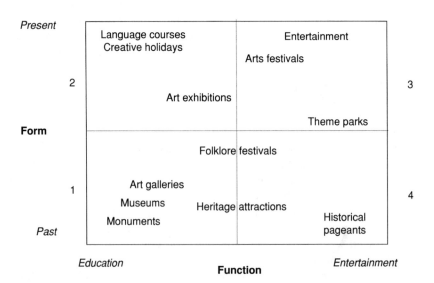

**Fig. 1.1.**   Towards a typology of cultural tourism attractions.

in his analysis of the Bonnefanten Museum in Maastricht (Chapter 5) for example, the increasing emphasis on dramatic architecture in modern museums means that many new museums act as monuments in themselves as well as repositories for artefacts. The Bonnefanten is also experimenting with different types of contemporary exhibitions in order to attract a wider audience, and in doing so is perhaps shifting towards quadrant 3 of the model. The typology should therefore be understood more as a dynamic field within which cultural attractions may position themselves than as a fixed classification.

The Glasgow case study compiled by David Leslie in Chapter 6 also illustrates the changing role of art museums, in this case the Burrell Collection. The pressures to develop new sources of funding have led the museum to challenge the original conditions of the Burrell bequest in order to be able to lend objects abroad. Increasing the international profile of the collection through such international activities has also become an important means of attracting international visitors.

In Chapter 7 Frances McGettigan and Kevin Burns demonstrate how Clonmacnoise, a remote religious attraction in the heart of Ireland, is facing increasing management problems as the stream of tourists grows. It has become difficult to reconcile the needs of visitors and local residents in this case, because the flow of tourists has to be constantly monitored and managed, leaving little room for constructive inputs from local people. One possible solution to this may eventually be to de-market the site to certain groups of tourists.

Sue Berry and Graham Shephard examine the market for heritage attractions across an entire region in Chapter 8. In the case of South-East England they demonstrate how the problems of heritage management can be very similar between different attraction types. The need to attract visitors in order to generate income may lead to cultural attractions clustering in quadrant 4 of the model, as they seek to become more visitor centred.

In Chapter 9, Michael Green assesses the effects of globalization and localization on the development of urban heritage tourism in three European cities. Tilburg (The Netherlands), Bilbao (Spain) and Leicester (UK) have all suffered decline in manufacturing industry, and in common with many other European cities are developing cultural tourism as a means of stimulating service sector employment. Green demonstrates that although global economic trends may be largely responsible for the development of cultural tourism in European cities, it is the interplay of both global and local factors that influences the development of cultural tourism attractions. It is also clear that these former industrial cities are struggling with the question of how to deal with their past, while trying to position themselves as modern, dynamic places. There are signs that cities are increasingly shifting the emphasis of cultural production away from the resources of the past shown in quadrants 1 and 4, towards the more contemporary cultural forms in quadrants 2 and 3.

Many areas have turned to event development as a means of addressing some of the problems posed by fixed attraction development. Events can present a constantly updated product, and do not usually demand the same amount of investment as fixed attractions. In Chapter 10 László Puckzó and Tamara Rátz examine the development of the Budapest Spring Festival and its attempts to develop an international cultural audience. They point out that the level of foreign visitation remains low, in spite of European reunification and the presence of world famous Hungarian performers at the festival. This indicates that the festival does not have enough 'globalized' cultural capital to attract a large international audience.

In the Polish case study presented in Chapter 11, Barbara Marciszewska points out that the cultural consumption and experience of Eastern Europeans can be very different from that of consumers in the West. Relatively low incomes contrasted with high levels of cultural capital in respect to high culture produce a different landscape of cultural consumption. Reviewing the market for cultural attractions as diverse as museums, galleries and a planetarium she demonstrates that these consumption practices nevertheless have just as much to do with status considerations and 'keeping up' with one's peer group as cultural tourism in the West.

In the final case study Caro Bonink and Erik Hitters (Chapter 12) examine one of the new breed of popular culture attractions being developed in European cities. The *Westergasfabriek* is a converted gas factory in Amsterdam, which is now a multifunctional cultural performance and production space. This attraction demonstrates a trend away from heritage attractions based on preserving the culture of the past, towards attractions based on creativity, typical of quadrants 2 and 3 in the model.

The different case studies presented in this volume therefore illustrate the range and diversity of cultural attractions across Europe, and at the same time demonstrate that many of these attractions are facing similar management and marketing problems. As the attraction stock of Europe grows, the problem of generating enough visits to meet policy goals and financial targets will also become more acute everywhere. The remaining chapters in Part 1 of the book consider the nature of the cultural visitor market and the way in which attractions are being created to meet the needs of this market.

## References

Advertising Association (1996) *Lifestyle Pocketbook 1996*. NTC Publications, Henley.

Bender, B. and Edmonds, M. (1992) Stonehenge: whose past? What past? *Tourism Management* 13, 355.

Bianchini, F. and Parkinson, M. (eds) (1993) *Cultural Policy and Urban Regeneration: the Western European Experience*. Manchester University Press, Manchester.

Bonink, C. and Richards, G. (1997) Attractiebezoek afgelopen tien jaar fors gestegen. *Recreatie en Toerisme*, 7(7) 6–8.

Boorstin, D. (1964) *The Image: a Guide to Pseudo-events in America*. Harper and Row, New York.

Bramwell, B., Henry, I., Jackson, G. and van der Straaten, J. (1998) A framework for understanding sustainable tourism management. In: Bramwell, B., Henry, I., Jackson, G., Goytia Prat, A., Richards, G. and van der Straaten, J. (eds) *Sustainable Tourism Management: Principles and Practice*, 2nd edn. Tilburg University Press, Tilburg, pp. 23–71.

British Tourist Authority (1989–1997) *UK Tourism Survey*. BTA, London.

British Tourist Authority (1997) *Overseas Leisure Visitor Survey 1996*. BTA, London.

Bywater, M. (1993) The market for cultural tourism in Europe. *Travel and Tourism Analyst* No. 6, 30–46.

Carroll, C. (1995) Tourism: cultural construction of the countryside. MA thesis, Programme in European Leisure Studies, Tilburg University.

Cloke, P. (1993) The countryside as commodity: new rural spaces for leisure. In: Glyptis, S. (ed.) *Leisure and the Environment*. Belhaven, London, pp. 53–67.

*Colors* (1999) Venice: how much? *Colors*, August–September.

Debord, G. (1995) *The Society of the Spectacle*. Zone Books, New York.

de Haan, J. (1997) *Het Gedeelde Erfgoed*. SCP, Rijswijk.

Dodd, D. (1999) Barcelona the cultural city: changing perceptions. In: Dodd, D. and van Hemel, A.-M. (eds) *Planning European Cultural Tourism*. Boekman Foundation, Amsterdam, pp. 53–64.

ECTARC (1989) *Contribution to the Drafting of a Charter for Cultural Tourism*. European Centre for Traditional and Regional Cultures, Llangollen, Wales.

Edensor, T. (1998) *Tourists at the Taj: Performance and Meaning at a Symbolic Site*. Routledge, London.

Edwards, J., Fernandes, C., Fox, J. and Vaughan, R. (2000) Tourism brand attributes of the Alto Minho, Portugal. In: Richards, G. and Hall, D. (eds) *Tourism and Sustainable Community Development*. Routledge, London, pp. 284–296.

English Tourist Board (1991) *Tourism and the Environment: Maintaining the Balance*. ETB, London.

European Commission (1998) *Culture, the Cultural Industries and Employment*. Commission Staff Working Paper SEC (98) 837, EC, Brussels.

Forni, G. (1999) Ethnographic museums in Italy: a decade of phenomenal growth. *Museums International*, 204, 47–52.

Glancey, J. (1999) That's enough culture. *The Guardian*, 27 December, p. 10.

Goedhart, S. (1997) 'New producers' in cultuurtoerisme. MA thesis, Tilburg University.

Gómez, M.V. (1998) Reflective images: the case of urban regeneration in Glasgow and Bilbao. *International Journal of Urban and Regional Research* 22(1), 106–121.

Grobler, J. (1998) The conflict between political correctness and cultural preservation at the Voortrekker Monument, South Africa. Paper presented at the ATLAS Annual Conference, Crete, October 1998.

Hall, C.M. and McArthur, S. (eds) (1993) *Heritage Management in New Zealand and Australia: Visitor Management, Interpretation and Marketing*. Oxford University Press, Oxford.

Hanna, M. (1998) The built heritage in England: grants, earnings and employment. *Cultural Trends* 32, 5–23.

Herrijgers, C. (1998) De culturele stedenreis. MA thesis, Tilburg University.

Hewison, R. (1987) *The Heritage Industry: Britain in a Climate of Decline*. Methuen, London.

Irish Tourist Board (1988) *Inventory of Cultural Tourism Resources in the Member States and Assessment of Methods Used to Promote Them*. European Commission DG VII, Brussels.

Jacobsen, J.K.S. (1997) The making of an attraction. The case of North Cape. *Annals of Tourism Research* 24, 341–356.

Janarius, M. (1992) A sense of place. *Leisure Management* 12(November), 34–35.

Kneafsey, M. (1994) The cultural tourist. In: Kockel, U. (ed.) *Culture, Tourism and Development: the Case of Ireland*. Liverpool University Press, Liverpool, pp. 100–116.

Leiper, N. (1990) Tourist attraction systems. *Annals of Tourism Research* 17, 367–384.

Lew, A. (1987) A framework of tourist attraction research. *Annals of Tourism Research* 14, 533–575.

Littrell, M.A. (1997) Shopping experiences and marketing of culture to tourists. In: Robinson, M., Evans, N. and Callaghan, P. (eds) *Tourism and Culture: Image, Identity and Marketing*. Centre for Travel and Tourism, University of Northumbria, pp. 107–120.

MacCannell, D. (1976) *The Tourist: a New Theory of the Leisure Class*. Macmillan, London.

Macdonald, S. (1997) A people's story: heritage, identity and authenticity. In: Rojek, C. and Urry, J. (eds) *Touring Cultures: Transformations of Travel and Theory*. Routledge, London, pp. 154–175.

Mowforth, M. and Munt, I. (1998) *Tourism and Sustainability; New Tourism in the Third World*. Routledge, London.

Munsters, W. (1994) *Cultuurtoerisme*. Garant, Apeldoorn.

Munt, I. (1994) The 'other' postmodern tourism: culture, travel and the new middle classes. *Theory, Culture and Society* 11, 101–123.

Murray, M. and Graham, B. (1997) Exploring the dialectics of route-based tourism: the Camiño de Santiago. *Tourism Management* 18, 513–524.

Pérez de Cuélla, J. (1996) *Our Creative Diversity*. UNESCO Publishing, Paris.

Picard, M. (1996) *Bali: Cultural Tourism and Touristic Culture*. Archipelago Press, Singapore.

Polácek, M. and Aroch, R. (1984) Analysis of cultural sights attractiveness for tourism. *Revue de Tourisme* 4, 17–18.

Pretes, M. (1995) Postmodern tourism: the Santa Claus industry. *Annals of Tourism Research* 22, 1–15.

Rásky, B. (1998) Cultural policy/policies in Europe. In: Ellmeier, A. and Rásky, B. (eds) *Cultural Policy in Europe – European Cultural Policy?* Österreichische Kulturdokumentation, Internationals Archiv für Kulturanalysen, Vienna, pp. 5–85.

Richards, G. (1996) *Cultural Tourism in Europe*. CAB International, Wallingford, UK.

Richards, G. (1999) European cultural tourism: patterns and prospects. In: Dodd, D. and van Hemel, A.-M. (eds) *Planning European Cultural Tourism*. Boekman Foundation, Amsterdam, pp. 16–32.

Richards, G. (2000) Cultural tourism: challenges for management and marketing. In: Gartner, W.C. and Lime, D.W. (eds) *Trends in Outdoor Recreation, Leisure and Tourism*. CAB International, Wallingford, UK, pp. 187–195.

Ritzer, G. (1999) *Enchanting a Disenchanted World: Revolutionizing the Means of Consumption*. Pine Forge Press, Thousand Oaks, California.

Roche, M. (1994) Mega-events and urban policy. *Annals of Tourism Research* 21, 1–19.

Samuel, R. (1996) *Theatres of Memory: Past and Present in Contemporary Culture*. Verso, London.

Shaw, S.J. and Macleod, N.E. (2000) Creativity and conflict: cultural tourism in London's city fringe. *Tourism, Culture and Communication* 2, 165–175.

Swarbrooke, J. (1996) Towards the development of sustainable rural tourism in Eastern Europe. In: Richards, G. (ed.) *Tourism in Central and Eastern Europe: Educating for Quality*. Tilburg University Press, Tilburg, pp. 137–163.

Towner, J. (1985) The Grand Tour: a key phase in the history of tourism. *Annals of Tourism Research* 12, 297–333.

Tunbridge, J.E. and Ashworth, G.J. (1996) *Dissonant Heritage: the Management of the Past as a Resource in Conflict*. Wiley, Chichester.

Urry, J. (1990) *The Tourist Gaze: Leisure and Travel in Contemporary Societies*. Sage, London.

van Elderen, P.L. (1997) *Suddenly One Summer: a Sociological Portrait of the Joensuu Festival*. Joensuu University Press, Joensuu.

Velázquez, T. (1996) Designing artifice for touring illusions: an analysis of visitor approaches to tourist attractions. MA thesis, Programme in European Leisure Studies, Tilburg.

Williams, R. (1983) *Keywords*. Fontana, London.

Wright, P. (1985) *On Living in an Old Country*. Verso, London.

# The Market for Cultural Attractions

## Greg Richards

*Tilburg University, Department of Leisure Studies, Tilburg, The Netherlands*

## Introduction

Cultural attractions and their visitors form an important element in the cultural life and the economy of many countries and regions. It is perhaps surprising that relatively little systematic research has been conducted on this important market. Many attractions conduct ad hoc surveys of their visitors, but these are often difficult to compare from one attraction to another. National surveys of domestic or international tourists rarely cover cultural tourism, apart from assessments of how many tourists visit cultural attractions.

This is slowly beginning to change, as more collaborative research is beginning to be undertaken by attractions and public sector tourism and cultural organizations. In the UK, for example, the Arts Council has researched the arts audience, including some information on the presence of tourists. The Museums and Galleries Commission (1999) has also examined the relationship between international tourists and museums, and they concluded that almost one-third of visitors to the UK are motivated to visit the country because of museums. In France, estimates have been made of the number of tourists visiting different types of attractions, and in Italy studies have been made of visitors to 'art cities' (van der Borg *et al.*, 1996). Usually these studies are guided by marketing or public policy considerations, as cultural attractions try to identify current audiences and look for new ones. Academic research covering more than one attraction is rarer, but developments are taking place in this direction too.

## Review of previous research and statistical sources

As noted above, most of the studies of cultural visitation are undertaken by or for individual cultural attractions. Such studies are often commercially sensitive, and therefore often remain confidential. Even where the results are made public, the surveys are usually specially designed for the attraction, and therefore difficult to compare with those conducted elsewhere.

Most academic studies of cultural tourism are descriptive, and are seldom based on empirical analysis of the visitor market. The emphasis of most research lies on examining the meaning of cultural tourism, either for the hosts or for the tourists. A recent collection of papers from a major international conference on tourism and culture held at the University of Northumbria (Robinson and Boniface, 1999), for example, contains 13 chapters, of which only three contain figures on tourism supply or demand. The only visitor research quoted is the number of visitors to museums in Greece. In none of these studies is any attempt made to gather information on cultural tourists or their behaviour. This is fairly typical of the literature on tourism and culture, which tends to be dominated by critical social science perspectives. The meaning of cultural tourism tends to be deduced from the interpretation of attractions and their presentation, rather than the behaviour or experience of visitors.

There seems to be a significant gap between the predominantly theoretical approaches to the study of the relationship between tourism and culture on the one hand, and the more practical, empirical studies of attraction visitors on the other. Much visitor research is undertaken from a marketing perspective, and is not usually designed to engage with the social science perspectives being put forward in the literature. This points to the need for more integration of theory and practice through the development of cultural and tourism consumption research above the scale of the individual attraction.

Most attempts to produce wider empirical insights into the nature of cultural tourism have been based on survey work at regional or national level. As Ganzeboom and Ranshuysen (1994) have noted, there are basically two methods of surveying cultural consumption: population surveys and visitor surveys. Population surveys attempt to discover the levels of cultural consumption in the population as a whole through surveys of representative samples of both visitors and non-visitors. This has the advantage that visitors and non-visitors can be compared, and reasons for non-visitation can be examined. In addition a clear picture of the proportion of different groups of the population making use of cultural facilities can be obtained. This is particularly useful where cultural attractions are trying to promote access under different segments of the population.

Most European countries have some form of omnibus survey which examines the cultural consumption patterns of the population, although the aspects of cultural visits are usually limited to levels of visitation and a basic profile of visitors and non-visitors. A further problem is that omnibus surveys carried out by different bodies often adopt differing definitions of cultural attractions and participation.

In the UK, for example, Davies (1994) compared the results of a number of omnibus surveys of visits to museums and galleries. Although the surveys all indicated that participation by UK adults was around 40% of the population per year, some of these surveys listed museums and galleries together, and others as separate categories. In estimating the number of visits generated by cultural visitors, the multipliers used to reach an aggregate figure also varied, between 0.8 visits per visitor per year for the General Household Survey to more than four visits. Davies himself established on the basis of site surveys that the average number of visits per participants was three per year.

Some of these omnibus surveys also provide information on non-visitors. For example Mintel (1993) found that cultural visitors were more likely to come from higher socio-economic groups than non-visitors, and that the 20–24 age group was particularly well represented among non-visitors. Kirchberg's (1996) study of museum visitors and non-visitors in Germany found that although non-visitors were more likely to be blue collar workers or those outside the labour force, a single clear distinction between visitors and non-visitors did not emerge. He identified a continuum of socio-demographic characteristics ranging from non-visitors through 'popular' museums (natural history and science) to 'high culture' museums (art and history museums). Davies and Prentice (1995) have also tried to conceptualize the 'latent visitor' and non-visitor from a theoretical perspective. As they point out, non-visitors have often been treated as an aggregate group, whereas there are significant differences between latent visitors who might be motivated to visit, and those non-visitors who are simply not interested in cultural attractions.

Some of the differences between omnibus surveys can be attributed to varying definitions of cultural attractions, usually depending on the interests of the sponsors. The studies reviewed by Davies, for example, were all based on museums and art galleries, as his research was conducted for the UK Museums and Galleries Commission. The Mintel study, on the other hand, includes historic properties as well as museums and galleries, but excludes the performing arts.

A much broader definition of 'arts tourism' was taken for figures emerging from the UK Tourism Survey (UKTS) on cultural visits by domestic tourists. The definition of arts tourism is where the main purpose of a trip is to attend a performing arts event (including the cinema) or to visit a museum, gallery or heritage attraction. The data indicate that 'arts tourism' accounted for 1.7% of all domestic holidays and 3% of all holiday expenditure in the UK in 1996. The longitudinal data generated by the UKTS show that expenditure on arts tourism has fallen in terms of constant 1996 prices from over £600 million (€850 million) in 1989 to less than £300 million

(€425 million) in 1996. Part of this fall may reflect an increase in cultural trips abroad by UK residents. However, it may also be the case that this specialist segment of the market is so small that sampling error may have a significant impact on the estimate of aggregate expenditure.

The solution adopted to this problem of small sample sizes in many population surveys is to use a very broad definition of cultural tourism in order to include larger numbers of respondents in the research. In US research on cultural visitors, for example, studies of 'cultural tourists' include all those visiting museums, monuments, historic sites and cultural performances and events (Travel Industry Association, 1997). Major European omnibus studies, such as the European Tourism Monitor, for example, do not specifically cover cultural tourism. The European Tourism Monitor asks a general question about city trips, which probably have a high cultural content, but no specific questions about cultural consumption on holiday. The EuroBarometer omnibus research by the European Commission, which covers tourism periodically, also generates no specific information about cultural tourism. The most recent EuroBarometer survey of tourism (European Commission, 1998) did contain a question on holiday motivations, however, which indicated that cultural heritage was not particularly important as a motivation. 'Culture' was only ranked fifth by Europeans as a motive for travel, and 'traditions' came in eighth place.

Because such population surveys usually contain a relatively small sample of cultural tourists, the information that can be generated about the specific motivations and behaviour of cultural visitors is limited. In order to obtain a reasonable sample of cultural visitors, therefore, the most cost-effective approach is to conduct site surveys. This is the strategy adopted in the European Association for Tourism and Leisure Education (ATLAS) Cultural Tourism Research Programme, on which this book is based. It is not surprising that many research studies conducted in the cultural visitor market are based on visitor surveys at cultural attractions.

A number of site-based surveys of attraction visitors have been carried out in recent years. For example, Light and Prentice (1994) carried out almost 4000 visitor interviews at 15 sites in Wales on behalf of Cadw, the Welsh Historic Monuments agency. This type of 'meso-scale' data collection allowed them to develop a detailed picture of the backgrounds, travel behaviour and site visits of heritage tourists. Prentice (1993) also carried out research at a number of sites in the Isle of Man, conducting 4000 visitor surveys between 1988 and 1991. He found that different groups of heritage visitors tend to seek different experiences and benefits when visiting attractions. In order to generate a picture of the arts consumption of tourists in Amsterdam, a study carried out for the Amsterdams Uit Buro (1996) included interviews with over 500 foreign tourists visiting the city. The research indicated that 70% of the visitors considered culture to be an important influence in their decision to visit the city.

Festivals and events have also become a major focus of academic research in recent years, and there have been a number of studies of visitors to cultural events, although the bulk of the research has been conducted in the US (Getz, 1991). In Europe, van Elderen (1997) has conducted a detailed longitudinal study of the Joensuu Festival in Finland, and examined how the audience has changed over the years. He found that the modernization of Finland has been accompanied by an evolution of the festival audience from 'cultural folk' through 'taste experts' into 'festival consumers', as the festival grew in popularity and the range of social groups increased.

In Italy, Formica and Uysal (1998) have surveyed the Spoleto Festival. They found the audience to be relatively young, with a high proportion of repeat visitors (59%). The motivations of the visitors were primarily an interest in the cultural forms presented at the festival, a desire to be entertained and to experience the atmosphere of the event. The audience could be divided into two primary segments: 'enthusiasts' and 'moderates'. The enthusiasts were more likely to be repeat visitors with higher incomes and education levels. Their motivations were more likely to be related to a thirst for culture, the desire to experience new things and a search for stimulation and excitement. This group might be broadly identifed as 'skilled consumers' (Richards, 1996a) and accounted for almost 80% of the festival-goers. The moderates were more likely to be 'unskilled consumers' with general leisure-related motivations.

One of the major problems of these studies is that they usually have different aims and adopt different methodologies which are specific to the site(s) being studied. This makes it very difficult to compare findings on an international or even national basis. In order to overcome some of the problems of comparability, it is important to use a common research methodology. This is the approach taken by the ATLAS Cultural Tourism Research Programme.

## The ATLAS Cultural Tourism Research Programme

ATLAS is an international association of higher education and other organizations which aims to develop transnational education and research in the tourism and leisure subject areas. ATLAS had some 250 member institutions in 45 countries at the end of 2000. The Cultural Tourism Research Programme was launched in 1991, with the support of DGXXIII (now the Enterprise Directorate) of the European Commission. The research focused originally on visitors to cultural attractions in the European Union (EU), but the scope of the research has increased to cover first Central and Eastern Europe and more recently Asia and Australasia as well.

The original aims of the research programme were to:

1. Devise definitions of the nature and scope of cultural tourism
2. Collect data on cultural tourism visits to European attractions

**3.** Assess the profile and motivations of cultural tourists
**4.** Develop case studies of cultural tourism management.

Many of these aims were at least partially fulfilled in the first phase of the research programme, which was undertaken in 1991–1993, and the results of which were published in Richards (1996b). The initial visitor surveys covered 6300 interviews with visitors to 26 cultural attractions in nine countries.

The visitor research was repeated in 1997 with over 8000 surveys at 50 sites in nine European countries. Some initial results of these surveys have been published in Richards (1998a, 1999). The 1997 research was expanded in scope to include countries outside the EU (Hungary, Poland) and to include more 'popular culture' attractions and events. The notion of 'culture' covered by the 1997 research is therefore somewhat broader than in the 1992 research.

A third survey was carried out in 1999/2000, and the scope of the research is again being expanded to include more information on marketing issues, and to include countries outside Europe for the first time.

The survey programme was originally designed to answer the basic question – who are the cultural tourists? The research programme has progressively addressed different aspects of cultural visitor behaviour. In 1997 the focus was on motivations, and the position of cultural visitation within overall leisure and tourism consumption. Statements relating to cultural motivations were added, which were developed through the study of 'new producers' by Saskia Goedhart (1997). The theoretical perspectives which were introduced into the research included Bourdieu's notion of cultural capital. Different aspects of Bourdieu's analysis of cultural consumption were operationalized in the motivational statements included in the questionnaire, including the effect of socialization and the link between occupation, cultural capital and cultural tourism. These relationships are dealt with in more detail in Chapter 3 of this volume.

For the research being undertaken in 1999/2000, it was decided to concentrate more on the marketing aspects of cultural visitation. Questions were added on sources of information about the attractions visited, and the point at which the decision to visit the attraction was taken. This last question was also added to examine the type of 'markers' being used by tourists in visiting cultural sites (Leiper, 1990).

Since 1994 the cultural visitor surveys have been supplemented by a series of specific studies on different aspects of cultural tourism, mainly conducted by students at Tilburg University, or participating in the Programme in European Leisure Studies (PELS). These studies have covered the motivation of cultural visitors (Roetman, 1994; van 't Riet, 1995), the role of new cultural intermediaries or new producers in the production of cultural attractions (Goedhart, 1997), the policies of European cities regarding cultural and heritage tourism (Green, 1998) and the role of tour operators in developing cultural destinations (Herrijgers, 1998).

The definition of cultural tourism has also evolved during the research programme, in line with the expanding horizons of our knowledge of cultural tourism consumption. Originally we began with a technical definition which facilitated the fieldwork. A conceptual definition was devised to describe the nature of cultural tourism itself, which we viewed as being focused on the motivations of tourists (Richards, 1996b, p. 24).

Technical definition:

> All movements of persons to specific cultural attractions, such as heritage sites, artistic and cultural manifestations, arts and drama outside their normal place of residence.

Conceptual definition:

> The movement of persons to cultural attractions away from their normal place of residence, with the intention to gather new information and experiences to satisfy their cultural needs.

Since these definitions were published there has been some comment made on them by other researchers. For example, Alzua *et al.* (1998, p. 3) have argued that because 'intention' is a complex concept to measure, that it would be better to use a scale of tourist motivations, such as that incorporated in Silberberg's (1995) definition 'visits by persons from outside the host community motivated wholly or in part by interest in the historical artistic, scientific or lifestyle/heritage offerings of a community, region, group or institution'. However, as our research has shown, it would be hard to find a tourist who is not interested at least in part in some aspect of the culture of the destination they are visiting. The point about using intent as a distinguishing feature is to differentiate between the 'culturally motivated' visitor, who makes a conscious, mindful decision to consume culture on holiday, and the 'culturally interested' visitor, who may be almost an accidental cultural tourist (Bywater, 1993).

Barbara Marciszewska has also suggested in Chapter 11 of this volume that the definition of cultural tourism should include a consideration of wants and desires as well as cultural needs. As Leiper has pointed out, needs are the underlying factors influencing tourist motivations to visit attractions. 'But a single need might be expressed in dozens of different motivations and wants and, conversely, a single want might reflect any of several different needs' (1990, p. 373). An analysis of wants and desires may be useful for a practical discussion about the consumption of individual attractions, but this does not provide a sound basis for the definition of the phenomenon of cultural tourism. The use of needs as the basis of motivations also relates more closely to the findings of tourism motivation studies, which have consistently identified the need for learning and new experiences as one of the core tourist motivations (Fodness, 1994; Moscardo, 1999).

## Research Methodology

As noted above, the research is based on surveys of visitors to specific cultural attractions. The research findings cannot therefore be considered to be representative of visitors to cultural attractions as a whole.

The research was organized on a devolved basis, which gave responsibility for the choice of attraction surveyed to the people conducting the research locally. This was partly on the basis that the people closest to the local situation would be able to choose the appropriate attractions to survey in their locations, and partly because of the limited funds available for the research programme. Cultural attractions had to be found that could be fitted into the existing research interests of the local partners. The attractions surveyed should therefore be considered a convenience sample rather than a representative sample of cultural attractions in Europe.

### Research instrument

The transnational nature of the survey meant that the development of a standard research instrument was crucial. The basic survey questionnaire was developed for the 1992 survey, and has subsequently been revised in the light of experience and as new aspects have been added to the research programme. The same basic questionnaire was used by all the survey participants. The English language questionnaire was used by the survey team to produce versions of the questionnaire in different languages. In 1997 the questionnaire was translated into Dutch, Finnish, French, German, Hungarian, Italian, Polish, Spanish and Swedish. The translations were made by native speakers who were also familiar with the research programme. In each case the wording and the order of the questions was left as close to the original English text as possible.

In order to facilitate comparison, standard classifications were used wherever possible. The employment question, for example, is based on standard ISCO occupation codes. This made the job of translation easier, since EU documents, such as the European Labour Force Survey, provide translations of the categories in different languages. The euro was also used as the basic monetary unit, with conversion scales being provided for the different language versions. Terms which might cause some differences of interpretation were also clarified in order to facilitate comparison. For example, references in the questionnaire to the 'area' in which the attraction was located were taken to mean the city or administrative region in which the respondent was being interviewed.

## Survey procedures

The questionnaire was designed to be used either by an interviewer or through self-completion. In most cases, however, the questionnaires were interviewer-completed, as this tended to give a higher degree of accuracy and generated a higher response rate.

The total visitor population in principle consisted of all visitors to the attraction or event being surveyed who were 16 years or older. In some cases, however, visitors younger than 16 were also interviewed, as it was difficult to judge the lower age limit visually. The sample obtained at each attraction depended to a large extent on local circumstances. Usually exit interviews were conducted, and visitors were sampled on a random basis, with the sampling interval being adjusted to the visitor stream. For groups of visitors the 'next birthday' principle was used to select respondents (Veal, 1992). Wherever possible, interviews were held over different days and time periods to ensure that all visitor groups were sampled. The questionnaire was deliberately kept as short as possible, to minimize problems of refusal. Visitors who could not speak the language of the country concerned or where the interviewer was unable to speak their language could often be offered a self-completion questionnaire in their own language. There is a likelihood, however, that Japanese and other Asian visitors will have been under-represented in the sample because of the lack of questionnaires in non-European languages.

For each survey site, information was also gathered on a number of background variables, including the date and times of interviews, details of sampling methods used and the number of face-to-face interviews and self-completion questionnaires gathered. A standard form was circulated to all survey participants for this purpose.

Although there are obviously problems involved with conducting a transnational research on this scale and without structural funding, there is no doubt that the project has generated important research data which are not available in any other way. The following sections examine the data generated by the visitor surveys in terms of visitor profile, motivation, activities and visit characteristics.

## A profile of cultural visitors

The following analysis of the cultural visitors to the attractions surveyed is based on surveys collected at all sites. Where references are made to significant differences, these have been calculated from chi-square or *t*-test statistics, with a confidence interval of 0.05.

## Gender

As with other surveys of cultural visitors, the majority of respondents (52%) were female in 1997. The proportion of women was slightly higher than that recorded in 1992. This tends to confirm the picture obtained from other studies of cultural consumption that cultural activities tend to attract more women, although the overall differences are not dramatic. In Poland, The Netherlands and Portugal men were in a slight majority, but in all other countries women predominated.

## Age

The 1997 research tended to confirm one of the major findings of the 1992 survey – that the cultural tourism market is younger than many previous studies have tended to suppose. Over 35% of respondents were aged under 30, and only 26% were over 50. The number of young visitors was slightly lower in 1997 than in 1992, which may relate to the fact that more surveys were held outside the main summer season, which would tend to increase the proportion of older visitors in the sample.

Not surprisingly the age profile of the respondents tended to reflect the age distribution in the destination country. So Sweden had a very high proportion of visitors over 50 (60%), compared with lower proportions in Poland (7%) and Portugal (19%).

## Education

Cultural visitors tend to be highly educated, with over 44% of respondents having a higher education qualification in 1997. This is slightly lower than the level recorded in the 1992 surveys (51%), probably because of the older age profile of the respondents. Even so, those with a higher education background are clearly over-represented among cultural visitors. Only 21% of the EU population had a higher education diploma in 1995.

## Occupation and status

Almost half of the respondents were employed, and a further 12% self-employed. Other important occupational groups were students (16%) and retired people (14%), again emphasizing the mixture of young and old in the cultural audience. The proportion of students tended to be highest at the Eastern European survey locations, and lowest in north-western Europe. The high proportion of students encountered at Eastern European sites is probably related to the rapid growth of the student population in recent years.

In terms of occupational status, almost 70% of respondents had a professional or managerial background. Professionals were particularly important, accounting for over half of the interviewees. Clerical and sales and service occupations accounted for a further 25% of respondents. The predominance of professional and managerial occupations in the cultural audience again contrasts sharply with the occupation profile of the EU workforce as a whole. The EU Labour Force Survey (EUROSTAT, 1995) indicated that less than 33% of the workforce were in managerial or professional positions in 1994, compared with 63% of the cultural visitors interviewed in 1997 (Fig. 2.1).

## Income

Not surprisingly, given the high status of the respondents, the majority had a relatively high income. For respondents interviewed in the EU, the median income lay around €30,000, some 30% higher than the EU average. In Poland and Hungary absolute income levels were much lower, with the median household income being about €6000. Even so, as Marciszewska (Chapter 11, this volume) indicates, this is higher than the average income in Poland, which is less than €5000 a year.

## Visitor origin

Almost 60% of visitors interviewed were tourists, and just over 40% were local residents. The proportion of tourists was slightly lower than in the 1992 surveys, mainly because the interviews were spread more evenly across the year. Of the tourists, about 90% were on holiday, and the vast majority were staying visitors – only 13% were day visitors to the survey region, and even some of these visitors were staying as tourists in another region.

Of the tourists interviewed, over half (55%) were foreign tourists. The country of origin of the tourists was strongly influenced by the survey locations, and cannot be said to be representative of the picture for Europe as a whole. In general, however, the major origin countries reflect the major tourist generating countries for Europe. The UK, Germany, France and Italy

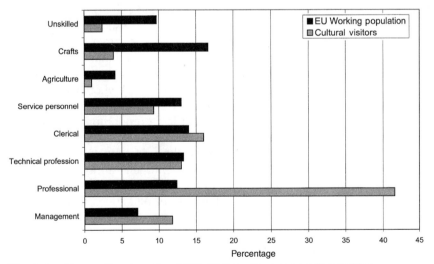

**Fig. 2.1.** Occupational profile of ATLAS interviewees and EU working population, 1997.

together account for over 40% of foreign tourists interviewed. American tourists were particularly well represented because of the large number of interviews conducted in the UK and Ireland, which accounted for 85% of American tourists in the sample. Tourists from other origin countries were generally more evenly distributed between the survey countries.

The proportion of cultural tourists among the foreign visitors varied considerably according to the origin country. The UK, for example, accounted for 20% of all foreign visitors interviewed, but only 9% of these saw themselves as cultural tourists. In contrast, both Belgium and Spain had more than 25% cultural tourists, and Austria, Denmark, France, Ireland, Italy, Switzerland and the USA had more than 20%. America, France and Germany therefore all generated more foreign cultural tourists than the UK, in spite of the large number of British tourists interviewed.

Australian and New Zealand tourists were predominantly on touring holidays. Because of the distance they have to travel to Europe, there is a tendency for these tourists to make long trips taking in several countries. For example, 83% of Australians interviewed were travelling for 3 weeks or more, compared with 26% of the respondents overall.

### Visit to survey attraction

Almost half of the visitors interviewed had visited the site or event before. Not surprisingly, local residents were more likely to have made a previous visit (72%) than visitors from outside the region (34%). The level of repeat visitation (33%) was relatively high even for foreign tourists, which suggests that cultural attractions do have the potential to generate repeat visits to a region or country. Those making a repeat visit to the attraction were significantly more likely than first time visitors to have a high income, a professional occupation and to have a job related to culture.

The ability of events to generate repeat visits is also illustrated by the fact that the proportion of repeaters at the events surveyed was 59%, significantly higher than the level of repeat visits to permanent attractions (47%). The level of repeat visits was significantly lower for tourists, 35% of whom were making a repeat visit to events, and 28% of whom were making at least their second visit to a fixed attraction.

The attraction visited was viewed by a large proportion of tourists as an important reason for travelling to the survey region. Almost 20% said that the attraction was 'very important' in their decision to travel, and a further 30% indicated that it was 'important'. In general, the remoter the attraction, the greater the importance of the attraction in stimulating travel. In major cities there is often a combination of attractions that generates travel rather than any specific attraction.

### Visits to other cultural attractions

Tourists were asked about their visits to other cultural attractions during their stay in the survey region. All visitors were asked about their visits to cultural attractions during their leisure time in the previous 12 months. This enabled a comparison to be made between cultural consumption on holiday and during 'everyday' leisure.

Although the average length of stay in the survey region was relatively low (2.6 nights), there was a relatively high level of visitation to cultural attractions, in addition to the attraction where the interview was held (Table 2.1).

As noted in previous research (Richards, 1996b) the frequency of visits to events, such as the performing arts and festivals, is far lower than for 'heritage' attractions. This is because the former require the tourist to obtain information about the staging of the event, acquire tickets, and in many cases also to have a command of the language.

Not surprisingly, the overall level of cultural attraction visitation is higher during leisure time than on holiday (Table 2.2). In particular, the proportion of respondents visiting the performing arts and festivals is more than double that on holiday. The only exception is monuments, which are visited by more people on holiday than during their leisure time.

For tourists, almost 40% of their visits to cultural attractions are undertaken on holiday. This emphasizes the important position that holidays have taken in total cultural consumption. For some consumers the holiday has taken on some of the functions that the weekend used to have, as their work

**Table 2.1.**   Visits to cultural attractions during stay in survey area (other than survey site).

| Attraction type | Per cent of tourists visiting |
|-----------------|-------------------------------|
| Museum | 49 |
| Monument | 39 |
| Art gallery | 28 |
| Historic house | 37 |
| Performing arts | 25 |
| Festivals | 13 |

**Table 2.2.**   Attractions visited in leisure time 12 months previous to the survey.

| Attraction type | Per cent visiting during leisure time in the previous 12 months (all respondents) |
|-----------------|-----------------------------------------------------------------------------------|
| Museum | 54 |
| Monument | 35 |
| Art gallery | 41 |
| Historic house | 37 |
| Performing arts | 55 |
| Festivals | 28 |

has become more pressured. Those visiting cultural attractions on holiday were significantly more likely to have a higher income, and to be employed in the cultural sector. Fewer differences were apparent in visits to cultural attractions during leisure time.

There were significant variations in audience composition according to the type of attraction visited. The survey sites could be roughly divided into museums, art galleries, heritage sites, industrial and crafts heritage, events and performance venues.

Younger visitors were particularly well represented at performance venues and events, middle aged visitors at museums and galleries, and older visitors at heritage sites (Table 2.3). Highly educated visitors tended to be found at museums and heritage sites, in line with previous surveys of cultural attendance (e.g. Merriman, 1991). Museums and heritage sites tended to attract those with high status occupations, whereas those in lower occupational groups were well represented at events and industrial and crafts heritage. Museums and galleries also attracted higher income groups.

Foreign visitors tended to be concentrated at heritage sites and galleries. Heritage sites are attractive because they are relatively easily accessible to foreign visitors, while the galleries surveyed tend to hold exhibitions that are potentially attractive to foreign visitors. In contrast, foreign visitors were under-represented at museums and performance venues. Arts performances tend to be oriented towards local audiences, and many of the museums featured in the survey have a more local or regional than international profile.

This confirms the profile developed by Richards (1999), which indicates that heritage attractions attract an older audience, that often has higher incomes and social status. Museums and cultural attractions based on contemporary cultural production, on the other hand, attract a younger audience, often with higher levels of cultural capital.

**Table 2.3.** Age group by attraction type (per cent of respondents).

| Age group | Events | Industrial and crafts heritage | Museum | Gallery | Heritage site | Performance venues | Total |
|---|---|---|---|---|---|---|---|
| 15 or younger | 12.5 | 7.5 | 22.5 | 12.5 | 22.5 | 22.5 | 100.0 |
| 16–19 | 30.8 | 3.0 | 13.3 | 21.3 | 14.0 | 17.6 | 100.0 |
| 20–29 | 26.7 | 2.9 | 14.1 | 23.4 | 16.8 | 16.1 | 100.0 |
| 30–39 | 19.5 | 11.8 | 15.8 | 20.4 | 20.4 | 12.1 | 100.0 |
| 40–49 | 23.3 | 8.4 | 19.5 | 18.2 | 23.5 | 7.1 | 100.0 |
| 50–59 | 23.3 | 8.7 | 23.3 | 15.9 | 25.9 | 2.9 | 100.0 |
| 60 or over | 30.3 | 7.3 | 16.9 | 14.6 | 30.1 | 0.8 | 100.0 |
| Total | 24.9 | 7.2 | 17.4 | 19.1 | 22.2 | 9.2 | 100.0 |

*Motivations*

The number of questions relating to motivation was expanded considerably in the 1997 survey, because the results of the 1992 survey had indicated a need to pay more attention to this issue.

One motivational question that was posed both in 1992 and 1997 was the type of holiday taken. In 1997 almost 22% of respondents indicated that they 'usually' took cultural holidays. Sun and beach holidays and touring holidays remain the most popular types of holiday taken, in line with the findings of the European Tourism Monitor. Countryside recreation and city breaks were also relatively popular holiday types among respondents, which is not surprising given the strong link between cultural tourism and urban tourism and the growing development of cultural tourism in rural areas.

When asked about the type of holiday being taken during their visit to the survey location, almost 20% of respondents indicated that they were on a cultural holiday. Because most of the surveys were conducted in urban locations, and many were held outside the main summer season, it was not surprising that the frequency of beach holidays was considerably lower than for the 'usual' type of holiday taken. This perhaps underlines the tendency for cultural holidays to be second holidays, taken alongside a long summer holiday which is more likely to be a traditional beach holiday.

Those classifying themselves as cultural tourists were significantly more likely to be older, better educated, in a professional occupation, to have a higher income and an occupation related to culture. This matches the picture of cultural tourists developed during previous research. There were, however, no significant differences between men and women in terms of cultural tourism participation.

A range of statements relating to the motivation of visitors for visiting the survey location was also included in the 1997 research (see Fig. 2.2). The motives rated most highly by respondents were experiencing new things, learning new things and relaxation. This tends to confirm the view that cultural tourists are motivated largely by a desire to learn about and experience other cultures, but it also underlines the fact that cultural tourism is no longer regarded as purely cultural – it has become a form of leisure as well. It is interesting to note that culture has become an almost compulsory part of tourism consumption for many. Almost half of those interviewed indicated that they 'always visit a museum' on holiday.

Cultural tourists were more likely to state that they were motivated by new experiences or learning and that they always visited museums on holiday. However, there was no difference from other tourists as far as relaxation or work motivations were concerned.

Far more significant differences in motivation were evident between tourists and local residents. Figure 2.3 indicates that tourists, perhaps not surprisingly, were more likely to be in search of new experiences and learning new things than local residents. Local people were also more likely than tourists to be making a visit connected to their work. One area where

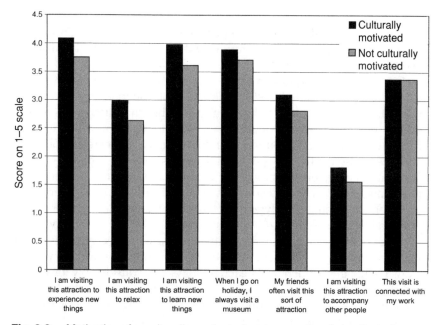

**Fig. 2.2.** Motivations for culturally motivated and non-culturally motivated visitors.

there was no significant difference between the two groups, however, was the search for relaxation.

An overall analysis of the motivations of visitors to cultural attractions reveals a distinct hierarchy of factors. The most important motivators are judged to be the experiential aspects of the visit, in particular experiencing new things, relaxation and learning new things. This tends to underline the assertion in the ATLAS definition of cultural tourism that motivations are related to gathering 'new experiences in order to satisfy cultural needs', but it also demonstrates the mixing of high culture 'learning' with popular culture and leisure 'relaxation'. The second group of motivations are rated as less important overall, and are those related to socialization – museum visiting as a habitual part of tourism experience, the occurrence of cultural visitation within one's peer group and travelling to accompany others. This indicates that individual motivations are more important for most people than collective motivations, although as van 't Riet (1995) has shown, the learning motivation may also be related to parents' desires to educate their children. The final motive, visitation connected with work, is not surprisingly rated relatively low – only the small proportion of those working in the cultural sector were likely to see this as an important reason for visitation. Tourists were significantly more likely than local residents to be motivated by learning or experiencing new things, whereas local residents were more likely to be visiting for social or work-related reasons.

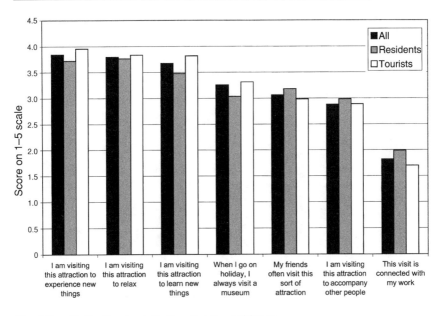

**Fig. 2.3.** Motivation to visit attraction by residence.

### Cultural destinations

A further question added to the 1997 survey related to cities which were ranked as the most suitable cultural holiday destinations by respondents. A list of 19 cities was constructed on the basis of the major cultural destinations in Europe identified by van der Borg (1994).

Analysis of the scores awarded by visitors indicated that people tended to score the city they were visiting significantly better than visitors interviewed in other cities. This indicates that visitation has a significant impact on the evaluation of the cities. In order to minimize this effect, respondents interviewed in one of the cities also listed as a cultural destination (Amsterdam, Budapest, Edinburgh and Munich) were omitted from the analysis for these cities.

The impact of previous visitation is still evident in the scores, however, as Paris, Rome and London scored highest, and these are cities that attract large numbers of international tourists (Fig. 2.4). Other cities, such as Florence, scored better than might be expected relative to their visitor volume.

In general, the rating of cities was strongly related to their stock of 'real cultural capital', or the number of cultural attractions available in the city. A correlation analysis of the visitor ranking of the cities and their stock of cultural capital as measured by the EU Inventory of Cultural Resources (Irish Tourist Board, 1988) indicated strong positive relationships for international, national and regional attraction categories (Pearson's $R$ 0.69–0.85: Richards, 2000). The level of correlation between the presence of these cultural cities

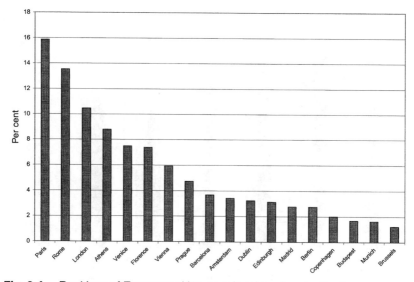

**Fig. 2.4.**  Rankings of European cities as cultural tourism destinations.

in tour operators' brochures in Europe (van der Borg, 1994) and their ranking as cultural destinations is much lower (0.25), primarily because the major cities tend to feature in all tour operators' programmes.

The perception of the different cities as cultural tourism destinations varied according to the background of the visitor. Rome, for example, scored better with women, Dublin with men. Athens, Barcelona, Berlin, Madrid, Rome, Paris and Venice were all significantly more popular with younger visitors, while Dublin, Edinburgh and Florence were more popular with the old. Those with a higher education were more likely to favour Dublin, Edinburgh, Florence, Paris and Prague, and those with lower educational attainment found Athens more attractive (this is because lots of students scored Athens high). Those with a professional or managerial occupation tended to score Florence and Paris high, and those in lower status occupations Athens, Edinburgh, Dublin and Munich. Those on lower incomes favoured Athens, Barcelona, Berlin, Madrid, Paris and Rome, and higher income groups Dublin, Edinburgh, Florence and Vienna.

The motivations of cultural tourists to choose a destination can be traced to a combination of factors, which together may be said to be related to the 'atmosphere' of a place. The importance of 'atmosphere' in tourist motivations to visit certain destinations has been underlined by a number of studies (Goedhart, 1997; Herrijgers, 1998). Atmosphere is of course very difficult to define, and may often be cited by tourists as a motivational factor because they are unable to describe the specific qualities of a place that motivates them. Leiper (1990, p. 376) suggests that the term atmosphere is 'not conducive to scientific understanding'. Instead, one should conceive 'atmosphere' as resulting from the clustering of nuclei, markers and tourists to 'create overlapping systems involving perceptions of atmosphere'. This is essentially what our research also suggests. Those destinations which are identified by tourists and cultural producers as having 'atmosphere' are in fact locations which are 'time-deepened' and rich in markers, nuclei and living culture.

## Holiday characteristics

In order to establish how cultural tourists travel, a number of questions were asked about their accommodation and travel arrangements, length of stay and group composition.

In spite of the image of cultural tourism as a short break form of tourism, the survey respondents tended to be staying longer than three nights away from home. Only 16% of tourists stayed one to three nights, and over half of the tourists were away for at least eight nights. Because of the high incidence of touring holidays, however, the length of stay in the survey region was considerably shorter. Over 50% of tourists stayed three nights or less in the region.

The most popular form of accommodation was hotels (33%), followed by staying with friends and relatives (19%). Self-catering accommodation or tent or caravan was used by just under a quarter of respondents. Self-catering accommodation and camping were particularly important in coastal and rural regions, whereas the majority of visitors to urban regions used hotels or stayed with friends and relatives.

Over half of the tourists had made their own travel arrangements, and a further 16% had made no prior arrangements or booking before travelling. A third of visitors made use of the travel trade to arrange either their transport or accommodation or both. All-inclusive packages (travel, accommodation and transfers) accounted for 16% of trips. The majority of respondents were travelling with their partner (38%) or with their family (28%). Less than 8% of all respondents and 16% of cultural tourists were travelling with a tour group.

Cultural tourists were significantly more likely to be staying in hotels (40%) and staying a relatively short period away from home. This tends to fit the picture of cultural tourists as short stay, high spend visitors. There were no significant differences in booking behaviour or party composition, however.

# An East–West Comparison

The inclusion of sites from Central and Eastern Europe in the 1997 surveys allowed comparisons to be made between cultural visitors in Eastern and

Western Europe. As noted in Richards (1996b), cultural consumption in Eastern Europe has suffered since the fall of the Berlin Wall from loss of public subsidies and falling incomes of local people. This has placed even more emphasis on the development of cultural attractions and events aimed at foreign visitors, with the aim of generating much needed income (see for example Puczkó and Rátz, Chapter 10 this volume). Because of the low purchasing power of people in the East, cultural consumption has been centred around relatively cheap forms of mass culture, such as video (Jung, 1994). High culture, which was promoted under Communist regimes, has tended to suffer from the absence of state funding. In addition, as Barbara Marciszewska points out in Chapter 11 of this volume, the idea that production is driven by consumption does not tend to apply in Eastern Europe, because of the low incomes and therefore limited commercial consumption opportunities for most people.

A comparison of cultural visitors in East and West shows a significant difference in motivations. Local residents in Eastern Europe are significantly more likely than their western counterparts to be in search of new experiences and to be accompanying other people. Their visit is also more likely to be related to their work, but they are less likely to visit museums as a matter of course when on holiday. Not surprisingly in view of the different structures of cultural attraction supply, respondents from Eastern Europe were far less likely to have visited art galleries and historic houses, although there was no difference in levels of museum and monument visitation. There were relatively few differences in cultural consumption levels during leisure time, although respondents from the East were more likely to have attended performing arts events. There was also no difference in levels of holiday taking between East and West.

Respondents from Eastern Europe were significantly younger, with 50% being under 30, compared with 28% of western visitors. This may have resulted from the 'popular culture' and performing arts nature of the Eastern European attractions. In spite of the younger age profile there were very small differences in the level of people with higher education qualifications. Eastern European sites attracted more students and fewer retired visitors. They also had more professional visitors and fewer clerical and sales and service staff. Far fewer of the Eastern European visitors had occupations connected with culture – indicative of the strong development of cultural employment in Western Europe in recent years (Bodo and Fisher, 1997).

In terms of favourite cultural destinations, there were also surprisingly few differences between East and West. Only Florence and Prague were rated significantly lower by those from the East than by western tourists. Prague still seems to have retained a bit of its cachet as a 'new' destination among western visitors, even though this may now be being eroded by easier accessibility to the city, and the consequent reduction in its scarcity value (Herrijgers, 1998 – see also Chapter 4 this volume).

The data from Eastern Europe underline the fact that many of the traditional images of the cultural visitor may be derived from a north-west European perspective. In our studies in Eastern Europe there is even less evidence of cultural tourism being dominated by older, wealthier tourists. The link between high levels of education and cultural consumption is clear in both regions, but cultural tourism in the East seems to be far less clearly linked to 'postmodern' styles of consumption, as Marciszewska emphasizes.

## An Overview of the Cultural Visitor Market in Europe

The picture that emerges of cultural tourists in the 1997 ATLAS survey is consistent with the picture obtained in 1992, and with other studies of the cultural tourism market. Cultural visitors tend to be better educated, have professional or managerial jobs and have relatively high incomes. In Western Europe at least, cultural visitors can be strongly identified with the 'new middle class', for whom cultural consumption is a means of consolidating their social position through the acquisition of cultural capital. In Eastern Europe the leading role played by the intelligentsia in cultural consumption (Jung, 1994) means that cultural visitors have similar levels of cultural capital to those in the West, but have far lower levels of economic capital.

Cultural tourists are shown to be heavy consumers of cultural attractions. Their attraction visits are often concentrated during their holidays, particularly as the increasingly time-squeezed new middle classes have less time available at weekends (Richards, 1998b). Cultural tourism seems to be particularly important for double income couples, who are often undertaking short break holidays. The indications are not so much that cultural holidays are replacing traditional beach holidays, but are becoming additional holidays or are being combined with sun, sea and sand products.

Learning and experiencing new things remain the most important motivations for cultural tourists, who are enthusiastic participants in the experience culture. It should be noted, however, that by no means all cultural visitors are tourists, and not all tourists have a cultural motivation. The culturally motivated cultural tourist remains a relatively small segment of the total tourism market, although undoubtedly a very important segment for cultural attractions in Europe.

In Chapter 3 consideration is given to the development of attractions for the cultural visitor market, particularly in the context of the growing 'experience industry'.

## References

Alzua, A., O'Leary, J.T. and Morrison, A.M. (1998) Cultural and heritage tourism: identifying niches for international travelers. *Journal of Tourism Studies* 9, 2–13.

Amsterdams Uit Buro (1996) *Appreciating the Arts: the Social and Economic Significance of the Professional Arts for Amsterdam.* Amsterdams Uit Buro, Amsterdam.

Bodo, C. and Fisher, R. (1997) *New Frontiers for Employment in Europe: the Heritage, the Arts and Communication as a Laboratory for New Ideas.* CIRCLE Publication No. 9, CIRCLE, Rome.

Bywater, M. (1993) The market for cultural tourism in Europe. *Travel and Tourism Analyst* No. 6, 30–46.

Davies, A. and Prentice, R. (1995) Conceptualizing the latent visitor to heritage attractions. *Tourism Management* 16, 491–500.

Davies, S. (1994) *By Popular Demand: a Strategic Analysis of the Market.* MGC, London.

European Commission (1998) *The Europeans on Holiday.* DGXXIII, Brussels.

EUROSTAT (1995) *European Labour Force Survey 1994.* EUROSTAT, Luxembourg.

Fodness, D. (1994) Measuring tourist motivation. *Annals of Tourism Research* 21, 555–581.

Formica, S. and Uysal, M. (1998) Market segmentation of an international cultural-historical event in Italy. *Journal of Travel Research* 36, 16–24.

Ganzeboom, H. and Ranshuysen, L. (1994) *Handleiding Publieksonderzoek Culturele Instellingen.* Boekmanstichting, Amsterdam.

Getz, D. (1991) *Festivals, Special Events, and Tourism.* Van Nostrand Reinhold, New York.

Goedhart, S. (1997) 'New producers' in cultuurtoerisme. MA thesis, Tilburg University.

Green, M. (1998) Urban heritage tourism: the global-local dialectic. A cross-national comparative study of Tilburg, Bilbao and Leicester. MA thesis, Programme in European Leisure Studies, Tilburg University.

Herrijgers, C. (1998) De culturele stedenreis. MA Thesis, Tilburg University.

Irish Tourist Board (1988) *Inventory of Cultural Tourism Resources in the Member States and Assessment of Methods Used to Promote Them.* European Commission DG VII, Brussels.

Jung, B. (1994) For what leisure? The role of culture and recreation in post-communist Poland. *Leisure Studies* 13, 262–276.

Kirchberg, V. (1996) Museum visitors and non-visitors in Germany: a representative survey. *Poetics* 24, 239–258.

Leiper, N. (1990) Tourist attraction systems. *Annals of Tourism Research* 17, 367–384.

Light, D. and Prentice, R.C. (1994) Market-based product development in heritage tourism. *Tourism Management* 15, 27–35.

Merriman, N. (1991) *Beyond the Glass Case: the Past, the Heritage and the Public in Britain.* Leicester University Press, Leicester.

Mintel (1993) Cultural visits. *Leisure Intelligence* 3, 1–28.

Moscardo, G. (1999) *Making Visitors Mindful: Principles for Creating Sustainable Visitor Experiences through Effective Communication.* Sagamore Publishing, Champaign, Illinois.

Museums and Galleries Commission (1999) *International Visitors to UK Museums and Galleries: an Analysis of the Museum Perspective.* MGC, London.

Prentice, R.C. (1993) *Tourism and Heritage Attractions.* Routledge, London.

Richards, G. (1996a) Skilled consumption and UK ski holidays. *Tourism Management* 17, 25–34.

Richards, G. (1996b) *Cultural Tourism in Europe*. CAB International, Wallingford, UK.

Richards, G. (1998a) Cultural tourism in Europe: recent developments. In: Grande Ibarra, J. (ed.) *Actas del Congreso Europeo sobre Itinereos y Rutas Temáticas*. Fundación Caja Rioja, Logroño, pp. 105–113.

Richards, G. (1998b) Time for a holiday? Social rights and international tourism consumption. *Time and Society* 7, 145–160.

Richards, G. (1999) Heritage visitor attractions in Europe: a visitor profile. *Interpretation* 4(3), 9–13.

Richards, G. (2000) The European cultural capital event: strategic weapon in the cultural arms race? *International Journal of Cultural Policy* 6, 159–189.

Robinson, M. and Boniface, P. (1999) *Tourism and Cultural Conflicts*. CAB International, Wallingford, UK.

Roetman, E.E. (1994) Motivatie in Retrospectief: een onderzoek naar motivatie voor cultuurtoerisme tijdens de Mondriaantentoonstelling te Amsterdam. MA dissertation, Tilburg University.

Silberberg, T. (1995) Cultural tourism and business opportunity for museum and heritage sites. *Tourism Management* 16, 361–365.

Travel Industry Association (1997) *Historical and Cultural Activities Report*. Travel Industry Association, Washington, DC.

van der Borg, J. (1994) Demand for city tourism in Europe: tour operators' catalogues. *Tourism Management* 15, 66–69.

van der Borg, J., Costa, P. and Gotti, G. (1996) Tourism in European heritage cities. *Annals of Tourism Research* 23, 306–321.

van Elderen, P.L. (1997) *Suddenly One Summer: a Sociological Portrait of the Joensuu Festival*. Joensuu University Press, Joensuu.

van 't Riet, S. (1995) Back to Basics: an analysis of tourist motivations for visiting cultural attractions. MA thesis, Programme in European Leisure Studies, Tilburg University.

Veal, A.J. (1992) *Research Methods for Leisure and Tourism: Practical Guide*. Longman, London.

# The Experience Industry and the Creation of Attractions

## Greg Richards

*Tilburg University, Department of Leisure Studies, Tilburg, The Netherlands*

The recognition of culture as an important motivation for tourism has stimulated a significant increase in the supply of cultural attractions. The growth in the number of cultural attractions is also part of a wider trend towards the production of experiences for consumers. The most important motivation for visiting cultural sites is 'to experience new things', and the growth in cultural visitation can be interpreted as an attempt to satisfy the 'experience hunger' which characterizes late modern society (de Cauter, 1996). Culture is arguably the most important raw material for the creation of experiences. As MacCannell (1976) notes, 'leisure is constructed from cultural experiences' (1976, p. 34) and 'cultural experiences are valued in-themselves and are the ultimate deposit of values, including economic values in modern society' (1976, p. 28). Creating cultural experiences, and particularly cultural attractions has therefore become a fundamental part of modern societies. This chapter analyses the changing nature of attractions, and examines their role in the experience economy.

## The Experience Economy

Services are dead – long live experiences. In their analysis of the evolution of the production process, Pine and Gilmore (1999) argue that the economy has gone through a transition from extracting commodities to making goods, delivering services and currently staging experiences as the primary arena of value creation. They argue that experiences are an economic offer distinct from services. Whereas services are delivered, experiences must be staged in a way which engages the customer to create a memorable event. Experiences are personal, and therefore no two individuals can have the same experience.

There is a growing number of examples of experiences being created to market products. In the case of the Niketown store chain, for example, Nike is creating an experience around its products which builds brand image and stimulates sales at other stores. In the experience economy, however, business will have to start charging for the experience they offer, rather than the services and products they sell. This may mean shopping malls charging an entry fee, for example. This inversion of the logic of the service economy will focus the minds of attraction managers on the experiences they offer – if the experience is not worth the admission fee, the customers will go elsewhere.

However, Pine and Gilmore's economic view of experiences has limitations. If an experience only becomes an experience if it is charged for, this means that the free goods that characterize the bulk of tourism consumption (such as most natural environments, many museums, cityscapes, etc.) do not offer experiences. In fact the experience is created by the visitor interacting with the offer – putting a price on the 'experience' simply tends to alter the perception of the economic value of the experience. But many experiences are beyond price, and may be extremely difficult to charge for. This does not reduce their value to the visitor, however. In fact, there may well be an opposite effect, as the most valuable and memorable experiences are often those which are unplanned and unexpected. It is likely that the perceived value of impromptu experiences in heterogeneous tourist spaces is often higher than those controlled experiences staged by the tourist industry in enclavic spaces (Edensor, 1998).

Whether we take a narrow economic view of experiences or a wider socio-economic view, there is little doubt that the growth of the experience economy can be linked to the increasingly experience hungry consumer, because as MacCannell (1976) notes the 'emerging modern mind is bent on expanding its repertoire of experiences'. Tourists, and particularly cultural tourists, play a major role in the development of the experience economy. This is largely due to '(T)he stridency with which many tourists have been willing to assert, or just assume, their right to experience' (Phipps, 1999, p. 75). 'Experience is an elusive quality which, regardless of its intangibility, is a powerful rationale for some of the otherwise inexplicably strange and dangerous pursuits of contemporary tourism, from bungee jumping to "disaster tours"' (Phipps, 1999, p. 79).

Entire tourist destinations are beginning to position themselves as 'experiences' in order to meet such demands. Britain, for example, is using the new-found popularity of 'Cool Britannia' to re-position itself as a country which offers 'a variety of experiences' as the British Tourist Authority *Annual Report* for 1998 is entitled. As the report says, 'visitors are discovering that Britain offers unique variety and real value for money. In this country they can encounter the traditional and experience the contemporary among some of the friendliest and most creative people in the world' (British Tourist Authority, 1998).

## The Emerging Experience Sector

Some of the fastest growing sectors of the global economy are related to the consumption of experiences. In addition to the widely cited rapid growth of the Internet, entertainment and tourism have been at the forefront of the development of the experience economy. In the UK car hire (+172%), novelties and souvenirs (+109%), cinema admissions (+94%) and photographic goods (+92%) have been among the major growth areas in consumer spending in the last decade (Advertising Association, 1999). Tourist attractions are also repackaging themselves as experiences, as the development of the 'White Cliffs Experience' in Dover and the 'Tower Bridge Experience' in London attest. In the experience sector, the emphasis of attractions changes from the physical resource to the 'story' attached to the attraction, or which can be created around the attraction.

Although the creation of experiences is often conceptualized as an activity of the commercial sector, much of the experience creation that is happening at present is driven by a desire of public authorities to develop the productive resources of their regions, particularly as traditional sources of income decline. The creation of cultural experiences has therefore become central to regional development strategies in Europe.

The attempt by policy makers to '(re)valorize place through its cultural identity' in the face of increasing globalization and economic integration is defined by Ray (1998) as the 'culture economy' approach to development. The idea of a culture economy stems from three sources: the changing nature of post-industrial, consumer capitalism; economic development policies; and the growth of regionalism as a global phenomenon. Culture has become a crucial resource in the post-industrial economy, as reflected in the use of cultural heritage in the development strategies of the European Union and other bodies, and culture is increasingly used by regions as a means of preserving their cultural identity and developing their 'socio-economic vibrancy' (Ray, 1998, p. 5).

In developing their cultural capital, regions mirror the efforts of entrepreneurs to capitalize on the intellectual property associated with their products – except that the intellectual property, or cultural capital is tied up in a particular location, effectively acting as a counterweight to the footloose existence of financial capital.

The attempts of regions to develop their local knowledge as a form of 'intellectual property' and cultural competitive advantage are however threatened by the tendency for such local knowledge to become incorporated into global systems of value creation. The consumer society is constantly searching for signs and symbols to valorize into commodities. As George Ritzer (1999) has argued, modern consumer society is characterized by a concentration on the 'means of consumption', which are stimulated in a 'dizzying proliferation of settings' which he terms the 'cathedrals of consumption'. The cathedrals of consumption include fast food restaurants, department stores, shopping malls, casinos, theme parks and 'eatertainment'. The cathedrals of consumption 'have an enchanted, sometimes even sacred, religious character for many people. In order to attract ever-larger numbers of consumers, such cathedrals of consumption need to offer, or at least appear to offer, increasingly magical, fantastic, and enchanted settings in which to consume' (Ritzer, 1999, p. 8).

The modern need for 'enchantment' is increasingly being met by culture, which is woven into the cathedrals of consumption through theming and storytelling – linking the local knowledge identified by Ray with the cultural needs of the global consumer (Gottdiener, 1997). The problem facing the cultural policy makers, therefore, is how to valorize the cultural value of local knowledge while at the same time protecting their intellectual property rights which give value to the specific location.

As Zukin (1996, p. 268) points out:

> In materialistic terms, emphasizing culture is a concerted attempt to exploit the uniqueness of fixed capital – monuments, art collections, performance spaces, even shopping streets – accumulated over the past. In this sense, culture is the sum of a city's amenities that enable it to compete for investment and jobs, its 'comparative advantage'.

Because such cultural capital is fixed, the consumer must be brought to the point of consumption. Attracting consumers therefore becomes one of the most important aspects of cultural development strategies. This applies even more strongly to economically deprived areas, since consumers with high spending power generally have to be attracted from elsewhere to stimulate the economy.

In many cities, the aim of attracting visitors appears to have been achieved. In the case of the European Cultural Capital event, for example, visitor numbers have shown significant growth during the cultural year itself, with increased visitor numbers of 12% in Copenhagen (1996) and Stockholm (1998), and a claimed threefold increase in the case of Antwerp (1993) (Richards, 2000a). This growing 'city marketing' emphasis in the role of the Cultural Capital event is arguably a result of the shift in cultural policy focus from educational policies and equality and equity in the 1970s to the new cultural politics of the 1980s which concentrated on 'building cultural capital by increasing access to the arts' (Zimmer and Toepler, 1996).

The cultural visitor, or cultural tourist has therefore become central to the success of cultural development strategies. As Bendixen (1997) points out, cultural tourism is a 'booming industry', which is thought to attract high spending, 'high quality' tourists. The number of tourists attracted is often one of the key indicators used to judge the success or otherwise of the event. But what is it that attracts tourists to particular sites in search of culture? There is a tendency for local policy makers to assume that since every city has its own unique culture, this must be attractive to tourists.

The enchantment of the cathedrals of consumption echoes the use of cultural tourism as a magical doctrine (see Chapter 1, this volume). The enchantment of the consumer is necessary for the spell to work. Creating enchantment is an art which has often been linked to the work of Disney and other 'dream factories'. It was precisely the power of the leisure industry to create such diversions from reality that led the Frankfurt School to identify the cultural industries as the ultimate manipulators of human consciousness. However, today it is not just the commercial leisure industry that uses culture to create experiences designed to lure the consumer. Increasingly the production of experiences is becoming central to the public policy arena as well. In the absence of production-related economic opportunities, both urban and rural areas are turning to the staging of experiences as a means of capturing the spending power of the mobile consumer.

## Experience Production Policies

In their review of European cultural policy, Ellmeier and Rásky (1998) emphasize the major shift that took place in the 1980s, when 'art and culture no longer served the individual or society, but had suddenly become a commodity, an economic product to be sold'. In the terminology of Pine and Gilmore (1999) of course, art and culture had become experiences for which a charge could be levied, and economic value extracted. This was not an activity confined to the commercial sector – as Gerhard Schulze (1992) emphasizes in his analysis of the *Erlebnisgesellschaft*, the economics motive for the development of culture was based on 'public experience production' and the creation of 'public experience amenities'.

Essentially, the production of experiences by the public sector and its commercial sector partners became a major means of combating the economic problems of many regions in Europe. The production of experiences such as festivals and events not only created employment directly by drawing visitors, but also enhanced the 'quality of life' for local residents as well. 'Whether a local authority succeeded in attracting and keeping better-off citizens was consequently also dependent on the public experience amenities, calculated in leisure-time values, that it could guarantee its citizens in the long term' (Schulze, 1992, p. 500). The happy coincidence of attractions for tourists and the economic and cultural benefits these offered to local residents ensured that the previous schism between the interests of tourists and local residents was diminished, and the rhetoric attached to tourism, cultural and leisure developments began to converge.

A large number of European cities have therefore begun to place experience production at the centre of their economic and cultural strategies. Initially it seemed that some cities were content to produce experiences in order to stimulate consumption, but in recent years experience production has been increasingly augmented by measures to stimulate cultural creativity in order to make the experience production system sustainable. Cultural events have been supplemented by Cultural Quarters and other areas in which small-scale cultural production can be encouraged. Attractions based purely on historic cultural production, such as heritage attractions, have been 'put on the back burner' (Boniface, 1998) in favour of creative activities and uses of urban space (Richards, 1999). As Bonink and Hitters show in Chapter 12 of this volume, there is a growing demand for small-scale cultural production spaces in cities such as Amsterdam. Amsterdam has recently adopted a policy of providing 'nursery' spaces for artists, who have often been forced out of their ateliers by commercial development (Wasmoeth, 1999). The local authority has recently decided to invest Fl 50 million (€23 million) in the provision of such spaces.

In effect, new experience production policies are beginning to treat the city as a stage on which experiences can be created. A whole range of spaces within the city, ranging from prescribed venues such as theatres to unbounded and impromptu stages fashioned from the city streets and open spaces, are beginning to be used as cultural production centres. The city becomes a stage, and the cultural life and everyday life of the city are developed into one extended festival. This 'festivalisation' process (van Elderen, 1997) is perhaps most clearly developed in cities which have a combination of a critical mass of real cultural capital and significant cultural production capacity.

Edinburgh is a prime example of the development of a city as stage. Edinburgh has the largest and longest running festival in the UK, but it has also used the Festival as a springboard to develop other events and attractions. The popularity of the Festival stems from the wide range of events held and the historic city centre which forms a backcloth to the Festival activities. In recent years, however, the previous 'high culture' image of the city as the cultural capital of Scotland has begun to change as more elements of popular culture have become associated with the image of Edinburgh. One example is the film *Trainspotting*, which has led to proposals for a 'Trainspotting Trail' in the city. In addition some of the 'villages' in the city, such as Leith and Portobello are being developed in terms of what Howie (2000) has called 'grey area' tourism, centred on the everyday life of the neighbourhoods and their inhabitants. The centre of the city has also been literally developed as a stage for the annual Hogmanay festival on New Year's Eve. The increasing popularity of the event saw the centre of the city being closed off, with ticket holders only being admitted. Although tickets for the event were distributed free to local residents, there was dissatisfaction among those unable to get tickets to celebrate the festival in their own city centre.

The considerable economic success of the Edinburgh Festival and other event-related initiatives in the city has stimulated others to adopt event-led development and marketing strategies. In the case of Glasgow, Leslie (Chapter 6, this volume) shows that such a 'second city' can successfully attract visitors by developing cultural events and attractions, although it is not always the traditional cultural attractions (for example museums) that benefit from increased visitor numbers (Richards, 2000a). Rotterdam, in a similar situation to Glasgow, has also adopted a culture-orientated experience development policy. Just like Glasgow before it, Rotterdam will host the European Cultural Capital event in 2001, and is hoping that this will attract even more visitors and improve the image of the city still further.

The weakness of Rotterdam has been its relatively poor supply of traditional cultural facilities, particularly on an international level, compared with cities such as Amsterdam. Rotterdam has therefore decided to project an image of being a modern art city, using its futuristic architecture as a spearhead for the campaign. Product developments undertaken in relation to cultural tourism include the opening of the National Architecture Museum and the Kunsthal, a gallery of modern art designed by Rem Koolhaas.

The event-led strategy of the city has been very successful in generating visits to Rotterdam. The number of event visitors in Rotterdam grew from less than 2 million in 1989 to almost 4 million in 1996, which was the highest rate of attraction growth achieved by a major city during this period (Bonink and Richards, 1997). This policy has been pursued further through the designation of Rotterdam as European Cultural Capital for 2001. The event is being used 'to show all inhabitants of the city, of the Netherlands, Europe and the rest of the world that Rotterdam is an unlimited, enterprising and unique city when it comes to culture in the broadest sense of the word'. The basic theme is that Rotterdam is many cities, including a pleasure city, a city of the senses, a transparent city and a cosmopolitan city.

However, experience production strategies based on cultural events do not always deliver long-term economic or cultural benefits, as Richards (2000a) has shown. The European Cultural Capital year has had a mixed effect on visitor numbers. Some cities have experienced significant rises in overnight visitors, but there have also been cases where the number of visitors has actually declined. The Cultural Capital event itself does not therefore necessarily lead to a long-term increase in staying visitors. The event is far more likely to produce a growth in day visitors, as recent events have shown. In Antwerp, for example, the increase in staying visitors was just over 10% in 1993, but the growth in total visitor numbers was estimated to be 218%. Although day visitors do generate economic benefits, these are far lower than for staying visitors. For example, the economic impact study for Glasgow indicated that only 20% of the economic impact of the event derived from day visitors (Myerscough, 1991).

It seems that events such as the Cultural Capital event are in themselves not enough to guarantee success in the highly competitive European cultural tourism market. Isolated events will generate short-term benefits, but in order to ensure long-term success the event needs to be integrated into a total cultural strategy. This can involve staging a series of events, in order to convince visitors that there is always 'something happening' in the city. This harbours the danger, however, that the city will become trapped on a treadmill of investment, requiring a constant supply of events to ensure the visitor flow. It should be much more effective to combine event based and attraction based strategies, as Glasgow has done. This can help to attract short-term attention to the city, at the same time as new cultural facilities are being developed to increase the 'real cultural capital' base of the city in the long term.

## Experience Factories – the Growth of Museums

Developing the real cultural capital of places usually involves the creation of amenities where cultural production and products can be displayed. This is often being provided by the growth of museums and other attractions, as described in Chapter 1 (this volume). The development of cultural attractions in general, and museums in particular has become a cornerstone of experience production policies. Museums play a particularly important role because they function as 'factories of meaning', developing cultural experiences for their visitors (Rooijakkers, 1999).

All over Europe there has been a veritable museum explosion. Germany in particular has led the way, with major cities such as Munich, Cologne, Stuttgart and Frankfurt competing with each other to develop the most sensational new museums. In Frankfurt 11 new museums have been built since 1983 (van Aalst, 1999). Not just the major cultural centres of Europe have been developing new museums. Some of the most notable new developments have been in relatively peripheral locations. In The Netherlands, for example, the most notable new museums in recent years have been the Groninger Museum in Groningen, designed by Alessandro Mendini and Aldo Rossi's Bonnefanten Museum in Maastricht (see Munsters, Chapter 5, this volume). The fact that these new developments are characterized by their dramatic architecture underlines the point that the content of such museums is no longer so important as the total experience offered by the combination of architecture, design and art.

Nowhere is this more obvious than in the development of the Guggenheim Museum in Bilbao. Frank Gehry's futuristic titanium-coated spacecraft which appears to have crashed into the centre of Spain's largest port cost almost €150 million to build, and was stocked with Guggenheim artworks for a further €25 million. The most dramatic thing about the museum is undoubtedly the building, which is now being widely promoted as a destination for architectural tourism in Spain. The futuristic look of the Guggenheim also gives Bilbao an image, which is becoming increasingly important in a postmodern world concerned with appearances, design and aesthetic value. Plaza (1999) argues that the non-reproducible Guggenheim building become a space for the elaboration of reproducible art, which in turn reinforces its image. Because reproducible art has economies of scale that are lacking in the production of the unique artworks displayed in the building and represented by the building itself, the reproduction of images associated with the museum is important in boosting the image of the city:

> Reproducible art consumption is highly addictive and, in this case, reinforces addiction to the Guggenheim-Bilbao museum, a non-reproducible artistic artefact . . . In other words, the diffusion of images of Frank Gehry's virtuoso architecture through reproducible art (printed and audiovisuals) is increasing addiction, which in turn is attracting more visitors (Plaza, 1999, p. 591).

The Guggenheim has certainly been successful in boosting visitor numbers to Bilbao. Spanish visitors from outside the Basque country increased by 20% in the first year of operation, and foreign visitors increased by 43% (Plaza, 1999). A total of almost 1.6 million visits were made to the museum between October 1997 and December 1998, and 1 million visits were recorded in 1999. The total economic impact of the museum since its opening is estimated to be ptas 72 billion (€430 million). Almost half of the total visits were made by foreign visitors, particularly from France, America and the UK (Anon., 2000).

Many other European regions have constructed museums and heritage attractions as a means of attracting visitors to less favoured locations. Many of these attractions are based on local culture but there have also been deliberate attempts to spread national cultural attractions to generate new visitor flows. In the UK, for example, outposts of the Tate Gallery have been developed in Liverpool and in St Ives, Cornwall. While some of these ventures have been successful, there have also been spectacular failures, such as the Royal Armouries Museum in Leeds. Purpose-built to house the armouries collection from the Tower of London, the museum was forecast to attract 1 million visitors a year. In fact, the visitor numbers have remained at a quarter of this level, and the museum has accumulated losses of £20 million (€31 million).

One of the problems for the Guggenheim and other similar regional developments is that they must function as largely isolated 'cathedrals of consumption'. In established cultural capitals, such as London and Paris, for example, the already rich and varied supply of museums and other cultural attractions is still being augmented. In addition to the 'must see' sights that draw tourists in the first place, these cities have innumerable other cultural attractions and most importantly a healthy dose of 'atmosphere' for visitors to experience. The wealth of experience that these traditional cultural capitals can offer is therefore far greater than their new competitors. Recent results from the European Association for Tourism and Leisure Education research indicate, however, that the newcomers, such as Barcelona, are gaining ground (Richards, 2000b).


## From Cultural Tourism to Creative Tourism

The idea of 'culture' as the main attraction for visitors is rapidly giving way to the idea that 'creativity' is what counts (Smith, 1998). One of the advantages that cities such as Barcelona and Milan enjoy is that they are centres of contemporary creativity and cultural production. The presence of fixed cultural attractions and the process of creation is an important indicator of the shift away from the museums and monuments approach to cultural tourism towards 'creative tourism'. In some respects, as the UNESCO report 'Our Creative Diversity' points out, this shift is bringing us full circle back to the idea of culture as the act of cultivation.

As Zukin points out, culture has demanded and attained more space in the urban economy in recent decades. In the 1990s, however, there was a shift in the use of this cultural space away from consumption towards production and creativity. Consumption of culture is no longer enough to guarantee success – cities must become centres of creative production as well. Creative production attracts enterprises and individuals involved in the cultural sector, generating important multiplier effects in the local economy, and raising the aesthetic value of creative production locations. Cultural production is also attractive because it is associated with dynamism and orientation towards the future, which is important in a climate of change surrounding the new millennium.

The development of creativity also places a location in a better position to generate new and innovative products for the consumer. As Poon (1993) has underlined in her concept of 'new tourism', innovation, new ideas, products and experiences are the order of the day. In Dumazedier's (1967) analysis of leisure experiences, two basic categories of experience can be identified. The more passive form of leisure experiences can be termed 'recreation leisure' which restores or 're-creates' the individual through rest and relaxation. On the other hand, 'creative leisure' brings about a new state by enabling the participant to develop new knowledge, skills and competences. The growth of 'skilled consumption' in modern society means that there is more demand for creative leisure. Creative leisure allows the individual to develop themselves and at the same time distinguish themselves from other consumers through the acquisition of consumption skills. Richards (2000c) has further argued that the growth of creative leisure and the rise of skilled consumption means that heritage tourism and cultural tourism are increasingly being supplemented by the advent of 'creative tourism' (Fig. 3.1).

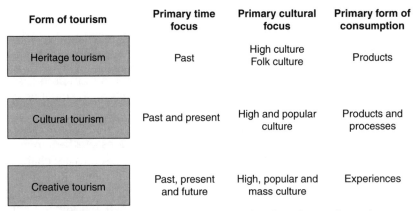

| Form of tourism | Primary time focus | Primary cultural focus | Primary form of consumption |
|---|---|---|---|
| Heritage tourism | Past | High culture Folk culture | Products |
| Cultural tourism | Past and present | High and popular culture | Products and processes |
| Creative tourism | Past, present and future | High, popular and mass culture | Experiences |

**Fig. 3.1.** Characteristics of heritage tourism, cultural tourism and creative tourism. (From Richards, 2000.)

Richards and Raymond (2000) have defined creative tourism as: 'tourism which offers visitors the opportunity to develop their creative potential through active participation in learning experiences which are characteristic of the holiday destination where they are undertaken'.

The key point about creative tourism, therefore, is that the consumption involved is active rather than passive, and is aimed at developing the potential of the individual. In place of the disconnected and disjointed 'experiences' offered by the experience economy, creative leisure and creative tourism offer people the chance to develop personal experience, in the sense of a coherent, cumulative build-up of experience.

Creative tourism is therefore related to self-discovery, but it is also related to discovering the world. Rather than the pre-programmed experiences provided by the tourist industry, creative tourism leaves the individual free to explore their environment in their own way. As Leiper has pointed out, 'some types of touristic experiences may be (more) pleasurable because they involve a tertiary nucleus, something discovered by the individual' (1990, p. 374). Individual freedom and the ability to determine your own role in the tourist performance (Edensor, 1998) is vital to the creative tourism experience.

Creative tourism is therefore about the creation of experiences, and the active involvement of the consumer in the production of those experiences. Holidays which offer tourists the opportunity to engage in some form of creative endeavour are now becoming increasingly common. The Disney Institute, for example, offers a wide range of creative courses to 'knowledge workers' and their families in the US. As well as such major players as Disney, there is also a growing range of specialist tour operators offering holidays involving activities such as painting, drawing, pottery, cooking, music and creative writing.

In the experience economy, passive consumption of cultural services will shift towards more participatory forms of consumption – interaction, learning, doing. This development is already evident in the rapid take-up of interactive interpretation by museums and other cultural attractions, and the increasing development of customized leisure and tourism products. In cultural tourism this is evident in the growth of products for the independent cultural traveller.

There also seems to be some recognition of the shift towards creative tourism in the way in which some cultural attractions are beginning to orientate themselves to their audience. A number of museums are changing their roles from being authoritarian 'factories of meaning' (Rooijakkers, 1999) to being interactive workshops where meaning is generated through co-makership between the museum and its visitors. There is a shift from providing visitors with answers to posing them questions. In the *Verzetsmuseum* (Dutch Resistance Museum) in Amsterdam, for example, a new exhibition installed in 1999 poses visitors the same questions as those faced by people living in The Netherlands during the Nazi occupation: Adapt? Collaborate? Strike? Report? Go into hiding? By placing the visitor in the position of making choices, the complex issues of resistance and collaboration are brought home, and at the same time brought up to date. Similar choices are faced daily by those caught up in modern conflicts around the world. The material culture of the Second World War can in this way be more effectively brought to life (Joke Bosch, personal communication, 2000).

This new approach poses cultural managers with a whole new set of problems. By giving the visitor more leeway to interact with the material being presented, and to generate their own meanings, the choice of perspectives becomes even more difficult. The problem becomes – whose narratives are acceptable? Are all narratives and interpretations equal?

The development of creative tourism is not therefore the easiest option open to cultural attractions and destinations, but nevertheless, creativity is becoming preferred to culture for a number of reasons:

**1.** Creativity can potentially create value more easily because of its scarcity. Creativity is an attribute supposedly possessed by relatively few people, whereas thanks to the broadening concept of 'culture', cultural products are ubiquitous. In the cultural tourism market cultural attractions of themselves no longer function as a means of distinction – every city has museums and monuments. The multiplication of cultural cities in Europe has meant that a new source of distinction had to be found in the 'creative city' (Landry and Bianchini, 1995).

**2.** Creativity allows destinations to innovate new products relatively rapidly, giving them a competitive advantage over other locations.

**3.** Creativity is a process, and creative resources are therefore more sustainable. Whereas physical cultural resources, such as museums and monuments, may wear out over time and become degraded, creative resources are arguably infinitely renewable. This rapid growth of cultural and arts festivals in Europe in recent years underlines this fact.

**4.** Creativity is mobile. Where cultural consumption is dependent on a concentration of cultural resources, creativity can become extremely mobile – arts performances and artworks can today be produced virtually anywhere, without the need for dedicated infrastructure.

These factors have tended to favour the development of creative resources from the supply side. At the same time, tourists themselves are becoming more active, and demanding new and involving experiences. Rapid market growth is evident in activity holidays, special interest holidays, health tourism and spiritual tourism, all of which may be linked to the growth of creative tourism in general. From the point of view of the tourist, they want to have holiday experiences which will change them rather than simply filling them with loose experiences.

Tourism must therefore have an impact on the tourist. There is evidence that cultural tourism is expanding beyond the mere contemplation of cultural objects. The tourist gaze (Urry, 1990), as a passive, contemplative pastime is being replaced by a reflexive stance, in which the tourist is at once the source and the object of the gaze, at once consumer and producer, at once audience and performer. As Mommaas *et al.* (2000) argue, the desire for experience is no longer restricted to the visual gaze, but all senses are now engaged. The tourist gaze has become a total tourist experience. Tourists are not just interested in the sights of modernity, but they want the sounds, smells, tastes and touch of a culture.

The question remains, however, who is going to create these new experiences for the tourist? Although creative tourism implies an active role on the part of the tourist, the tourist usually has to be provided with the cultural raw material to create their own experiences. This is where the role of the cultural producers is crucial, as we will see in the following chapter.

## References

Advertising Association (1999) *Marketing Pocket Book 2000.* NTC Publications, Henley.

Anon. (2000) El Museo Guggenheim, motor económico. *Editur* no. 2094/5, p. 39.

Bendixen, P. (1997) Cultural tourism – economic success at the expense of culture? *Cultural Policy* 4, 21–46.

Boniface, P. (1998) Are museums putting heritage under the domination of the tourist industry? *Nordisk Museologi* 1, 25–32.

Bonink, C. and Richards, G. (1997) Attractiebezoek afgelopen tien jaar fors gestegen. *Recreatie en Toerisme* 7(7), 6–8.

British Tourist Authority (1998) *A Variety of Experiences, Annual Report.* BTA, London.

de Cauter, L. (1996) *De Archeologie van de Kick.* Garant, Leuven.

Dumazedier, J. (1967) *Toward a Society of Leisure.* Free Press, New York.

Edensor, T. (1998) *Tourists at the Taj: Performance and Meaning at a Symbolic Site.* Routledge, London.

Ellmeier, A. and Rásky, B. (1998) *Cultural Policy in Europe – European Cultural Policy?* Österreichische Kulturdokumentation, Internationals Archiv für Kulturanalysen, Vienna.

Gottdiener, M. (1997) *The Theming of America: Dreams, Visions, and Commercial Spaces.* Westview, Boulder, Colorado.

Howie, F. (2000) Establishing the common ground: tourism, ordinary places, grey-areas and environmental quality in Edinburgh, Scotland. In: Richards, G. and Hall, D. (eds) *Tourism and Sustainable Community Development.* Routledge, London, pp. 101–118.

Landry, C. and Bianchini, F. (1995) *The Creative City.* Demos, London.

Leiper, N. (1990) Tourist attraction systems. *Annals of Tourism Research* 17, 367–384.

MacCannell, D. (1976) *The Tourist: a New Theory of the Leisure Class.* Macmillan, London.

Mommaas, H., van den Heuvel, M. and Jansen, J. (2000) *Vrijetijd door Stad en Land: een Studie Naar de Opkomst en Dynamiek van de 'Vrijetijdsindustrie' in Nederland.* SDU, Den Haag.

Myerscough, J. (1991) *Monitoring Glasgow.* Glasgow City Council, Glasgow.

Phipps, P. (1999) Tourists, terrorists, death and value. In: Kaur, R. and Hutnyk, J. (eds) *Travel Worlds: Journeys in Contemporary Cultural Politics.* Zed Books, London, pp. 74–93.

Pine, B.J. and Gilmore, J.H. (1999) *The Experience Economy.* Harvard University Press, Harvard.

Plaza, B. (1999) The Guggenheim-Bilbao Museum effect: a reply to María V. Gómez' 'Reflective images: the case of urban regeneration in Glasgow and Bilbao'. *International Journal of Urban and Regional Research* 23, 589–592.

Poon, A. (1993) *Tourism, Technology and Competitive Strategies.* CAB International, Wallingford, UK.

Ray, C. (1998) Culture, intellectual property and territorial rural development. *Sociologia Ruralis* 38, 3–20.

Richards, G. (1999) European cultural tourism: patterns and prospects. In: Dodd, D. and van Hemel, A.-M. (eds) *Planning European Cultural Tourism.* Boekman Foundation, Amsterdam, pp. 16–32.

Richards, G. (2000a) The European cultural arms race. *International Journal of Cultural Policy* 6, 159–181.

Richards, G. (2000b) Development and evolution of cultural tourism in Europe. Paper presented at the Cultural Tourism Expert Meeting, Barcelona, April 2000.

Richards, G. (2000c) World culture and heritage and tourism. *Tourism Recreation Research* 25(1), 9–18.

Richards, G. and Raymond, C. (2000) Creative tourism. *ATLAS News* No. 23.

Ritzer, G. (1999) *Enchanting a Disenchanted World: Revolutionizing the Means of Consumption.* Pine Forge Press, Thousand Oaks, California.

Rooijakkers, G. (1999) Identity factory southeast towards a flexible cultural leisure infrastructure. In: Dodd, D. and van Hemel, A.-M. (eds) *Planning European Cultural Tourism.* Boekman Foundation, Amsterdam, pp. 101–111.

Schulze, G. (1992) *Die Erlebnisgesellschaft: Kultursoziologie der Gegenwart.* Campus, Frankfurt.

Smith, C. (1998) *Creative Britain*. Faber and Faber, London.

Urry, J. (1990) *The Tourist Gaze: Leisure and Travel in Contemporary Societies*. Sage, London.

van Aalst, I. (1999) Nieuwe musea in de stad: tussen kunst en kitsch. *Agora* June, 8–9.

van Elderen, P.L. (1997) *Suddenly One Summer: a Sociological Portrait of the Joensuu Festival*. Joensuu University Press, Joensuu.

Wasmoeth, H. (1999) Broedplaats Amsterdam: crèche or crash? *Agora* June, 12–13.

Zimmer, A. and Toepler, P. (1996) Cultural policies and the welfare state: the cases of Sweden, Germany and the United States. *Journal of Arts Management, Law and Society* 26, 167–193.

Zukin, S. (1996) *The Cultures of Cities*. Blackwell, Oxford.

# The Cultural Attraction Distribution System

## Greg Richards[1], Saskia Goedhart[2] and Carla Herrijgers[3]

[1]Tilburg University, Department of Leisure Studies, Tilburg, The Netherlands; [2]LA Group, Leisure and Arts Consulting, Amsterdam, The Netherlands; [3]Pelikaan Reizen, Zevenbergen, The Netherlands

Although the cultural production system is busy creating cultural experiences and manufacturing meaning (Rooijakkers, 1999), such growth of attractions can only be sustained by ensuring a continuing flow of visitors. The visitor industry has increased significantly in recent years as tourism has expanded in size and scope. But as the supply of cultural attractions has also grown, all attractions have to work harder to distribute their products to the tourism market. Cultural destinations seeking to attract both domestic and international visitors must increasingly make use of a series of tourism intermediaries, whose function is to distribute their cultural tourism products to potential visitors.

The major intermediaries between cultural attractions and the tourism market are Destination Marketing Organizations (DMOs) and tour operators. DMOs include local, regional and national organizations whose task is to market the destination product to visitors. In Europe such bodies are often public or voluntary sector organizations, usually working in collaboration with commercial sector tourism firms in their region. The basic problem for all such organizations is that they have no direct control over the tourism or cultural products they are trying to market. The product comprises a vast array of heterogeneous services provided by a wide range of different suppliers, usually with very different aims, aspirations and modes of operation. This is certainly true of the development of cultural tourism products, where lack of cultural knowledge on the part of many tourism organizations is matched by a lack of awareness of tourism on the part of many cultural organizations. In fact the attitude of some attractions can be antagonistic, because they do not see their role as catering to tourists.

There is little doubt, however, that DMOs are beginning to use cultural attractions more actively in their tourism marketing strategies. One feature of recent years has been the production of specific brochures promoting cultural attractions in different European countries. For example the Deutsche Zentrale für Tourismus produced a brochure entitled 'Experience Culture 1999', which lists a wide range of cultural events, including the Goethe year, the Weimar Cultural Capital programme, historic festivals and art exhibitions, along with many other events. The British Tourist Authority has bundled a number of cities together under the banner of British Art Cities, which in addition to London, which profiles itself in the brochure as 'the cultural capital of the world' also features cities such as Glasgow, Leeds, Manchester, Bristol and Cardiff. Turespaña, the Spanish tourism promotion agency, also produces a brochure entitled 'Art in Spain' which provides an historical overview of the cultural heritage of the country.

All these brochures attempt to give (potential) visitors an impression of what the destination has to offer the cultural tourist. National and regional tourist offices have an important role to play in creating an image of the cultural tourism product and bringing that to the attention of the visitor. However, these brochures also underline one of the major problems faced by the DMOs in developing cultural tourism. They can rarely give the visitor direct access to the products they are seeking. For information on individual attractions, their programmes or tickets, visitors usually have to approach the attractions directly, or find other intermediaries who can provide access to these services. However, existing cultural distribution systems tend to be geared to the local, or at most national market. International tourists must make use of the same systems that are used by locals. The fragmentation of the cultural attraction market, poor development of distribution channels and the resulting lack of access to cultural products for tourists have been identified as key problems in the European tourism industry.

The current lack of distribution systems is being addressed by a growing number of commercial providers, including ticket brokers, cultural information service providers and tour operators. For example, ArtBase, an international cultural listings company based in Amsterdam, has a database of over 200,000 cultural events at 25,000 cultural venues worldwide. For a large number of these events consumers can book tickets online. ArtBase is now working together with the Dutch tour operator NBBS to develop flexible cultural tourism products which give the consumer the possibility of booking a holiday or weekend break together with the cultural event of their choice. The Art Cities in Europe initiative, launched with 30 cities in 11 countries in the early 1990s, now includes 43 cities in 16 countries. Visitors can book a wide range of events via any travel agency linked to the START ticket reservation system, thanks to the involvement of the German tour operator IfB in the programme.

The increasing interest of tour operators in the cultural market has posed them with a particular problem. Because the products offered by the cultural sector are not specifically tourism products, these have to be adapted to the needs of the tourist. In this respect, it is interesting to investigate whether tour operators are acting merely as distributors of cultural products to tourists, or if they are creating entirely new products.

## Tour Operators and Cultural Tourism

Tour operators have been identified as the vital link between supply and demand in tourism (Ioannides and Debbage, 1997). Tour operators package the different elements of the holiday product and distribute these to the consumer, either directly or through the retail trade. Although tour operators do not provide the majority of holidays in Europe, they account for a sizeable proportion of the market in the major generating countries, and exert a substantial influence on the market as a whole. The development of new destinations by tour operators can provide a market for new airline routes, for example, which can open those destinations up to individual travellers as well. Tour operators are also increasingly moving away from their image as inflexible providers of standardized, Fordist tourism products. Recent years have seen a substantial growth of small specialist tour operators offering more flexible products, and this has in turn forced the larger companies to increase their range of products as well, particularly through mass customization.

Tour operators have played a role in the development of cultural attractions since Thomas Cook began taking groups of tourists to Egypt and the Middle East in the 1860s. The British middle classes were eager to see the treasures of antiquity being unearthed by archaeologists in the region at that time (Swinglehurst, 1982). Although tour operators have continued to distribute cultural products since that time, the explosion of mass tourism from the 1960s onwards tended to dwarf the relatively specialist cultural tourism market. Specialist cultural tour operators began to emerge in the 1950s, particularly in the German-speaking countries and The Netherlands. As Roth and Langemeyer (1996) indicate in their case study of Studiosus, currently Germany's largest specialist cultural tour operator, these companies catered for a small and exclusive market. The emphasis was on tours to classical destinations, such as Italy and Greece. This product emphasis is illustrated by the name of the oldest specialist in The Netherlands, Antieke Wereld, which like Studiosus was formed in 1954.

It was only in the 1990s that mass-market tour operators really began to pay attention to the expanding cultural tourism market. In particular, the extension of information technology allowed major tour operators to engage in the mass customization of products, including cultural attractions and events. As the mass-market operators began to identify the cultural tourism market as potentially profitable, they began to move into the niche formerly occupied by the small specialist companies. Initially these developments were limited to the production of city break programmes, which provided little more than the chance to visit cultural destinations relatively cheaply. More recently, however, the city break products have been enhanced by the addition of specific cultural elements, such as visits to art exhibitions, the theatre, musicals and opera. Some major operators have also begun to produce specific brochures related to cultural events, such as TUI in Germany.

In spite of the entry of the larger players in the market, specialist operators have continued to grow and prosper. The leading German cultural tourism specialist Studiosus, for example, has increased its client numbers from 50,000 clients in 1988 to almost 100,000 in 1999.

The role of tour operators in developing the cultural tourism market has been the object of specific studies carried out under the European Association for Tourism and Leisure Education (ATLAS) Cultural Tourism Research Project in recent years. These studies have covered the role of specialist tour operators (Goedhart, 1997) and the relationship between specialist operators and mass market tour operators (Herrijgers, 1998).

Saskia Goedhart's analysis of the role of cultural intermediaries in the production of cultural tourism experiences is based on the work of Bourdieu (1984) and Zukin (1996). Both of these authors identify key groups within the new middle classes who are crucial to the cultural production process. According to Bourdieu, the 'new petite bourgeoisie' attempt to increase their economic capital through valorizing their cultural knowledge. This is no longer possible through the traditional high cultural channels, so they seek new areas in which their cultural capital can be legitimized. One of the areas in which this has happened is tourism. Through the professionalization of tourist consumption processes the 'new petite bourgeoisie' tries to create economic opportunities for itself.

In this role the 'new petite bourgeoisie' can be referred to as the 'new cultural intermediaries' because they fulfil the role of intermediary between the producers and consumers of art and culture. This is not simply a transmission role, but also involves the transformation of the dispositions of the old 'petite bourgeoisie' by dictating the 'taste' of cultural consumers. Zukin (1996) refers to the same group as the 'critical infrastructure', whose function is to transmit information over new cultural goods and services. The critical function of these cultural intermediaries can influence both the supply of cultural services and at the same time make the audience self-conscious of their own consumption. Their critique allows the consumer to choose more easily the valuable elements of culture out of the growing stream of mass produced and mass distributed cultural offerings. This enables consumers to distinguish themselves from others, not just through the consumption of elite culture, but also in the way in which they use popular culture and mass culture. The need for distinction is at the root of the modern class struggle, as it forms the means to raise one's social position relative to other class factions.

The need for distinction means that as soon as the new cultural products are discovered by the mass of consumers they lose their distinctive value, and the new cultural intermediaries need to maintain their cultural leadership by generating new ones. In this way, Bourdieu argues, there is a competitive search for newer, rarer and more distinctive cultural products. The critical infrastructure assumes a key position in this process because they offer the consumer the means of decoding the cultural value of different forms of cultural consumption.

The new cultural intermediaries therefore exercise a great influence on the taste and behaviour of others. These are the people who according to Richards (1996) possess the necessary skills and cultural competence to develop products for the new middle class consumer. In cultural tourism it seems that similar processes are at work to those described by Munt (1994) in the context of tourism in developing countries. Munt argues that the new middle class has appropriated a number of tourism practices in order to distinguish themselves from tourists from other social classes. Munt recognizes the advent of 'the Other postmodern tourism' as a reaction to tourism that is characterized by hyperreality and simulation. The Other postmodern tourism comprises individualized products compiled by specialized producers with a postmodern de-differentiation between elements such as tourism, sport, archaeology, ecology and anthropology, and increasing combination of work and leisure. Munt argues that the new middle class fulfils an important role as both consumer and producer of these products. Through both the production and consumption roles the new middle class can achieve distinction and secure their social position. Urry (1990) also maintains that this process also affects tourist destinations: certain destinations are visited not only because they offer a higher quality of tourism product, but also because of the status that visiting them confers on the visitor. As soon as such destinations are discovered by the mass market, however, they lose their distinctive power and the elite tourists must seek new destinations.

The search for new destinations is influenced by the fact that cultural capital also has a spatial component (Zukin, 1996). Unique architecture, historic buildings and monuments or important cultural venues are all spatial representations of cultural capital that give specific locations a symbolic value. According to Zukin these cultural features constitute the 'real cultural capital' of a location, which in turn can shape the lifestyle and cultural consumption of its inhabitants. The new cultural intermediaries can utilize the real cultural capital present in cities by living or establishing businesses in locations high in real cultural capital. Therefore, Goedhart (1997) argues, the 'new producers' often live in the cultural or historic centres of European cities. These locations not only support the lifestyle of the new producers by offering a wide range of cultural consumption opportunities, but the location itself becomes an important element of that lifestyle. Goedhart's research in Amsterdam posed the question – to what extent can the new producers be identified in the field of cultural tourism? Related to this central question are issues surrounding the lifestyle choices of the new producers. What role does the consumption and production of cultural attractions play in the lifestyle of the new producers? How far can their cultural productive and consumptive activities be distinguished from one another, and what influence does such activity have on the behaviour of other cultural tourists?

The research adopted both quantitative and qualitative methodologies. Depth interviews were conducted with people who could be regarded as 'new producers'. The six interviewees worked for various organizations directly or indirectly related to cultural tourism. These included two specialist cultural tour operators, a guide lecturer on cultural tours, two journalists writing about cultural tourism and a museum director. The new producers were identified on the basis of their lifestyle, occupational profile and area of residence. The quantitative element of the research consisted of two surveys. The first was a postal survey undertaken among a group of 60 new producers, identified in the same way as the interviewees. The second was administered via personal interviews with 250 cultural tourists visiting the Van Gogh Museum in Amsterdam. Both surveys contained a number of common questions to allow direct comparison between the two survey groups. In the following summary of the research, the letters in brackets refer to the individuals interviewed.

## The production of cultural tourism: the 'work' of the new producers

The interviewees indicated that it is difficult to find work in the traditional cultural sector. One of the respondents who could not find work in the sector made an explicit link between this and his decision to establish a cultural tour company:

> Two of us established the company. The company was started partly to create work for ourselves and also for other art historians, because it is very difficult to find work in the cultural sector and we wanted to increase the possibilities. What we had in mind ideally was to make use of our specialist knowledge and to find work in our sector. That is very difficult in the current market. There just isn't any work. People who have a job just sit tight. The art history world is completely blocked up – you just can't find work as an art historian any more . . . that is basically why we started (A).

Creating work for themselves was the primary motivation for the interviewees working with cultural tour operators. In addition to work, the combination of culture and travel in their lifestyle was also an important reason to start a tour operation:

> I loved travel, in fact it was a sort of hobby gone wild. Actually it seemed like a nice lifestyle to me. And that's true, you work between business and culture, you travel a lot, you meet lots of different people in different situations and you come across things that you otherwise wouldn't experience. It's a rich life (F).

It is the cultural capital that these two interviewees possess that enabled them to professionalize their knowledge through cultural tourism. However, all the interviewees were able to use their cultural and social capital as an information source for their work. Most had an art history, history or archaeology education. In addition, the consumption of cultural tourism is increasingly accepted as a valuable form of cultural capital and a means of expanding your own cultural competence. The interviewees gained ideas from their own holidays that were used to further develop their products. Their tourism consumption thus becomes a means of production.

The choice of a holiday destination, or the decision to develop a destination as a cultural product is based on a combination of cognitive and affective factors. Personal feelings are particularly important in the decision to feature a particular destination or activity in a tourism programme. The destinations that appeal personally to the interviewees tend to be the first destinations to be featured in their products:

> [the destinations] are dependent on personal preferences, mine in particular. And that is based on a sort of 'instinct' that the client also needs (A).
>
> I was recently in Budapest. I raced through all twelve museums in one day. And then I know exactly which ones I want and which ones I don't. For example the Museum of Applied Art is housed in a very beautiful building, has a wonderful East European atmosphere, and that I will use. There are other art museums where the collection isn't great and the museum is stuffy. That isn't really interesting – so I dump it. A Franz Liszt Academy with a small, stuffy, but great museum is however very interesting, because it is charming, because it touches you or it has something beautiful (F).

The activities during a cultural tour are mainly linked to high culture. Sometimes popular culture elements are also included, such as a visit to a market or a camel ride. Through the specialist guides that the cultural tour operators offer, they can distinguish themselves from other tour operators who offer the same countries or destinations. One of the interviewees indicated that because the tourists experience popular culture activities in their other holidays they want their cultural holidays to have 'very cultural activities':

> I shouldn't say this, but it is becoming more and more a cafeteria, it is eclectic. The people who go with us to St Petersburg, they also go to Ibiza for a week to chill out and eat well, and then they go to France for two weeks to visit some museums, but they'll take the tent. They are increasingly . . . yes, how can I put it? Yes, postmodern tourists (F).

It seems that the new cultural producers are aware that they are dealing with an increasingly culturally omnivorous market. As Bonink and Hitters indicate in Chapter 12 of this volume, the distinctions between 'high' and 'popular' culture are becoming increasingly vague, and consumers switch increasingly easily between the two. Learned codes of cultural behaviour therefore become less important in consumption choices, and the arbiters of taste and fashion, such as the media and tour operators, become increasingly important. The choices made by the new producers in the selection of products grow in importance as well.

Some of the interviewees were aware that subjective choices are sometimes made in assembling a cultural tour, a brochure or articles for a newspaper. However, particularly those involved in writing brochure descriptions or newspaper articles try to be as objective as possible. This sometimes conflicts with their own preferences:

> Sometimes you have to send people to places where you would rather not have them. I don't put my favourite little restaurant in the guide book – otherwise next time you go their will be 30 Dutch tourists there. You don't want that (C).

Finding 'authentic' places is therefore crucial for the new producers because authentic experiences provide some compensation for their lack of economic capital (Munt, 1994, p. 108). Knowing where to find authentic places or activities makes the cultural producer a specialist and also offers the possibility to distinguish themselves from other tourists or tour organizers. If they describe these places in their brochure or in an article, however, this can mean that more tourists go there, that other tour operators decide to feature the destination, which then loses its distinctive qualities. The most valuable experiences are those which the tour operator has sole rights to. For example the Spanish specialist Iverus has just signed a deal with the Archbishop of Barcelona giving the company unique access to the 14th century cloisters of Sant Anna. This delivers a strong spatial claim, because of the exclusivity that this tour operator has. Privileged access to 'backstage' areas has a powerful symbolic value, particularly in view of the tourists' desire for authentic experiences.

Not every tour operator is able to transform their vision of culture into a spatial claim. The ability to make such a claim rests with the cultural capital required to construct a vision of what a 'good' cultural tour should contain, and the knowledge of the tour operator of what places are interesting to visit and why. This also requires social capital because the producer needs access to a network of contacts to make their vision a reality.

## Leisure and tourism as part of a cultural lifestyle

Culture has an important place in the lifestyle of the interviewees. Their work and their leisure and tourism consumption are infused with culture. One of the interviewees even indicated that almost all the activities that they undertook were related to culture in some way, and to art history in particular. This was also the case for their leisure time. The idea of a life drenched with culture was also a reason for one of the interviewees to look for other hobbies. About these leisure activities that were not related to culture he said:

And that has the consequence that in my private life I am also concerned with art, because it is my whole life. It is just everywhere, it is automatic actually. It is just second nature to me. But if you look at what you do in your own time, would you visit all the exhibitions as well? I would like to do that, but I don't have the energy. You're just busy with it all day, and that is great, but I can't face going to an exhibition in the weekend as well. It happens sometimes, but less than I would like. But that's because I can't face it. I work on the car . . . I want to do something else. So the need is there but I can't combine it with my work any more (A).

Another interviewee indicated that they had reached a similar saturation point: in his leisure time he didn't visit many museums because he did that frequently for work. The saturation point seemed to be quite high, however, because he immediately named three exhibitions he was planning to visit in the near future during his leisure time. The other interviewees had other activities in addition to their cultural consumption, such as gardening, watching TV or going to the pub. But they don't see this as a deliberate attempt to do something uncultural.

All six interviewees indicated that they undertake cultural activities in their leisure time, but they don't perceive themselves as frequent cultural consumers. This is remarkable in view of the fact that three of them were planning to visit at least one exhibition the following week. Other cultural activities undertaken included visits to museums, concerts, the opera or the cinema. Two indicated that they went to a concert at least once a month and all six visit a museum a few times a year. In comparison with the average cultural consumption in The Netherlands, the new producers are relatively frequent cultural consumers. Only 6% of the Dutch population visits a museum more than four times a year (de Haan, 1997).

It seems that they gauge their own cultural consumption not with reference to the average cultural visitor, but to members of their peer group – other cultural producers. They have a 'habitus' in which culture is highly valued and is almost taken for granted. They move in a cultural field where culture is a source of power.

In this field, leisure time is in any case in short supply. Most of the interviewees said that they were pressured for time in general, and that they had very little leisure time. One commented 'I don't have leisure time'. When asked what they did in their leisure time during the week, the reaction was an uncomprehending 'during the week?', as if the question of having leisure time other than at the weekend had never occurred to them.

The holidays of the interviewees were similar to their leisure time – rest and cultural activities were central. The most common form of long annual holiday was a combination of rest, sunbathing, swimming and culture. Cultural activities were usually of secondary importance to rest and relaxation. Two of the interviewees didn't fit this pattern, however, because they indicated that they soon got tired of the beach, and that cultural activities were therefore very important. Short holidays are mainly weekend trips abroad, often to a specific exhibition, or combined with a longer work trip. These trips are often seen as 'cultural holidays', and usually consist of a mixture of activities such as museum visits, trips to markets and café terraces. The survey results indicate that the 'new producers' undertake far more activities during their cultural trips than other cultural tourists. Their activities also exhibit more diversity, and are more likely to be related to city trips. City trips in particular are suitable for the combination of different cultural and non-cultural activities.

In addition to holidays abroad, the interviewees all travel several times a year for work, for example to prepare or lead cultural tours. As a result of work pressure, one of the interviewees had not taken a holiday in the previous 2 years, although he travelled at least once a month for his work.

## Cities as cultural destinations

The new producers were asked to compile a list of their top five cultural destinations. Rome, Paris, London and Berlin were named by almost all respondents. Rome is the most popular city, and for many was the natural choice as the most important cultural destination in Europe. 'Rome is compulsory', 'Rome in any case', 'if Rome isn't the cultural capital of Europe, then no other city can be', 'Rome is the starting point'. The amount, quality and diversity of the cultural capital present in Rome are the bases for the high opinion of Rome as cultural destination. It is particularly the presence of 'real cultural capital', such as monuments and museums that distinguishes Rome from other destinations.

The choice of cultural destinations was strongly influenced by 'atmosphere'. This is a very difficult concept to define, as Leiper (1990) has noted in the context of attractions (see Chapter 1, this volume). This is also evident from the responses of the new producers – their descriptions of the atmosphere of a destination varied considerably. For one respondent Rome had an atmosphere that is characterized by the liveliness of the city, the food and the language. For another:

> It is not my favourite city, certainly not . . . It is a city full of churches,
> monuments, administrators and priests. It has no real 'life', only history.
> I don't feel it is a living organism that can care for itself (E).

After Rome, London and Paris were mentioned almost in the same breath. For both cities the high quality of art, the large number of museums and historical significance are reasons to take a cultural holiday there. Which city is placed higher depends again on the atmosphere of the city, although the opinions are also here divided.

Berlin came next in the pecking order, largely because of the historic character of the city and its blossoming cultural 'scene'. However, some of the respondents don't see Berlin as a beautiful or lively city. As one of the respondents remarked, it is a city full of contradictions that you either love or hate, but it is difficult to ignore.

Beyond these four cities, a number of other destinations were named in the top five, such as Madrid, Barcelona, Vienna, Venice, St Petersburg and Amsterdam. None of these cities was chosen by more than two of the interviewees, however. Even though the interviewees all live in Amsterdam, only two named Amsterdam spontaneously as a favourite cultural city. When asked why they had not chosen Amsterdam, the usual response was that they had overlooked their home city, but on reflection would tend to put Amsterdam in the top five. This is perhaps because the respondents don't see themselves as consumers of their own cities, but in fact have chosen to live there because of the cultural attractions of the city.

A comparison of the city rankings of the interviewees with the surveys of cultural producers and cultural tourists reveals some interesting differences (Fig. 4.1). For example, Berlin hardly rates with the other cultural producers or the cultural tourists. They are, however, much more likely to select Florence, although this was not named by one of the interviewees. This is remarkable because Florence has a wide reputation as a cultural destination and contains a large amount of 'real cultural capital' (Richards, 1996; van der Borg, 1994). This might indicate the importance placed by the interviewees on atmosphere. Support for this interpretation can be drawn from the attitude of most of the interviewees, who see Rome as a compulsory destination because of its real cultural capital, but decry its lack of atmosphere. For the 'new producers' high culture is not enough on its own – elements of

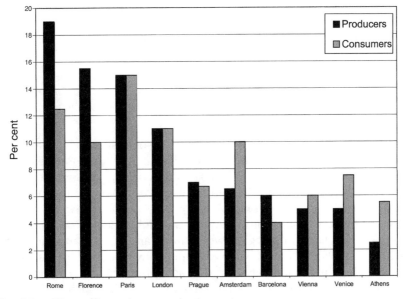

**Fig. 4.1.** City rankings of new producers and consumers.

popular culture play an important role in their destination choice and in their consumption of the destination. Rome and Florence are seen as having less to offer in terms of popular culture, and the interviewees don't see Florence as a 'must see' destination on the basis of its real cultural capital alone.

## The distinction between work, leisure and holiday

All the new producers indicated that work and leisure and holidays often spill over into each other. The degree to which this happens varies, but none of the respondents was able to make clear distinctions between these elements of their lives:

> Yeah, my holidays and my work are actually an extension of each other – that is sometimes annoying and sometimes not (F).

> Yes, as I already told you about the art historians, we have actually made our hobby into a job (E).

The absence of a division between work and leisure is experienced as positive and negative. One negative aspect is that the respondents are never free from their work. However, some ask themselves if there is any longer a difference between work and leisure, particularly because their work is 'fun':

> For example my holiday in France. I discovered a really great little museum run by this guy with a great storyline. It would be a pity not to use that, so I made notes as he was talking. That became a short piece in the newspaper (B).

Although this interviewee was conscious of the fact that work and leisure run into one another, for most of the new producers this de-differentiation is mainly unconscious. One tour operator who travelled with his own company made a point of telling his fellow-travellers that the trip was a holiday for him. But in fact work kept creeping in:

> The only aspect that you maybe wouldn't see as pure holiday is that you are looking out for things the whole day. I sit there the whole day not really looking at the contents of the trip, but thinking in the back of my mind about the structure of the trip – is this good, is that good? (A).

The division between work and leisure is in some situations clear. New producers who guide groups of tourists indicate that this is for them work and not leisure. Another respondent said that visiting a museum in leisure time was different to making the same visit for work. Work and leisure don't influence each other so strongly that the new producers would go to a particular holiday destination because it is useful for their work. But when they are on holiday in a region where there are cultural attractions that might be useful for their work, they will almost always go and have a look. A similar lack of distinction between work and leisure has been identified by Rojek (1999) who examined the leisure of the super rich, such as Bill Gates and Warren Buffet.

Goedhart (1997) summarizes the relationship between work and leisure for the new producers as a form of 'gaze' (Urry, 1990). The gaze exercised by the new producers places the leisure or holiday environment in the context of their work. One of the interviewees, for example, visits hotels in his holiday region and collects folders for possible later use in a tour programme. But even when they are not specifically thinking about work, the gaze is so constructed that leisure is experienced through the lens of work.

The new producers are therefore an influential group of cultural intermediaries who manufacture cultural tourism products based on their own tastes and interests. Their own consumption, and therefore their leisure activities are important in this regard. They see no clear distinction between work and leisure, because they have made their hobby into their work. By exploiting their cultural capital to develop cultural tourism they can increase their economic capital, as well as creating a means of distinction.

## Specialist and Generalist Tour Operators

The 'new producers' studied by Goedhart can be found mainly in specialist tour operating companies, where their cultural competence is essential to the production process. As larger tour operators move into the cultural market, however, the production of 'cultural holidays' is also being undertaken by people with less specialized cultural knowledge. Herrijgers (1998) studied the product development and marketing strategies of specialist and generalist tour operators in The Netherlands in order to analyse this process.

The basic aim of this research was to provide insights into the factors that play a role in the development of cities into cultural tourism products for general and specialist tour operators. An initial survey of general tour operators selling cultural city trips through the retail trade yielded a total of 11 operators, of which the top four companies were selected. Four specialist cultural tour operators were selected from a list of operators compiled by Goedhart (1997). For each company the managing director or marketing director was interviewed and a brochure analysis was made. The brochure analysis was focused particularly on the coverage given to cultural destinations and the textural and visual markers used to present those destinations.

Very clear distinctions emerged between the general and specialist tour operators in terms of their organizational characteristics and the personal background of the people responsible for developing cultural programmes. In general the specialist tour operators tended to have a similar background to the new producers identified by Goedhart, whereas the general tour operators were more likely to have a tourism industry background, and a vocational rather than an academic education (Table 4.1). The general tour operators tend to focus much more strongly on the commercial aspects of the product, and the theming of the product which will make it more

**Table 4.1.** Profile of specialist and general tour operator staff interviewed. (From Herrijgers, 1998.)

|  | General tour operator | Specialist tour operator |
| --- | --- | --- |
| Function | Product manager | Director |
| Tasks | Marketing | Based on intuition |
| Education | Polytechnic | University |
| Work experience | Diverse | Tour leader |
| Travel experience | High | High |
| Division between work and leisure | Yes | No |

marketable to the non-cultural consumer. Specialist operators tended to pay more attention to the purely cultural aspects of the destination.

Not surprisingly the general tour operators saw themselves primarily as travel specialists. They aim at the mass market, but for city trips they recognize that the clients are often young couples with double incomes or older 'empty nesters', a profile which is close to that for cultural tourists in general (see Chapter 2, this volume). These tour operators provide not just complete packages with Dutch guides, but also more flexible products for experienced travellers who may have visited a city several times before.

The cultural specialists, on the other hand, tend to provide guided tours using guides with specialized cultural knowledge. Most of these tours are only run once or twice a year, and often contain elements not available to other tour operators.

> For example, we organise tours to Russia for musicians, which includes a visit to a rehearsal at the Bolshoi. Afterwards they can talk to the ballerinas and visit one of the musicians at home. Everybody can visit Russia and buy a ticket to the Bolshoi, but they can't experience these things. This is in fact the added value that we sell.

Because these companies have such specialized products, they also usually sell their products direct, rather than through the travel trade. This is changing, however, as the specialists have noted that the travel agents exert an important influence over the destination choice of their clients, but most sales are still made direct. The basic target group for the specialists is older culturally interested couples. They describe their market as 'cultural tourists' but they recognize that the interests of this group include not just high culture but also popular culture as well. 'I think a cultural holiday must be more than art and history, it must also include contemporary culture. How do people live? What do they eat?'

The specialists are convinced that using the word 'culture' in the name of their companies distinguishes them from the mass market operators, and they can therefore avoid direct competition. The cultural edge is maintained through the cultural background of the people working in the organization, most of whom have an arts or cultural education. Just like the 'new producers' interviewed by Goedhart (1997) these people see little distinction between their work and their leisure, but feel rather that they have made a business out of their leisure.

## Cities as Cultural Tourism Products

The way in which urban destinations are packaged and presented by the specialist and general tour operators reflects to a large extent their differing backgrounds and modes of operation. The general tour operators view a city more in terms of accessibility and tourist facilities, whereas the specialists are guided more by a 'feeling' for a specific city.

One general tour operator commented: 'A city is attractive for us if it is of a certain size, has a certain number of cultural attractions and a number of standard facilities, such as shops, restaurants and hotels'.

In contrast, 'atmosphere' seems to play a more important role in the decisions of specialist tour operators: 'A city must of course have enough cultural attractions, but in addition it must have atmosphere. A place has to radiate liveliness'.

The cultural aspects of the city are also more emphasized by the specialists, whereas the general tour operators are more concerned with the 'commercial' aspects of the product, such as accessibility and market potential. This difference is perhaps not surprising given the mass-market nature of their operation – they have to attract enough clients to make the product viable. Specialists, operating with small groups, can visit less accessible and less well known cities (Table 4.2).

These factors affect the cities that are included in the brochures. Figure 4.2 shows that Florence was the only city included in seven of the eight brochures. All the respondents regarded Florence as a 'real cultural city' (Herrijgers, 1998, p. 49). One of the specialist tour operators remarked: 'Italy is the basis of our culture. Now we can look at all sorts of other cultures, but ultimately we will all want to see Italy'.

The attitude of the specialist tour operators to the selection of Florence therefore matches the view of the 'new cultural producers' that Italy is the source of western culture. For the general tour operators, however, Florence is not always a success. Two of the general tour operators noted that Florence was not booking well, partly because of problems of accessibility. There are also signs that Florence may be less popular with the specialists in future. One operator had already decided to drop Florence, on the basis that his clients wanted something new: 'We don't have Florence in our brochure any more, because our clients are more taste makers than cultural followers. They have already visited that sort of city'.

The search for something new probably also explains why Rome is only featured by four of the operators, in spite of the general agreement among

**Table 4.2.** Characteristics of cities as cultural tourism products according to general and specialist tour operators. (From Herrijgers, 1998, p. 37.)

| Items | General tour operators | Specialist tour operators |
|---|---|---|
| Commercial factors | | |
|    Potential | ✓✓✓✓ | |
|    Accessibility | ✓✓✓ | |
|    Market recognition | ✓ | |
|    Fashion | ✓✓✓ | |
| Facilities | | |
|    Hotels | ✓✓✓✓ | ✓✓✓✓ |
|    Restaurants | ✓✓ | ✓✓ |
|    Public transport | ✓ | |
|    Shops | ✓✓✓ | |
| Cultural factors | | |
|    Cultural attractions | ✓✓✓✓ | ✓✓✓✓ |
|    Cultural themes | | ✓✓✓ |
|    Places of worship | | ✓✓ |
|    Architecture | | ✓✓✓ |
| Themes | | |
|    Cultural Capital of Europe | ✓✓✓✓ | ✓✓ |
|    Festivals and events | ✓✓✓ | ✓ |
|    Musicals and theatres | ✓ | |

respondents that Rome is a prime cultural destination. New destinations, such as Budapest, Seville, Salamanca and Prague feature much more prominently in the tour operators' brochures than in the perception of the new cultural producers of the top European cultural destinations. The established cultural capitals such as Rome, Paris and London remain undisputed market leaders, and take up far more brochure space than other cities, but the search for new products creates a constant undercurrent of 'new' destinations which surface in the brochures, particularly among the specialist operators.

Herrijgers (1998) observes that the Spanish cities in particular have experienced a significant growth in recent years. Spain is therefore viewed by her respondents as the top European city destination for the near future. A specialist tour operator remarked:

> When I started with Spanish cities, I got a lot of comments like 'you are a cultural operator – what are you doing in Spain?' And look at it now – the Spanish cities are no longer poor relations of the Italian cities. Spain is now after Italy our second most important destination. Together they account for half our turnover.

The newly-popular destinations need to be careful that they do not lose their attractiveness as 'new' or 'exclusive' destinations, as one specialist operator has seen in the case of Prague:

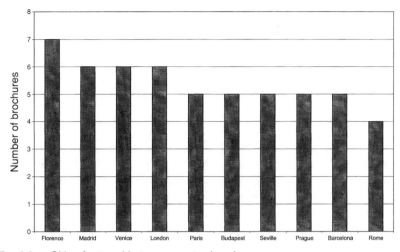

**Fig. 4.2.** Cities featured in tour operator brochures.

> Prague was really nice while the Iron Curtain was closed. After the Berlin Wall
> fell, there was an enormous hype for Prague, because it became accessible
> to the mass market. A tourism explosion followed, with new hotels and
> restaurants. And now Prague is a fantastic example of a declining cultural
> good. What was once an exclusive cultural destination you can now visit for
> €90 with the bus. So it isn't worth it any more – our target segment is looking
> for something new again.

Tour operators do pay some attention to major events such as the European
Cultural Capital. However, in the case of such non-recurring events the host
cities tend to be featured in the programme during the year itself, and then
the operators move on to the next Cultural Capital the following year.

The general conclusion drawn by Herrijgers (1998) is that tour operators
play an important role in the creation of urban cultural destinations in
Europe. Different types of tour operators can, however, have different roles
in the destination development process. It is the specialist tour operators that
tend to go in search of 'new' or 'unique' destinations or product elements. In
this search they are usually guided by the presence of 'real cultural capital'
in the destination, just as Goedhart (1997) concludes for the new cultural
producers as a whole. For the general tour operators the presence of real cultural capital is just one of the factors that they take into consideration, along
with other elements such as accessibility and the presence of shops, restaurants and suitable accommodation. In the development of new cultural
tourism destinations, therefore, the specialist cultural tour operators tend to
adopt a pioneer function, seeking out new destinations with which they can
distinguish themselves from other suppliers. Once a city proves popular with
the specialists, however, it may well be taken up by the larger tour operators,
on the basis that it has become 'fashionable' and there is a sufficiently large

market to make it worth their while. This may well mean that cities wishing to establish themselves in the cultural tourism market may have to think twice about their tendency to target promotional efforts at attracting larger operators, and rather use the specialists to develop the market first.

## Conclusions

The role of tour operators in the European cultural tourism market should not be overestimated. According to the ATLAS research in 1997, only 16% of cultural tourists were travelling on fully-inclusive tours. However, the research by Goedhart and Herrijgers has indicated that the cultural producers in general, and tour operators in particular have an important role to play in developing new destinations and in informing the tastes of other tourists.

The specialist operators in particular seem to fulfil a pioneer role in the market, opening up new cities to cultural tourism before they are discovered and taken up by the major tour operating companies. The tour operators keep a close eye on market trends, and are quick to spot potential new destinations and develop them. This means, however, that destinations can just as quickly fall out of favour. The recent shift between the classic cultural product of the Italian cities towards the 'new' cities of Spain is indicative of the effect of changing fashions. This is particularly evident with event-based cultural tourism, which seems to have little lasting effect beyond the event itself.

In ensuring that a destination is taken up in the cultural tourism distribution system it is important to ensure that all the elements of the cultural tourism product are present. Today this means not just a plentiful supply of real cultural capital, but also living culture, popular culture and a creative base to support them. All of these elements not only serve to attract tourists, but they also help to create and support the 'atmosphere' which has such an important role in tour operators' decisions to feature the destination.

The previous chapters have summarized some of the major trends in the cultural tourism market as a whole. In Part II of the book, more attention is paid to the development and marketing of individual cultural attractions, and the problems that they face in managing the growing flows of visitors.

## References

Bourdieu, P. (1984) *Distinction: a Social Critique of the Judgment of Taste*. Routledge & Kegan Paul, London.

de Haan, J. (1997) *Het Gedeelde Erfgoed*. SCP, Rijswijk.

Goedhart, S. (1997) 'New producers' in cultuurtoerisme. MA thesis, Tilburg University.

Herrijgers, C. (1998) De culturele stedenreis. MA thesis, Tilburg University.

Ioannides, D. and Debbage, K. (1997) Post-Fordism and flexibility: the travel industry polyglot. *Tourism Management* 18, 229–241.

Leiper, N. (1990) Tourist attraction systems. *Annals of Tourism Research* 17, 367–384.

Munt, I. (1994) The 'other' postmodern tourism: culture, travel and the new middle classes. *Theory, Culture and Society* 11, 101–123.

Richards, G. (1996) *Cultural Tourism in Europe.* CAB International, Wallingford, UK.

Rooijakkers, G. (1999) Identity factory southeast: towards a flexible cultural leisure infrastructure. In: Dodd, D. and van Hemel, A.-M. (eds) *Planning European Cultural Tourism.* Boekman Foundation, Amsterdam, pp. 101–111.

Rojek, C. (1999) *Leisure and Culture.* Routledge, London.

Roth, P. and Langemeyer, A. (1996) Cultural tourism in Germany. In: Richards, G. (ed.) *Cultural Tourism in Europe.* CAB International, Wallingford, UK, pp. 165–181.

Swinglehurst, E. (1982) *Cook's Tours: the Story of Popular Travel.* Blanford, Poole.

Urry, J. (1990) *The Tourist Gaze: Leisure and Travel in Contemporary Societies.* Sage, London.

van der Borg, J. (1994) Demand for city tourism in Europe. *Annals of Tourism Research* 21, 832–833.

Zukin, S. (1996) *The Cultures of Cities.* Blackwell, Oxford.

# Case Studies of European Cultural Attractions

# The Bonnefanten Museum, Maastricht

## Wil Munsters

*Hoge Hotelschool Maastricht, Maastricht, The Netherlands*

## Introduction

The cultural attraction dealt with in this case study is the Bonnefanten Museum, a fine art and archaeology museum located in the city of Maastricht in the extreme south of The Netherlands. In order to be viewed in the proper context the discussion of the survey data is preceded by a brief characterization of the museum providing essential information about its collection, housing, revenues as well as its place within the local and regional tourism product.

This chapter centres on the analysis of the visitor market of the Bonnefanten Museum carried out in the framework of the European Association for Tourism and Leisure Education (ATLAS) survey in the spring of 1997. One of the main reasons for the Bonnefanten Museum to participate in the ATLAS Cultural Tourism Research Project was that the management of the museum was faced with an alarming drop in visitor numbers, and did not have any market data at its disposal to explain this development or to underpin a change in policy. Later in the chapter it is made clear how the museum staff, using the information gathered during various market researches, developed an appropriate marketing policy in order to attract more visitors.

By definition a case study is focused on the peculiar aspects of the study object. It gains in interest and in significance if these peculiarities can be interpreted as being exemplary for general developments within the field of research. As the last part of the chapter illustrates, the Bonnefanten Museum faces the dilemma with which all museums are confronted in positioning themselves between two extremes: splendid isolation in an ivory tower versus opening the gates for the cultural entertainment of the masses.

## The Bonnefanten Museum as element of the tourism product

How interesting a place, object or event is for tourists depends not only on the qualities it possesses *sui generis*, but also on the supply of additional services, infrastructure facilities and other artificial or natural attractions together with which it forms a complete tourism product (Munsters, 1997). This applies likewise to the Bonnefanten Museum which as a cultural attraction is part of the urban tourism product offered by the city of Maastricht.

The capital of the Province of Limburg with about 120,000 inhabitants, Maastricht is an old monumental town whose history goes back to Roman times. Since 1991 the city has become widely known thanks to the European Unification Treaty bearing its name. The tourism product the visitor finds in Maastricht is rich and varied:

- *Tourist attractions*
  - Artificial attractions: monuments (Romanesque and Gothic churches, a classical city hall, mansions, historic squares, fortifications), ancient street patterns, museums (art museum, treasure houses, natural history museum), art galleries, theatres, cinemas, annual events (carnival, an international arts and antiques fair, a festival of religious music, a gourmet fair, cycle races for professionals).
  - Natural attractions: the River Meuse (boat trips, aquatic sports), hilly surroundings (the natural monument Mount St Peter), marl caves.
- *Service providers*
  - Tourist organizations: the tourist office of Maastricht offering a wide range of services (information, reservations for hotels and bookings for events, convention service, guided walking tours, day programmes, package tours, souvenir shop).
  - Primary tourism enterprises[1]: chain hotels as well as small downtown hotels, an exhibition and conference centre, a bungalow park, a four star camp site and a youth hostel.
  - Secondary tourism enterprises: bars, pavement cafes, fast food and culinary restaurants, chain stores, boutiques, shopping arcades, outdoor markets.
- *Transport infrastructure*
  - Accessibility by car or coach (international motorway, parking route), train (national main station) and aeroplane (regional airport); availability of a city bus service.

---

[1] Primary tourism enterprises have first of all tourists as customers, secondary tourism enterprises offer products and services for the local inhabitants but which are also used by tourists.

- An extra footbridge over the river Meuse will in the near future directly connect the Right Bank where the Bonnefanten Museum is located with the historic city centre on the other bank (VVV Maastricht, 1999).

This tourism product secures Maastricht a strong position in the markets of – in the order of importance – shopping tourism, cultural tourism and congress tourism. With regard to incoming urban tourism in The Netherlands the city of Maastricht occupies the third position behind the capital Amsterdam and The Hague, the seat of government (Nederlands Bureau voor Toerisme, 1998). In the period August 1995 to July 1996 2.6 million day-trippers visited the town generating a turnover of Fl 221 million (€100 million). In 1995 tourists booked 302,000 overnight stays in hotel accommodation, which represents a turnover between Fl 84 million and Fl 94 million (€38–43 million) (Lagroup, 1997). Given the steadily growing tourist attractiveness of Maastricht, the development of visitor management as part of a quality tourism policy is being considered in order to preserve its image as a hospitable historic city full of atmosphere (VVV Maastricht, 1999).

## The Bonnefanten Museum collection

The Bonnefanten Museum is the museum for fine art and archaeology of the Dutch province Limburg. Well over 100 years old, it owes its name to an ancient convent in Maastricht where nuns used to bring up orphan children called 'les bonnes enfants' by the local inhabitants.

The fine art collection encompasses on the one hand old masters in the field of medieval religious sculpture, early Italian painting (14th to 16th century) and southern Netherlandish painting (16th to 17th century) with Pieter Brueghel the Younger as the key figure; on the other hand select contemporary works focused on minimal art, Arte Povera, conceptual art and fundamental painting, streams represented among others by Beuys, Broodthaers, Dibbets, Fabro, Kounellis, LeWitt and Serra. The archaeology collection consists of finds from Limburg dating from 250,000 years BC to the Modern Era, in particular from the Stone Age, the Roman period and the early Middle Ages.

The museum has an exhibition programme in which a number of presentations and collections alternate simultaneously with each other.

## Housing

In 1995 the museum moved from the old town centre of Maastricht to the new Céramique District located on the East Side of the River Meuse. The site was home to the potteries of the Société Céramique since 1859. In the near future it will house an urban ensemble of dwellings, offices, shops, cultural centres, hotels, parks, squares and avenues designed by international architects under the supervision of their Dutch confrere Jo Coenen.

The Bonnefanten Museum consists of a new building designed by the Italian architect Aldo Rossi and the historic Wiebengahal. Rossi's creation is in the shape of a lying, symmetrical 'E' attempting to embrace a striking dome tower, the distinguishing mark of the museum on the right bank of the Meuse (Fig. 5.1). The building is made of traditional materials (brick, stone and wood) and is designed to admit a great deal of daylight, giving the interior an ambience of natural brightness.

Because logic and simplicity have been guiding architectural principles, the four floors are all identical. The ground floor consists of the entrance hall, the museum shop and the Grand Café on the Meuse; the first floor houses the archaeology and old masters collection, besides the library and the auditorium; the second floor contemporary art, both displays from the collection and temporary exhibitions; the third floor the print room. The tower room is used for special projects.

**Fig. 5.1.** Bonnefanten Museum Maastricht: the museum from the riverside (photograph courtesy of K. Zwarts).

Next to the museum building is the Wiebengahal, an earthenware factory constructed in 1912. A reminder of the industrial past of the Céramique district, it is one of the first examples of concrete frame construction. After having been restored to its original state, this monument of industrial archaeology now houses contemporary sculpture, permanent installations as well as temporary exhibitions. So the Wiebengahal is among the many examples of monuments that have been developed as a museum and/or exhibition space after the model of the Louvre, former palace of the Kings of France. Conversely, the new museum building of Aldo Rossi has the potential to become a monument of modern architecture just as happened to the Centre Georges Pompidou in Paris (Munsters, 1997). In other words, the complex in its entirety offers a unique permanent interaction between museum and monument functions (Fig. 5.2).

With regard to its surface area, the Bonnefanten Museum is one of the ten biggest art museums of The Netherlands, belonging to the second rank group after the internationally renowned Rijksmuseum and Van Gogh Museum in Amsterdam.

**Fig. 5.2.** Bonnefanten Museum Maastricht: front side with Wiebengahal on the right (photograph courtesy of K. Zwarts).

## Sources of revenue

The principal financier of the Bonnefanten Museum as a provincial institution is the Province of Limburg which contributes by means of structural subsidies to the yearly operating costs (60% of the budget as of 1999) and who also paid the construction costs of the new building.

The second source of revenues consists of the income generated by the museum itself through admissions revenue and merchandising, lending or leasing works of art and letting the Grand Café, the auditoriums and the library.

Finally, the museum depends for its funding and especially for the extension of the collection on sponsor gifts from private Maecenas and cultural foundations as well as commercial companies.

# Analysis of the Visitor Market

### Evolution of visitor numbers (1993–1996)

While the number of museum visitors amounted to 45,000 in 1993, the last year the old building was open, it quadrupled – and even more than that – in 1995 under the influence of the so-called 'new building effect': 175,000 people found their way to Rossi's art temple, 50,000 of them within the 6 weeks after the opening for the public on 9 March. The decrease of this effect was one of the reasons why in 1996 the visitor numbers dropped to 129,169 (Nederlands Bureau voor Toerisme, 1999). For 1997 the museum expected 100,000 visitors. Basic market data making it possible to explain this evolution were missing. At the same time the provincial authorities of Limburg were dissatisfied not only with the fall in visitor numbers in general, but especially with the low number of regional visitors in view of the function of the Bonnefanten Museum as art centre for the inhabitants of Limburg. Furthermore, the drop in visitor numbers stood in the way of the privatization policy the province was considering pursuing by reducing the amount of subsidy in order to compel the museum to generate more own revenues. So the Bonnefanten Museum is facing similar problems to many other public cultural institutions in The Netherlands and other European countries: rising costs, tighter government funding and a need to prove their social value by increasing visitor numbers. These pressures are forcing them to change from product orientation to market orientation as a policy guideline (Richards, 1996).

Reasons enough for the management of the Bonnefanten Museum to be interested in participating in the ATLAS European Cultural Tourism Research Project in 1997. The analysis of the survey data could contribute to developing an appropriate marketing policy aiming to gear the supply of the museum to the demand of the market in order to increase visitor numbers.

## The visitor survey

The visitor interviews took place in the entrance hall and in the Grand Café of the museum. Interviewing occurred during the last week of April 1997 and the first week of May 1997 in order to include a mixture of weekends and weekdays in the sample. In total, 388 questionnaires were processed, 384 being the minimum amount of respondents necessary for a representative sample of museum visitors with a 95% reliability level and a 5% confidence interval.

The data were gathered, processed and analysed by a group of students of the Hoge Hotelschool Maastricht within the framework of a management research project carried out in the fourth and final year of their study (Albers *et al.*, 1997).

## Cultural participation of the visitors

The main motives for visiting the museum were holiday making (75%), relaxation (73%), experiencing new things (65%) and learning new things (56%). Of all respondents 89% had been on a holiday in the past 12 months. The holidays they usually take are mostly cultural holidays (17%), city trips (14%) and touring holidays (12%). In their leisure time during the preceding year, 91% of the respondents visited cultural attractions and events, such as museums (91%), monuments (58%), historic houses (43%), art galleries (51%), performing arts (66%) and festivals (27%). In the opinion of the Bonnefanten Museum visitors, the five most interesting European cities for a cultural holiday were Paris (13%), Rome (10%), Florence (10%), Amsterdam (9%) and London (8%).

## Holiday pattern of the tourist visitors

Almost two-thirds (63%) of the respondents were overnight tourists. They described their current holiday as a city break (29%), a cultural holiday (29%), a health/sport-orientated holiday (19%) or a combination of these (14%). For a quarter of this visitor category, the presence of the Bonnefanten Museum was important in their decision to come to Maastricht, for 55% it was of minor importance. Nearly half of them have visited other cultural attractions in Maastricht and its surroundings during their stay.

Of the overnight tourists 37% were staying at a hotel, 23% in self-catering accommodation, 24% were camping. Half of them were staying for a period of four to seven nights and 41% for one to three nights. The majority (58%) organized the holiday by themselves and 21% did not arrange anything in advance. The tourist visitors mainly go on a holiday with their partner (57%) or their family (22%).

## Visitor expectations and satisfaction

When the visitors were asked which particular aspect had pushed them to come to the museum, 33% answered 'the museum as a whole', 16% 'the architecture of the museum' and 13% 'the reputation of the museum'.

The respondents were most unanimous in their appreciation of the architecture of the building (73%). Both the archaeology collection and the old masters collection matched the expectations of 55% of the visitors (versus respectively 9% and 13% of visitors who were disappointed), while the modern art department was appreciated the least: 43% were satisfied, but for 36% it fell short of expectations.

The general impression of the Bonnefanten Museum as a whole was positive for 67% of the visitors. They specially appreciated the beautiful and spacious building, the well-ordered presentation of the collections and the variety of exhibits. The 8% of visitors who did not appreciate the museum as a whole thought above all that the quality of the art displayed was not high.

## Visit patterns

Almost 75% of the respondents were visiting the new Bonnefanten Museum for the first time. The first time visitors were particularly attracted by the museum as a whole (36%), its architecture (16%) and its reputation (15%). The repeat visitors also came for the museum as a whole (23%) and its architecture (15%), but they were much more likely to be interested in the temporary exhibitions (16% of repeat visitors compared with 3% of first time visitors). The majority of both first time visitors and repeat visitors stayed 1 to 2 h (48 to 49%) or 2 to 3 h (31 to 32%).

It should also be observed that the more someone returns to visit the museum, the bigger the chance that he or she will come back again: 81% of the repeat visitors against 51% of the first time visitors. The principal reasons for these repeat visits were future exhibitions (33%) and the museum as a whole (24%).

## Profile of the visitors

Visitors to the Bonnefanten Museum came mainly from The Netherlands (88%), with a minority from Belgium (4%) and Germany (4%). The proportion of men and women among the visitors is almost equally divided: 49.5% of the visitors were male and 50.5% were female. Most of the visitors (56%) were aged between 35 and 54, with 23% being younger than 35 and 21% older than 54.

Nearly 70% of the visitors had a higher educational qualification. Of all visitors 55% were employees, most of them being professionals or office employees. On average 15% of the visitors had occupations linked to the world of arts, museums or monuments. The median gross income per household was Fl 80,000 (€36,000) a year, significantly higher than the national average (Albers *et al.*, 1997).

# First Steps Towards a New Marketing Policy

## The Bonnefanten Festival

As expected by the management of the Bonnefanten Museum, visitor numbers fell in 1997 (reaching 102,800), which was partly due to the limited interest in the temporary exhibition held that year (though it should be noted that this matched the prognosis of 100,000 visitors a year made in the planning of the new museum). The financial year closed with a loss of Fl 400,000 (€180,000).

In order to turn the tide, the Province of Limburg decided at the beginning of 1998 to increase the yearly operating subsidy of Fl 6.3 million (€2.9 million) by an additional amount of Fl 1 million (€450,000), despite its privatization policy. The money should be used to develop a new policy with the help of external management consultants. Anticipating one of the recommendations of the consultancy bureau, the museum staff organized from September 1997 to February 1998 the *Bonnefanten Festival*, a special project to attract the regional public so as to meet the concern of the provincial authorities about the low proportion of Limburgers among the visitors. Besides the temporary exhibition of 33 visual artists having ties with Limburg, this cultural experience consisted of music, theatre, dance, cabaret and other performances by regional bands, companies and artists in the museum rooms on 19 consecutive Sundays. The aim was that the cultural activities should serve as an attraction factor making the exhibition of young modern art accessible for a wider public. The festival was a success, attracting 19,000 visitors over the 19 Sundays. During the period of the event, the museum received in total more than 45,000 visitors, of whom 40% came from the region. One-third of the visitors came especially for the festival and four out of five visitors said they intended to return to the museum.

## Fabrica, Colors of Benetton

In May 1998 another successful event was launched: *Fabrica, Colors of Benetton*, a special exhibition devoted to the communication activities of the Italian clothing firm, based on the controversial photographs taken by Oliviero Toscani for Benetton. After having been prolonged until the end of September, the exhibition attracted well over 80,000 people, twice as many as expected, and it is the most popular exhibition held at the Bonnefanten Museum to date.

A market research study was commissioned by the museum management from the ETIL bureau to measure the satisfaction of the different visitor segments during the Benetton exhibition. The main results of this research are as follows. More than 50% of the respondents came to the museum specifically to visit the Benetton exhibition, 40% of them being first time visitors, 60% repeat visitors. Of the other visitors almost 20% came for the museum as a whole and 10% out of curiosity: 80% of these were first time visitors, 20% repeat visitors. The majority of the repeat visitors were from Maastricht and the Province of Limburg and they came for the exhibition rather than for the permanent collection they had already seen. They made a shorter visit to the museum than the first time visitors who mostly came from other provinces and tended to see the whole museum. In total almost half of the visitors stayed at least 1.5 h in the museum.

The image of the Bonnefanten Museum is vague: many visitors do not associate the museum with a specific type of art. Any associations tend to be with modern art and, to a much lesser degree, with old art and archaeology. More than half of the visitors are of the opinion that modern art fits the museum most and archaeology the least. They are surprised about the combination of the three collections in one museum building.

The most important conclusions of the research are that nearly three-quarters of the respondents judge their visit positively and that almost two-thirds of them intend to visit again, especially for an interesting exhibition. The fact that 69% of the 'Benetton visitors' intended to return compared to 59% of the other visitors led the researchers to conclude that special exhibitions and events generate repeat visits (ETIL, 1998).

It is interesting to compare some of the findings of the ETIL research with those of the ATLAS survey. The most notable difference was a shift in the proportion of first time visitors versus repeat visitors: from 75% : 25% (research period 1997) to 60% : 40% (research period 1998). This evolution can be attributed to both the decline of the 'new building effect' and the attraction of the special character of the Benetton exhibition for previous visitors. Other factors have remained fairly constant, however. First time visitors continue to be attracted by the museum as a whole. Repeat visitors are much more than first time visitors interested in events like temporary exhibitions. Two-thirds of the visitors in both surveys also intended to return to the museum for another visit and mentioned future exhibitions as visit motive.

## Market growth

The objective of both events to generate more (regional) visitors to the museum can be defined more specifically in marketing terms as growth of the market (share). This means that these marketing actions can be described

| Product ▶ Market ▼ | Existing products | New products |
|---|---|---|
| Existing markets | Market penetration | Product development |
| New markets | Market development | Diversification |

**Fig. 5.3.** The product/market expansion grid of I.H. Ansoff. (From Kotler *et al.*, 1996.)

according to the marketing growth strategy-grid proposed by Ansoff (Fig. 5.3).

The question is whether it is the product offered by the museum and/or the market targeted by the museum that have been changed to attract more people. The *Bonnefanten Festival* as well as the exhibition *Fabrica, Colors of Benetton* can be qualified as new, original, consumer-oriented marketing initiatives of the museum staff using the event as attraction factor. On the other hand, the public targeted by these new products is still the same as before: the well educated regional and (inter)national art lover. So the product/market combination is a new product for the existing market and the marketing growth/strategy is product development. This provided a fruitful strategy because in 1998 the museum broke out of the negative spiral and a favourable reversal occurred: the Bonnefanten Museum received 155,500 visitors and occupied the eighth position in the visitor numbers ranking of Dutch art museums (Nederlands Bureau voor Toerisme, 1999). And that is not all: what also should be taken into account is the positive underlying effect of the repeat visits that both events will probably generate in the next few years.

## The Bonnefanten business plan 1999–2002

As foundation for its policy in the near future the management of the museum has drawn up a business plan based on the various market researches conducted since the opening of the new building and on the advice of external management consultants. The points of departure of the business plan are that the museum will need more funds and personnel to be able to carry out its tasks and that the archaeology department and the Wiebengahal will probably be hived off.

The Bonnefanten Museum aspires to be a leading international museum with a catchment area radius of 200 km covering the local region, the west of The Netherlands and neighbouring regions of Germany and Belgium. The museum aims at receiving a minimum of 125,000 visitors yearly. Beside the existing target group, those interested 'by nature' in art, both young and old, the museum will aim at a new segment consisting of youth and young families. This matches national cultural priorities which will target additional subsidies at those institutions which can attract more young visitors or ethnic minorities. In order to attain these goals, the museum wants to distinguish itself from other museums that are its competitors by a branding focused on quality, personal experience and freshness (new, youthful and experimental art). Furthermore, the presentation of art to the public will be based on a balance between, on the one hand, educational information by means of the permanent collection and, on the other, experiencing art by means of cultural events and projects for the new young target groups. According to the product/market expansion grid of Ansoff (Kotler *et al.*, 1996) this implies developing new products for new markets and choosing diversification as a market growth strategy (Fig. 5.3).

The output of public relations and marketing must also be increased in order to become more independent of subsidies by generating sufficient revenues from the activities of the museum itself (events, museum shop, merchandizing, lending of art, catering, letting of rooms) and by attracting sponsors for events and special projects. The marketing policy therefore has to be professionalized and fleshed out by a new Department of Commercial and Public Affairs, which was set up in 1998. The new department aims to take advantage of market trends, attract more visitors and expand sales in order to fulfil the ambition of the Bonnefanten Museum to be the spearhead of cultural tourism in the region (Bonnefanten Museum, 1998).

## General Issues

### The cultural tourism field of tension

The case of the Bonnefanten Museum is representative of major trends within the museum sector. Many art museums are facing the same kind of difficulties and are searching for similar remedies to overcome them. The whole problem can be reduced to one basic dilemma: how can the art museum perform its traditional tasks (collection, conservation, exhibition) and, simultaneously, meet the requirements of earning capacity and market orientation imposed by the authorities who lend weight to their demands by withdrawing as main financier and making way for the mechanisms of the free market?

The field of tension between the cultural and the commercial approaches is represented in Fig. 5.4, which shows how the interests of the parties involved can conflict. The figure illustrates the most striking example within the museum sector: a so-called blockbuster exhibition of masterpieces of world-famous painters. Thanks to their uniqueness these mega-events attract masses of cultural tourists supplied by tour operators for

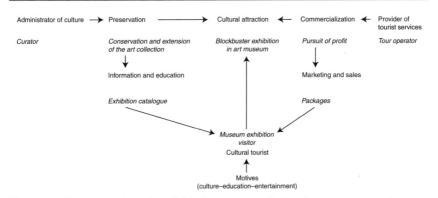

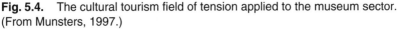

**Fig. 5.4.** The cultural tourism field of tension applied to the museum sector. (From Munsters, 1997.)

whom cultural packages are a lucrative business. The adverse consequence is often the overcrowding in the museum rooms, which makes it impossible to consider attentively the works of art in spite of visitor management measures. The commercial success of these kinds of exhibitions is indisputable but the informative and educational tasks of the museum may well suffer. Furthermore, the organization of exhibitions often happens at the expense of caring for the permanent collection because the resources and the time reserved for preservation and research are used to set up crowd pulling events.

## The museum as a cultural enterprise

The Bonnefanten Museum will not run into this extreme situation not only because it is a regional museum without blockbuster aspirations but especially because the museum now regards itself as a 'cultural enterprise'. This expresses the symbiosis between its function as a cultural institution and the commercial approach of the museum management required by its main financial backer, the Province of Limburg. This philosophy is coming to the fore in the formulating of a real business plan (qualifying collections, exhibitions, events, shop, catering and building as a 'set of products and services'), the creation of a Department of Commercial and Public Affairs and the appointment of a marketing manager. All this must not conceal an essential difference between a commercial enterprise and a cultural enterprise emphasized by the director of the Bonnefanten Museum: the former is by definition profit seeking whereas the latter develops commercial activities only with a view to covering deficits or keeping the budget balanced (van Grevenstein, 1999).

The gradual change of policy of the Bonnefanten Museum can be described in terms of the dialectical process: any tensions between the

seemingly incompatible objectives of preservation (= thesis) and commercialization (= antithesis) of art are neutralized in the new well-balanced
organizational structure (= synthesis) of the museum. Instead of just defend-
ing one's own interests, complementarity and synergy characterize the
cooperation between the department of curators and that of marketeers both
united by the same enterprise mission. The art-orientated curators have the
knowledge necessary to meet the information need of the highly educated
visitor. The marketeers master the techniques appropriate to canvass the
market and are familiar with the provision of services which contribute to
the tourist attractiveness of the museum. Moreover, the cooperation benefits
from the affinity with art and culture that is required for the staff members of
the commercial department.

     On further consideration, it is possible to represent the organizational
structure of the enterprise Bonnefanten Museum as a linear input–output
model describing the commercial transformation process the art collection
undergoes as basic product in order to become a cultural attraction meeting
the needs of consumers (Fig. 5.5). In short, a productive harmony model has
taken the place of the unproductive conflict model in the cultural tourism
field of tension (Fig. 5.4).

## The interaction between museum and event

The Bonnefanten Museum possesses the people and the means to adopt
creative and professional approaches to the development and marketing
of the museum as a cultural tourist attraction. Within this framework the
event occupies a privileged position as an effective medium to experience
art. In the Bonnefanten business plan, events are defined as literature, music,
theatre and film activities apart from visits to the permanent and temporary
exhibitions. These activities are organized in cooperation with regional
institutions and are meant for the general public (Bonnefanten Museum,
1998). Evidently, the *Bonnefanten Festival*, which was so successful with
the regional public, has served as a model for this component of product
development.

     By defining the term *event* in the usual, broader sense as a 'public
happening of limited duration', it is also possible to consider temporary
exhibitions as events. An example of these mentioned by the Bonnefanten
business plan are the recurring summer exhibitions on modern art entitled
*Points of Contact*. Inspired by the success of the Benetton exhibition, these
exhibitions are focused on creativity in social and cultural mediums other
than the visual arts, like publicity and pop music. The projects intend to
give visitors the opportunity to experience art for themselves (Bonnefanten
Museum, 1998). The exhibition *On Taste* set up by the Bonnefanten
Museum during the autumn and winter of 1999 was also in line with
this policy. In this exhibition the concept of 'taste' was presented as a

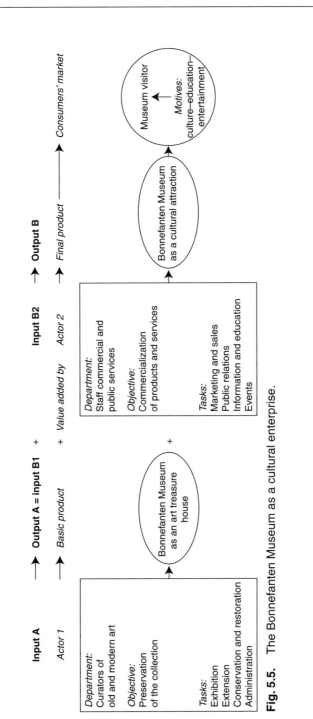

**Fig. 5.5.** The Bonnefanten Museum as a cultural enterprise.

kaleidoscope of fashion and media, trends and mass customization, food and scents as well as extraordinary art collections. Visitors played a key role by tasting, sampling and participating in events such as demonstrations, performances and discussions.

No matter in which sense the term *event* is defined, the preceding examples clearly show how a museum – just like a monument – can be used as décor for cultural or other activities which attract a broader public than the usual visitor who comes for the museum or the monument itself. The dynamics of the event can be an enticement for the less interested consumer who associates culture with the static remnants of the dim and distant past, such as 'stuffy' museum collections. Since an event implies by definition that something is happening, it is a proper instrument to bring art and heritage to life and to stimulate the cultural participation of a broader public. Conversely, the background of the museum or monument adds a special dimension to the event (Munsters, 1996, 1997).

## An alliance of elite and popular art

The launching of events like the *Bonnefanten Festival, Points of Contact* and *On Taste* leads undeniably to a broadening of the museum public. The Bonnefanten business plan itself contends that the target group of *Points of Contact* is different, because it will consist of younger visitors up to 30 years as part of the diversification strategy aiming new products at youth and young families. The Benetton exhibition set the tone for this policy: the age of the public attracted by this event was younger than that of the usual museum visitor (ETIL, 1998). This is not surprising for Benetton clothes are a mass product for the young public promoted by worldwide advertising campaigns. The photographs of Oliviero Toscani aim to arouse the interest of as many potential buyers as possible. From this angle, *Fabrica, Colors of Benetton* can be qualified as a popular art project in the same way as the planned events on pop(ular) music.

At the same time, being a fine art museum, the Bonnefanten Museum keeps on aiming at the existing target group of art lovers, those consumers interested 'by nature' in art, who couple a high curiosity and inquisitiveness with a preference for confrontations (Bonnefanten Museum, 1998). These museum visitors correspond with target group 1 of the typology of the cultural tourist[2]: highly educated tourists who want to discover, experience and broaden their knowledge of art (Table 5.1). The new market of youth and young families whom the Bonnefanten wants to attract matches with target group 2 of the typology: cultural tourists who go to a museum from

---

[2]  By *cultural tourists* are meant tourists, over-night tourists as well as day-trippers, visiting cultural attractions.

**Table 5.1.** Typology of the cultural tourist. (From Munsters, 1997.)

| Target group | Level of interest | Motive | Education |
| --- | --- | --- | --- |
| 1 | High | Culture | High |
| 2 | Average | Education and entertainment | High |
| 3 | Latent | Entertainment | Secondary |

time to time and who are searching for a combination of education and entertainment, or 'edutainment' (Table 5.1).

In the short term, the broadening of the public with new target groups implies that the museum staff must be prepared for any clash of the different categories of visitors emanating from their various motives (Munsters, 1996). The classic culture seeker and the culture-cum-leisure tourist come to the museum with different needs and expectations and this will manifest itself in their visit behaviour. The trick is equally satisfying both target groups so that they might become repeat visitors or at least ambassadors for the museum. Visitor management offers a range of possibilities varying from targeted information to spreading of visitor streams in order to avoid tensions between the target groups.

In the long term, the challenge for the Bonnefanten Museum – whose situation is representative of that of many other museums – will be to stick to its fundamental scientific, cultural and educational mission. In this respect, further reduction in the level of public funding as part of the privatization policy seems to be the major threat because it could lead to more commercialization in order to increase visitor revenue and other self-generated income. The worst case scenario would be the situation in which the quantity of visitors becomes more important than the quality of the visitor apparent from the ATLAS survey. Such a shift from quality cultural tourism to mass cultural tourism would bring closer a spectre for many museum staff: the art museum as a cultural amusement park offering to the visitor a mixture of 'edutainment', merchandizing and blockbuster exhibitions.

But it is more likely that the museum staff will succeed in turning the threat of privatization into an opportunity by making a virtue of necessity: a greater proportion of own revenues and more control over own expenditure means more freedom of movement towards subsidizers. The Bonnefanten Museum can take advantage of this relative financial independence by maintaining an autonomous fine art policy for which success with art lovers and art critics will be a more decisive performance indicator than high visitor numbers or self-generated income. None-the-less, the fact remains that the museum as a fully subsidized art enclave for a select public seems a paradise forever lost.

## Acknowledgements

The author wishes to thank the following persons who were helpful in supplying assistance and information for the research project presented in this chapter:

- Ton Quik, Esther Saris and Ger Minkman, members of the Bonnefanten Museum staff
- Wim Weijnen, Director of the Department of Economy, Province of Limburg
- Wilco de Jong, Director of the Maastricht Tourist Office
- Myrthe Albers, Saskia Baggen, Marjolein de Best, Simone Bregman and Roy Eitjes, members of the management project group Bonnefanten Museum of the Hoge Hotelschool Maastricht.

## References

Albers, M., Baggen, S., de Best, M., Bregman, S. and Eitjes, R. (1997) *Come Across the Bridge. Survey About the Profile of the Visitors of the Bonnefanten Museum.* Management project report, Hoge Hotelschool Maastricht, Maastricht.

Bonnefanten Museum (1998) *Bonnefanten Ondernemingsplan 1999–2002.* Bonnefanten Museum, Maastricht.

ETIL (1998) *Het Bonnefanten, van Vele Kanten.* ETIL, Maastricht.

Kotler, Ph., Bowen, J. and Makens, J. (1996) *Marketing for Hospitality and Tourism,* 1st edn. Prentice Hall, Upper Saddle River.

Lagroup Leisure & Arts Consulting (1997) *Economische Betekenis van het Toerisme voor de Stad Maastricht en een Geïntegreerde Marketingstrategie voor de Stad Maastricht,* Lagroup, Amsterdam.

Munsters, W. (1996) The strategic development of heritage tourism: the Dutch approach. *Managing Leisure* 1(3), 139–151.

Munsters, W. (1997) *Cultuurtoerisme,* 2nd edn. Garant, Louvain-Apeldoorn.

Nederlands Bureau voor Toerisme (1998) *Toerisme, Goed Bekeken. Het Nederlandse Aanbod door een Buitenlandse Bril,* NBT, Leidschendam.

Nederlands Bureau voor Toerisme (1999) *Bezoekersaantallen Toeristische Attracties 1993–1998.* NBT, Leidschendam.

Richards, G. (1996) Cultural tourism in The Netherlands. In: Richards, G. (ed.) *Cultural Tourism in Europe.* CAB International, Wallingford, UK, pp. 233–247.

van Grevenstein, A. (1999) Overheid moet duidelijk museumbeleid voeren. *NRC Handelsblad* 19 March, 7.

VVV Maastricht (1999) *Marketing Activiteitenplan.* VVV Maastricht 2000. Maastricht.

# Urban Regeneration and Glasgow's Galleries with Particular Reference to the Burrell Collection

## David Leslie

*Department of Hospitality, Tourism and Leisure, Glasgow Caledonian University, Glasgow, UK*

## Introduction

The latter part of the 20th century has witnessed a myriad of changes; 'The times they are a changin', to quote Bob Dylan and 'the old order is rapidly fadin . . .'. There are many factors influencing these changes of which the development of mass tourism is but one. Tourism is recognized as a force for change, evidence of which is manifest most tangibly at the local level. The situations selected to illustrate such change more often than not relate to the negative impacts of tourism on the physical and, to a lesser extent, socio-cultural environment in lesser developed countries. In contrast, attention to the positive dynamics of tourism invariably focuses on the perceived economic benefits. But tourism is just one vector of change in a complex social system which itself is increasingly influenced by international factors. Therefore whether the impacts of tourism are positive or negative (more often a combination of both), realizing the potential economic benefits necessitates comprehensive planning and controlled development. However, tourism can be utilized, in combination with other strategies, as a tool to aid economic development. This is nowhere more apparent than in post-industrial cities where tourism is increasingly an element of an overarching strategy to address socio-economic problems. Basically, tourism is seen as having a potentially key role in the regeneration of a city in economic decline.

The role of tourism in urban regeneration received little attention prior to the 1990s (see Vandermey, 1984) since when attention has substantially increased (Richards, 1996a), particularly for economic motives (see

Bianchini and Parkinson, 1993; Hall, 1996). In the context of the UK, consideration of tourism and urban regeneration essentially involves attention to those cities built up around traditional industries of the 19th and early 20th centuries, such as Liverpool, Belfast and Glasgow (see DoE, 1990; Leslie, 1991; Fladmark, 1994). In such contexts urban tourism amounts to the marketing of cities as tourist destinations – a growing phenomenon of the late 20th century (see Gold and Ward, 1994; Gunn, 1997). In effect, as David Harvey wrote '. . . cities no longer are setting themselves as places of production but as places of consumption . . .' (quoted by Law, 1998). That tourism can play such a role is largely due to their undoubted potential to attract tourists (Zeppel and Hall, 1992) which arises due to their historic development and purpose; i.e. 'The city's primary function is to act as a service centre for the hinterland economy . . . supplying it with central goods and services . . . and . . . many central services are of a cultural nature . . .' (Richardson, 1969, pp. 157–158).

The development of urban tourism is primarily based on the presence of such 'central services of a cultural nature' unique to the locale. Such resources, and their promotion through tourism, are significant as they can be seen as counteracting globalization and loss of place identity and increasing homogeneity through creating new images and identity of place (Chang *et al.*, 1996). However, tourism's potential in urban regeneration is by no means limited to historical attractions; as Richards (1996a) argues: 'The consumption of culture is increasingly used as a means of economic regeneration, and the creation of cultural facilities is an important weapon in the competitive struggle to attract inward investment to European cities'.

Furthermore, comparatively few cities can rely solely on their heritage. In general, a gallery will not draw *tourists* but needs to be part of a more diverse product. New attractions need to be developed which often means the development of museums and galleries, and exhibitions, which will renew interest, and prompt repeat visits and, more significantly, generate new visitors (see Coutts, 1986; Richards, 1996a).

The key role player in urban tourism in the UK is the local authority (see Richards and Wilkes, 1990; Bianchini and Parkinson, 1993; Charlton and Essex, 1996). Apart from their central role in tourism *per se* they are also the stewards of most of the cultural facilities of a city. The most common cultural attractions are museums, the provision of which is a statutory duty of local authorities under the 1845 Museums Act. It is not surprising perhaps that more than 60% of local authorities consider the arts to be very important or important for attracting tourists to the area (see Huber *et al.*, 1992). At this juncture is would be useful to clarify what is encompassed by the term 'museum' or 'arts' in this context. According to the Museums and Galleries Commission (MGC, 1998, p. 1) the definition of museums includes art galleries; '. . . the word "museum" is used to embrace museums, galleries and other institutions – an institution which collects, documents, preserves, exhibits and interprets material evidence and associated information for the public benefit'.

Generally, local authorities perceive heritage tourism, which encompasses museums and historical architecture and sites, as more important than arts tourism (i.e. performing arts). This is justified by the findings of the European Association for Tourism and Leisure Education (ATLAS) research in Glasgow: 63% of respondents visited museums on holiday compared with 14% who attended performing arts. This is not intended to play down the importance of tourism to the performing arts, which is itself very significant (see Chapter 10, this volume).

While the local authority invariably is the initiator and facilitator of urban tourism development, the realization of the potential benefits to the local community overall is very much a function of private sector involvement (see Imrie and Thomas, 1993).

## Cultural Tourism in the UK

A degree of caution should perhaps be exercised in establishing the level of demand for cultural tourism given the absence of a technical definition. However, in general it is seen as encompassing that demand which is 'motivated wholly or in part by interest in the historical, artistic, scientific or lifestyle/heritage offerings of a community, region, group or institution.' (Silberberg, 1995). Further complications arise in this field as cultural tourism is as complex and heterogeneous as that of tourism itself (Cohen, 1993, p. 2).

In worldwide terms the World Tourism Organization estimates that cultural tourism accounts for 37% of all tourism trips and that demand is growing by 15% a year. In the UK, cultural tourism has long been recognized as a substantial factor; for example, in 1990 it was 'considered to account for 27% of Britain's tourism earnings.' (Crawford, 1990, p. 1). +ve In 1998, it was estimated that 401 million visits to tourist attractions were culture based (English Tourist Board, 1999). It is significant that the key agencies involved in tourism and arts in Scotland launched a development strategy for 'Tourism and Arts' in 1991 and in 1998 changed the title to 'Cultural Tourism' – 'In order to ensure that the full range of cultural activities are covered . . .' (Scottish Tourist Board, 1998a, p. 2).

With the growth of cultural tourism has come varying 'profiles' of the cultural tourist which attempt to define the 'type' of person more likely to participate in cultural tourism (see Richards, 1996a). The key characteristics identified include that they are mainly visiting for another reason and while there take in a cultural attraction. Secondly, the general socio-economic profile leads to speculation that cultural attractions still predominantly attract the more 'elite' tourists as in the days of the 'Grand Tour' (see Pick, 1988). Further, the growth in cultural consumption has been aided by the growing trend for short-break (three nights or less) holidays, especially in urban areas. In the 1997 ATLAS survey, 37% of all respondents were staying in the survey region for three nights or less (see Averill *et al.*, 1997).

Pick (1988) argues that the financing of 'Arts' in the form of funding is based on value for money rather than any aesthetic or cultural reasons. Tourism readily lends weight to such arguments about the value of the Arts. However, the benefits arising from cultural tourism are difficult to quantify accurately not only because tourist numbers are hard to measure, but also due to multiplier effects of visitors to the locality. Assessment of the value of cultural tourism gained little attention prior to the 1980s (Vandermey, 1984) since when it has become a major area of study, in spite of the remaining difficulties (see Page, 1995; Richards, 1996a).

As well as generating visitor expenditure, tourism creates jobs. Employment studies consistently find that capital investment in tourism generates more employment opportunities than equivalent sums invested in other areas; estimates suggest that an additional investment of £2500 (€3500) will generate one new tourism related job (Adams, 1994). In terms of urban regeneration we can identify the following direct and indirect effects of cultural tourism development:

- Employment in attractions, provision of amenities and supporting services.
- Revitalization of buildings and localities.
- Improvements in environmental quality.
- Creating a positive 'image' of the area.
- Improving the quality of life of the community.

*+ve*

The contribution of cultural tourism to the local economy is therefore more pervasive than many realize. It is for these very reasons that tourism is utilized as a tool to alleviate the socio-economic problems of the UK's industrial cities.

## Glasgow

In the past Glasgow was largely perceived as being a city of heavy industry and crime, hence the reason for the 'no mean city' tag it acquired. This is in contrast with the image of its rather more refined 'cousin' Edinburgh in the 'cultured' east of the country. Glasgow, although having a wealth of cultural attractions, never quite managed to shake off this 'hard' image. Generally it was thought that if it was 'culture one wanted, one visited Edinburgh'. As with many cities whose development and growth were based extensively on the activities of its port, coal mining and steel production, Glasgow witnessed a substantial decline in the traditional sectors of its economy from the 1960s. The locality gradually moved into decline as alternative

industries did not develop sufficiently to combat this problem. Little attention was paid to the negative factors and the concomitant social problems
until the early 1980s when the city undertook decisive action to address the
socio-economic problems of the area. The strategies formulated recognized
and gave due attention to the potential of tourism to aid the objective of
regeneration. Glasgow readily developed its tourism strategy based on the
arts. The rich cultural resources of the city give a sense of identity and
enhance its attractiveness. Arguably, it was one of the first British cities to
develop a regeneration strategy which had a clear emphasis on the role of its
cultural facilities (Boyle and Hughes, 1994).

That Glasgow has managed to shake off its undesirable image is largely
due to what Boyle and Hughes (1994) describe as 'urban entrepreneurialism'. Urban entrepreneurialism basically involves using local resources to
attract investment by private capital, thus stimulating economic regeneration. In adopting this approach the council sought to regenerate Glasgow
in a way that was similar to the regeneration happening in Liverpool, at
roughly the same time. Without doubt, the Council succeeded in changing
Glasgow's traditional image, largely through tourism promotion heralded
through the 'Glasgow's Miles Better' campaign which ran for 7 years from
1983 to 1990. The annual arts festival 'Mayfest' was also launched at
this time which further enhanced Glasgow's 'new, clean' reputation.
This success was built upon at the end of the 1980s and into the early
1990s when Glasgow was host to the International Garden Festival in
1988 and with the opening of The Royal Concert Hall in 1990, which Boyle
and Hughes (1994) describe as '. . . one of the most important capital
events . . .'.

It was during the 1980s that Glasgow's popularity as a cultural destination started to really develop. The city's leaders and champions of tourism,
such as Pat Lally (Leader of the Labour Council and Lord Provost for many
years) and Eddie Friel (Chair of the Tourist Board) successfully generated £2
billion (€2.8 billion) of investment in the city through partnerships between
public and private sector bodies (Stammage, 1990, p. 11) (for a detailed
discussion of the factors behind the emergence and development of the
Council's overall approach prior to and during the 1980s, see Booth and
Boyle, 1993). The designation of Glasgow as 'European City of Culture' in
1990 further marks the substantial progress achieved in the arts and tourism
field as well as being a watershed in the city's progress towards resolving the
socio-economic problems of the 1970s.

There were, however, critics of the City of Culture award. Many citizens
of Glasgow felt that it was not Glasgow's culture that was being represented
but the culture on show was being bought in, expensively, from elsewhere
(see Boyle and Hughes, 1994). The bid was therefore seen very much as
a part of tourism development planning and aimed to bring visitors
from England (Myerscough, 1990). In this latter aspect it was successful;

according to Myerscough (1990) it generated approximately £11–£15 million (€15–21 million) in additional revenue for the city after allowing for the substantial public sector costs involved. The contribution to establishing Glasgow's new image was significant. The award of City of Culture status for 1990 in itself demonstrates the perceived change in Glasgow's image. From the 'hard image' of the early 1980s, and earlier: 'to one of the UK's first post industrial cities, basing its economy around the service industries and most notably around the arts' (EC News, 1990: quoted in Zeppel and Hall, 1992, p. 53).

Irrespective of the controversy surrounding the Council's programme of events for the year, the fact remains that the Council succeeded in promoting Glasgow as a cultural destination. Undoubtedly, the status of 'City of Culture' was a significant watershed because all previous Cities of Culture were capital cities, recognized as important cultural destinations, while Glasgow was not considered to be 'one of the established cultural destinations of Europe' (Richards, 1996a, p. 27). This is further reinforced by the substantially high positive perceptions of Glasgow by residents in London and the south-east of England (see Law, 1995). Subsequent initiatives in the arts include the establishment of the Gallery of Modern Art (if, once more, somewhat controversial), gaining permission for lending overseas of items from the Burrell Collection (see below) and designation of City of Architecture and Design in 1999.

Glasgow recognizes that destinations cannot afford to stand still. Many new attractions have therefore been developed, starting with the Burrell Collection and subsequently the Garden Festival in 1988 and City of Culture in 1990, the new Concert Hall, Citizens' Theatre, Scottish National Opera, St Mungo's and most recently the Gallery of Modern Art. These have been factors in maintaining and helping to promote Glasgow's position as a major tourist destination city.

However, the development of cultural attractions is only one part of a more comprehensive tourism strategy. Substantial attention has also been paid to developing the retail and conference markets to draw visitors and complement its cultural elements creating a more diverse tourism product. Major developments include the launch of Princes Court which, after initial difficulties, is now a highly successful 'retail attraction' and most recently the opening of Buchanan Galleries. In total the retail sector is considered to account for annual spending of £2.5 billion (€3.5 billion) (Glasgow Development Agency, 1999). Further reflecting this success is the appointment of a City Centre Director to improve the management, quality of environment and promotion of the commercial heart of the city. The position, a multi-partnership funded post, evidences Glasgow's continuing success in building and developing partnerships between the key role players in the city who have formed the City Centre Partnership. The promotion and development of conferences and conventions, a major element of the Council's tourism strategy, was also initiated in the 1980s.

## Conference/convention market

Conferences are of potentially substantial value to the local economy, especially if international in their representation (see Opperman, 1996; Richards, 1996b). It has been estimated that conference delegates spend up to three times more than the average overseas leisure tourist. In 1994 the average residential delegate spend was estimated at £164.26 (€230) per day (Vidal-Hall, 1996). Studies suggest that approximately 50% of delegate spend is accounted for by hospitality, retail, entertainment/attractions and local transport (Henley Centre, 1996; Vidal-Hall, 1996; Dorsey, 1998).

Glasgow's commitment to such an approach was heralded by the establishment of the Convention Bureau well in advance of most others in the UK and, more importantly, has demonstrated the ability to compete well in the international marketplace. The continued development of Glasgow as a conference venue is manifest in the following points:

- The Convention Bureau was voted best UK Convention Bureau in 1994 and 1995.
- Glasgow was ranked eighth in the UK as a conference venue in 1995.
- The value of conferences to the city was estimated at £33 million in 1995 and £54 million in 1996.

The commitment of Glasgow City to this area is well exemplified by the infrastructure that has been developed, most recently evidenced by the expansion of the Scottish Exhibition and Conference Centre (SECC), now one of the leading venues in the UK.

Key factors influencing conference organizers in their choice of location are appropriate facilities and accessibility. Further, when comparing suitable venues, sights of interest and cultural attractions become important elements in deciding between comparative locations. Therefore the status of Glasgow as a primary destination renowned for its cultural attractions is a highly influential factor.

## Tourism demand

Tourist data for Glasgow in the 1990s are presented in Table 6.1. Growth in the number of tourists while not dramatic has been consistent. Between 1991 and 1998 domestic tourism grew by 88% and overseas tourism increased 30% between 1991 and 1997. Glasgow Airport is the major entry/exit point for overseas visitors accounting for 20% of trips to Scotland and 30% of trips to Glasgow (Leslie and Craig, 2000). Two-thirds of these visits take place between April and September. Once in Scotland the main transport category is the hired car, accounting for 23% of trips (Scottish Tourist Board, annual). Over 50% of overnight stays are in hotel/guesthouse accommodation (UKTS, annual). Overall, Glasgow has outperformed the

**Table 6.1.** Volume and value of domestic and overseas tourism to Glasgow. (From Glasgow Development Agency, 1999.)

| Year | Domestic trips (million) | Domestic expenditure (£million) | Overseas trips (million) | Overseas expenditure (£million) |
|------|---------|---------|---------|---------|
| 1991 | 0.8 | 102 | 0.43 | 82 |
| 1992 | 0.7 | 94 | 0.46 | 101 |
| 1993 | 0.8 | 100 | 0.44 | 105 |
| 1994 | 0.8 | 114 | 0.49 | 151 |
| 1995 | 1.0 | 112 | 0.49 | 155 |
| 1996 | 1.2 | 132 | 0.50 | 159 |
| 1997 | 1.4 | 163 | 0.56 | 166 |
| 1998 | 1.5 | 183 | – | – |

rest of Scotland in overseas visitors, the main market segments of which are the USA and Germany; Germans consider Glasgow second only to London in the UK (Leslie and Craig, 2000).

On average, 50% of all holiday trips are for three nights or less whilst overseas visitors to the Greater Glasgow and Clyde Valley (GGCV) area average 5.5 nights per trip. The proportion of short stays (53%) is higher than the average for Scotland (43%), indicating the popularity of the area as a business and short stay destination. The area is also more popular as a destination for visits while on a touring holiday (17% of visitors compared with 15% nationally).

Glasgow is the main business area and largest urban destination in Scotland, and now is second only to Edinburgh as the most important localized destination for tourists (Leslie and Craig, 2000). It is also one of the most popular UK destinations for overseas visitors ranked third, after London and Edinburgh (see Table 6.2).

## The ATLAS survey (1997) and the cultural tourist in Glasgow

It is clear from the findings of the 1997 ATLAS survey (see Averill *et al.*, 1997) undertaken in Glasgow, and earlier studies (see Richards, 1996a) that the desire to experience (65% of visitors) and learning new things (60% of visitors) are still prime motivators for the majority of cultural tourists. Interestingly, just over half of all respondents said that they always visit a museum when on holiday, yet according to Silberberg's definition most of these visitors must be classed as being motivated only 'in part' by culture as 28% of respondents describe their normal holiday as 'sun/beach'.

When asked how important the attraction was in their desire to visit the area, only one in nine visitors regarded it as being important or very important. This would indicate that the majority of tourists visiting these attractions are in the 'accidental' category. This may be linked to the absence of admission charges; people may be more inclined to 'wander in' particularly as major attractions are readily accessible to people already in the central areas.

The one major variance of significance in comparison to the main findings of the full ATLAS survey was that the connections between working in the 'culture sector' and visits to cultural attractions are less apparent in the case of Glasgow, thus supporting the view that the attractiveness of Glasgow's cultural attractions appeals to a wider audience. Other variances relating to key aspects of the socio-demographic profile of cultural tourists in general, as identified by Richards (1996a), compared with the cultural tourist in Glasgow are presented in Table 6.3. Significantly, Glasgow's cultural visitor tends to be younger and is a little less likely to be in a professional or technical occupation. Table 6.4 presents a general profile of the cultural tourists to Glasgow's galleries.

**Table 6.2.** Top ten overseas tourist destination cities in the UK 1998. (From Anon., 1999.)

| City | Number of tourists |
|------|--------------------|
| London | 13,460,000 |
| Edinburgh | 1,100,000 |
| Glasgow | 560,000 |
| Birmingham | 490,000 |
| Manchester | 470,000 |
| Oxford | 450,000 |
| York | 380,000 |
| Cambridge | 370,000 |
| Bath | 350,000 |
| Brighton | 310,000 |

**Table 6.3.** Key demographic factors: comparison between findings of main ATLAS survey and Glasgow.

| Key aspects: main survey | Glasgow |
|--------------------------|---------|
| Visitors earn higher than average incomes | Yes |
| Visitors are more highly educated than average | Yes |
| Visitors tend to be in the older age groups | Only approx. 20% were 'over 50' while approx 50% were in the '20–39' age band |
| Visitors tend to be in professional/technical occupations | Less evident |

**Table 6.4.** Comparison of visitors to the Burrell Collection with total visitor survey: key characteristics.

| Factor | Visitor response (%) | |
|---|---|---|
| | Burrell Collection | Main survey |
| Experience new things | 60 | 64 |
| Less likely to be in the company of others | 50 | 64 |
| Less likely to be 'just to relax' | 41 | 52 |
| Visits a museum while on holiday | 43 | 52 |
| Take a cultural holiday | 5 | 18 |
| Involved in some aspect of 'culture' in work | 9 | 19 |
| Recommend friends to visit | 25 | 36 |
| Visit one or more art galleries per year | 64 | 72 |
| Visit one or more museums per year | 21 | 32 |
| Intend to visit a 'festival' | 0 | 8 |

## Glasgow's main galleries

The influence of Glasgow's galleries during visits to Glasgow has long been recognized. For example, in the late 1980s Myerscough (1990) estimated that 34% of all trips to Glasgow were arts related tourism. This strength was recognized by the Council and in their commitment to the supply and development of its galleries, which are substantially dependent on the Council for funding. Council funding represents approximately 88% of their income – £9.55 million (€13.4 million) in 1995 which supported 689 direct jobs (Glasgow City Council, 1998). In 1998 Glasgow's museums and galleries received 3,125,524 visitors (Table 6.5). A profile of the major galleries in Glasgow (except the Burrell Collection, which is dealt with in more detail later) is presented below.

### Kelvingrove Art Gallery and Museum

This gallery is one of only two attractions in Scotland which consistently attract over 1 million visitors a year (the other being Edinburgh Castle).

One of the aims of the first of Glasgow's Great Exhibitions (1888) was to finance a new Art Gallery, Museum and School of Art. Kelvingrove Art Gallery and Museum was '. . . seen as necessary to reflect the city's growing stature' (Kinchin and Kinchin, 1989, p. 19). It was completed in time for the 1901 Great Exhibition, opening in its present form the following year. It now houses displays on natural history, archaeology, history and ethnography and what is considered to be 'Britain's finest civic collection of British and European paintings' (Greater Glasgow Tourist Board, 1996, p. 17).

Kelvingrove Art Gallery is currently seeking £20 million (€28 million) from Lottery funding for a major refurbishment (due to commence in 2001).

**Table 6.5.** Visitor numbers (,000) to Glasgow's Galleries. (From Glasgow City Council.)

| Year | Attraction[a] | | | |
|------|-------------|---------|------|----------|
|      | Kelvingrove | Burrell | GOMA | St Mungo[b] |
| 1990 | 1016 | 878 | – | – |
| 1991 | 906  | 486 | – | – |
| 1992 | 875  | 425 | – | – |
| 1993 | 796  | 362 | – | 159 |
| 1994 | 904  | 336 | – | 147 |
| 1995 | 992  | 294 | – | 154 |
| 1996 | 1060 | 279 | 561 | 158 |
| 1997 | 1054 | 331 | 410 | 130 |
| 1998 | 1128 | 343 | 453 | – |

[a]Visitor numbers rounded to nearest thousand.
[b]St Mungo is included to provide a comparison.

But refurbishment will involve closure for 18 months, which, given the gallery's position as *the* visitor attraction in terms of numbers, holds potentially serious impacts on visitor demand. It will be interesting to see if visitor numbers to the other galleries decline during the planned closure period.

### Gallery of Modern Art (GOMA)

The GOMA opened in March 1996, and is housed in a building that dates back to 1780. The gallery is set on four floors reflecting the elements of fire, earth, water and air, with a collection of works from the 1950s to the present. It received its millionth visitor in January 1998.

### The McLellan Galleries

The McLellan Galleries are mentioned here because of two key differences to the other galleries in Glasgow. First, the attraction is based on exhibitions which are often very diverse in content (e.g. the James Bond exhibition in 1998) and secondly, it is the only council gallery which charges for admission.

The McLellan Galleries were initially opened in 1854, but following a fire in the mid-1980s, complete refurbishment was required and the 'new' McLellan Galleries were officially opened in March 1990. The galleries are now recognized as: 'the largest, most exciting, touring exhibition venue in Britain outside London' (Glasgow City Council, 1994). The level of visitor interest is very much a function of an exhibition's attractiveness, e.g. in 1996 it received 215,684 visitors and in 1997 only 39,774 visitors.

In addition to the above attractions, Glasgow also has:

- The Museum of Transport (approx. 440,000 visitors in 1998).
- The People's Palace, Glasgow's social history museum which under-
  went refurbishment and reopened in summer 1998 (approx. 442,153
  visitors since reopening).
- St Mungo Museum of Religious Life and Art: the most controversial and
  unique museum in Glasgow opened in 1993. It is the first museum of
  religion in the world, incorporating an exploration of different faiths
  through paintings and religious artefacts.
- The Scotland St School Museum of Education (approx. 60,000 visitors in
  1997).
- The House of an Art Lover, which is on the south side of Glasgow
  (approx. 22,000 visitors in 1997).

One other major collection bears mention: the Hunterian Museum at
Glasgow University (some commentators might argue that this is one of
Glasgow's better kept secrets!) which received approx. 67,000 visitors in
1997. Renovations are currently being undertaken, supported by a £2.4
million (€3.4 million) Heritage Lottery grant.

## The impact of tourism/cultural tourism

Glasgow is unique in Scotland in terms of its array of substantial cultural
attractions, predominantly of historic importance, which for the past decade
have gained considerable and consistent numbers of visitors. The importance of these attractions collectively in terms of drawing people to Glasgow
cannot be overstated (Leslie, 1997).

While it is difficult to quantify accurately the impact of tourism on
Glasgow the following paragraphs serve to demonstrate that it does have
a substantial direct impact in terms of revenue and employment and
additional significant benefits compared with more traditional sectors of
the economy. Even so this hardly conveys the actual and potential
domino effects of visitors to the locality. Visitors to urban environments have
generated additional demand on general services such as transport, e.g.
public transport and taxis, retail outlets and entertainment with additional
and positive impacts on suppliers to the main tourist amenities and services.

There are potentially strong interrelationships between tourism
development (a key element of the main strategy formulated by the city
in the early 1980s to address and promote urban regeneration) and
perceptions of image, quality of environment and general well-being on
the part of the community. Evidence of these interrelationships is clear
from the success that the city's strategy has achieved over the last 15 years;
witness the position of Glasgow as a leading short-break destination and
attractive location for new business. In addition to its growing profile in
developing and promoting itself as a major tourist destination, it has been

very successful in attracting new business development (see Boyle and Hughes, 1995; Leslie and Craig, 2000).

The development of tourism demands a quality environment and thus provides impetus to such campaigns as cleaning buildings, retaining historical building façades, revitalizing buildings of high visual amenity, reducing pollution through, for example, traffic and improving public transport. Further, there are developments in the streetscape such as pedestrianization, attractive lighting systems, enhancement of walkways (for instance, introduction of attractive seating and hanging baskets) and so forth. These initiatives make the locale all the more attractive to shoppers and thus promote demand for retail space and the development of retail based attractions such as Princes Court and most recently Buchanan Galleries (Shopping Mall). Collectively, this generates an attractive destination drawing more visitors. The reality of this is evident in a number of ways, not least in the accommodation sector which has grown and is still expanding with major new hotel developments, particularly in the closing years of the millennium (Leslie and Craig, 2000).

### Revenue

Additional to the tourist expenditure noted in Table 6.1, almost 140 million excursionists spent £1400 million (€1960 million) in the city in 1998, which accounts for more than 25% of total expenditure for all Scotland (Glasgow Development Agency, 1999).

### Employment

There are an estimated 21,000 tourism related jobs in Glasgow, and 45,984 jobs overall in the GGCV area, accounting for approximately 7% of all employment in the area (Glasgow Development Agency, 1999).

The overall level of visitor demand for the city bears witness to the success of the strategic initiatives launched in the early 1980s; an approach comparable with other cities in Europe which have a substantially higher presence of cultural and symbolic capital (see van der Berg *et al.*, 1995). Further recognition of its 'Arts Tourism' strategy is evident from the city's designation as one of the British Arts Cities – 'Cities of Excellence for Arts and Culture', established in 1996. The other cities are: Edinburgh, Bath, Bristol, Brighton, Birmingham, Cardiff, Leeds, Liverpool, London, Manchester and Newcastle.

## The Burrell Collection

The gifting of the Burrell Collection in 1944 to the city presented the council with a major problem for many years, primarily due to the absence of a suitable venue. However, establishing the Collection in a suitable venue became very much a part of the Council's agenda in the mid-1970s. As

Daiches wrote at the time of the presentation of the plan for housing the Collection: '. . . amid the fierce debates about high-rise flats and grandiose plans for urban renewal, Glasgow has been quietly establishing its right to be considered as a great city of the arts' (Booth and Boyle, 1993, p. 31).

The outcome of the Council's deliberations was the establishment of 'The Burrell Collection' in Pollok Park in 1983 – a timing which bears witness to the substantial expansion of 'heritage attractions' in the 1980s. This custom-built museum, designed by Gasson, houses the eclectic collection of Sir William Burrell, which includes medieval, oriental and classical art. In itself, it is an unusual collection compared with the national museums of renown which developed in the 19th century and designed, to quote Richards, 'to provide comprehensive collections spanning all epochs and cultures' (1996b, p. 273). It is located on the south side of Glasgow, isolated from the other major attractions located on the north side across the River Clyde, approximately 3 miles from the city centre and is accessible by bus and rail link. It is close to the M77 and M8 motorways and easily accessible by car from the city centre.

The delay between the gifting of the collection and its eventual display was due to the inability of the city to find a suitable location that fitted the stipulations of the will. One of Burrell's concerns was the potential damage to the collection from the air pollution of the city at the time. This hurdle was overcome by the improvement in air quality after the 1950s and the decision to establish the collection in 361 acres of parkland in the grounds of Pollok House; itself bequeathed to the people of Glasgow by Sir John Maxwell in 1966.

Due to the extensive nature of the Collection, it is not possible to display all items. This, along with the decline in visitor numbers, led to the controversy regarding the lending of artefacts outwith the museum (see below).

The position of the Collection in marketing terms cannot be overstated. It is an integral part of the tourism product of Glasgow and is a unique facet. As an attraction away from the City centre it holds a number of advantages in the context of tourism, e.g.:

- Visitor demand for local transportation will increase.
- The length of stay will be extended due to the increased length of time taken by visits. This in turn will give rise to additional visitor expenditure.

## Demand

The visitor figures for the Collection are presented in Table 6.5. Although the numbers have been declining, the Collection has consistently been in the 'top twenty' for admissions to Scotland's free attractions. It is notable that the visitor profile is more diverse than that of the other galleries in Glasgow which indicates a wider appeal to a greater cross-section of society and thus visitor type (ATLAS Survey, 1997). This implies that there is a higher proportion of 'accidental tourists' which may be a function of its location within Pollok Park, with some visitors being primarily motivated by the attractions of the park and/or Pollok House itself.

### Socio-demographic profile

Visitors to the Collection are likely to be younger than at other cultural sites, with less than 3% of visitors aged 60 or over, compared with 13% for the survey sites as a whole. Education is another factor which stands out when analysing the socio-demographic profile of 'Burrell visitors'. There is a lower percentage of visitors who have studied at 'higher and postgraduate' levels of education (35%) compared with the overall analysis (47%). However, the visitors were found to be not substantially less interested, or motivated, in 'learning new things' when compared to the main survey (see Table 6.4).

### Reasons for decline in tourist visits to the Collection

The fact that visitor figures are not reported in detail makes it difficult to account for the evident decline in visitor numbers in recent years. However, a number of factors have been suggested:

- Decline in local, regional and Scotland based visitors due to many having already visited the Collection.
- Decline in domestic visitors outwith Scotland due to previous visits and lack of promotion.
- Lack of awareness on the part of domestic visitors on developments over time.
- Lack of awareness of changes in exhibits.

However, interest by overseas visitors should not have declined to such a notable extent due, in many cases, to an absence of prior experience. Only 14% of overseas visitors had visited the Burrell Collection previously, compared with 33% repeat visitors among foreign tourists at other attractions surveyed. In fact 30% of visitors to the Burrell Collection came from overseas and 'The Burrell' is invariably cited as *the* attraction to visit when overseas visitors enquire about places to visit (Leslie, 1997).

## Overseas lending

Glasgow's galleries are an integral and substantial component of the city's attractiveness as a tourist destination. Consequently displaying renowned elements of the Collection in museums and galleries abroad contributes to the marketing and promotion of Glasgow overseas. However, this was not possible until late 1997 (see below).

Glasgow's appeal as a city destination will vary over time. It is thus important that new products are developed, such as the Gallery of Modern Art. But also it is important for new approaches to be adopted in the

promotion of existing facets of the city's tourism product. The popularity of
the Burrell Collection in the 1980s bears witness to both factors. However,
with the decline in visitors in the 1990s it was considered that it was important to promote the Collection more widely, thereby stimulating renewed
interest among previous visitors, attracting new visitors and more importantly to promote the Collection to a wider international audience. Thus,
displaying elements of the Collection outside of Britain was seen as a way of
promoting the Collection and Glasgow to a far wider audience and potentially thereby encourage visits to the Burrell Collection. Secondly, through
displays elsewhere the image of the City of Glasgow would be usefully promoted. Partly in recognition of such factors the council decided to seek to
overturn the stipulation in Burrell's bequest that items for the Collection may
not be lent outside of mainland Britain. The primary argument presented by
the Council was that this stipulation was made at a time when the world was
a very different place (i.e. during the Second World War) and shipping valuable and fragile items was by no means as safe or secure as it is in the 1990s.

As this is a substantial management issue and of importance to a large
number of attractions, the matter is discussed further in the following
section.

## Management issues

A key management issue, if not the most important issue for all galleries, is
funding. There have been a number of recent government initiatives on
funding in England and Wales, which are also of significance to Scotland as
they will undoubtedly be very influential in the deliberations of the Scottish
Parliament on developments in this sector in Scotland. Therefore attention
is given here to ways in which galleries can address problems arising
from declining funding, commencing with the Burrell Collection and
the controversial initiative by the council to challenge one of the main
stipulations of the bequest.

## The Burrell Collection and lending rights

The Burrell Collection has and is experiencing a continuing problem in
attracting visitors and, along with the other galleries in Glasgow, declining
funding from the Council. The Council claimed that part of the problem at
The Burrell was its inability to display pieces outside of mainland Britain
(due to conditions of the will), while the trustees, and others who oppose
further manipulation of the stipulations of the bequest, felt not enough
was being done to promote the Collection (Burrell Inquiry, 1997). Some
commentators felt that this was a dangerous precedent, as it may discourage
similar bequests.

The council's main argument was that in 1944 at the time of Sir William
Burrell's death the world was a very different place. Burrell's involvement in
shipping meant that he was all too well aware of dangers to cargoes during
transit. This action was opposed by the Trustees and a Parliamentary

Commission was established (Burrell Inquiry, 1997). A significant aspect of the Council's rationale as to why lending overseas would be a benefit to the city involved its contribution to tourism and thus a specialist witness (the author) in this field was called to give evidence to the Commission[1]. The underpinnings to the Council's action were: first, that the possibility of lending items from the Collection abroad will generate income; for example, the loan of material for exhibits from the Kelvingrove Gallery to Japan for 6 months raised £100,000 (€145,000). Secondly, the publicity which potentially surrounds such loans will contribute to promoting the source of the exhibits and more importantly Glasgow's image. Further, it has been argued, that such promotion and greater awareness of Glasgow as a 'cultural destination' may influence those persons influential in the decision making process as to where to locate their next international conference (Burrell Inquiry, 1997).

The points made in the preceding sections will have conveyed the complexity of tourism and related demand. In some ways, cities may be seen as products – tourism products. If we take the view that a city can be a product in tourist terms then we can develop this perspective into the realms of product marketing and, for example, draw comparisons with the marketing of other popular consumer goods. There is a need to maintain a level of market awareness of the product, but such campaigns are often expensive and well beyond the means of the city. However, the staging of exhibitions of artefacts from the Collection elsewhere when coupled with the potential promotional exposure that could be achieved might justifiably be seen as having a very similar effect. Arguably, overseas loans could promote Glasgow more effectively than advertising through general media channels and generate more publicity.

The Commission found in favour of the Council with the exception of the loan of lace and similar material.

## Funding

An obvious response in the face of decreasing public sector funding is to introduce charges – a highly controversial debate in the UK. However, it is only the national galleries, as noted earlier, which are for the most part funded directly by central government which may introduce charges. This happened in 1998 in Scotland, earlier in England and Wales. However, the Government is arguably backtracking on their original support for the introduction of charges. It has allocated £99 million (€140 million), over 3 years, to the national museums and galleries and a further £7 million (€10 million) from the Heritage Lottery Fund to promote access to new audiences. This

---

[1]  The author was the specialist witness in tourism at the Burrell Collection (Lending) Draft Provisional Parliamentary Inquiry in September 1997.

money is primarily aimed at improving access and to enable admission charges at national museums and galleries in England and Wales to be discontinued by 2001. Scotland will almost certainly follow this lead.

Those galleries which come under local government may not introduce charges. Beyond their role in contributing to the tourism product of a destination and as such present a valuable economic argument to counter reductions in their funding they have but limited options in terms of generating income. Limited because a number of potential opportunities will conflict with their primary purpose, create tension and generate controversy (for example, see Pick, 1988; Evans, 1995).

Essentially, to increase income galleries need to obtain more funding from private sector. To aid such an approach the Association for Business Sponsorship of the Arts (ABSA) was founded in 1976, and serves to provide a conduit between galleries and business to help develop potential partnerships. In 1996/97 the organization contributed £95.6 million (€137 million) (ABSA, 1997). A more recent initiative was the launch of the Arts in Action Award for business in partnership with the Arts launched by Arts and Business. This award is designed to recognize a business programme which demonstrates the use of arts to promote social and economic regeneration. In both cases, the support is basically sponsorship and, as such, is subject to the vagaries of perceptions as to what is 'appropriate' and 'high Art' etc.

An alternative and potentially lucrative source of additional income is to market the venue as an attractive location in which to stage a business meeting, conference or dinner. Venues, e.g. Kelvingrove Art Gallery, which have such potential, present the council and Tourist Board with additional elements in their bids to attract conferences and, for example, as venues for hosting civic receptions.

Another potential opportunity is to introduce a loyalty credit card whereby the organization receives a royalty every time the card is used, as some of the national museums in London have done (Seward, 1995).

The Lottery has been a major source of funding for attractions (Scottish Tourist Board, 1998b), but such funding has been for capital costs and not income related. However, there are clear indications that this orientation is shifting from capital investment to be more project based. However, there are a number of developments which hold potentially significant implications in accessing Lottery funding in future.

- The Government has called for local authorities to develop local cultural strategies which include libraries, parks, playgrounds, museums and arts and other cultural activities (Department of Culture, Media and Sport, 1999). The first development of this initiative is now being piloted by 14 local authorities in England. Although the focus is on England this initiative is likely to be taken up by the Scottish Parliament. Further, the cultural strategy should link with the proposed Regional Cultural

Consortia; both of which will be explicitly influential in levering funds from the National Lottery.

- The Government has produced revised projections of the available Lottery funding for the Arts sector for buildings for the period to 2006 – from £1 billion to £630 million. This ties in with the Government's aim that projects seeking support from the Lottery should be considered in the regional context and related cultural strategies. To quote the Secretary of State for Culture – 'Public subsidy for the arts is vital to encourage participation but needs to be firmly controlled' and further 'Public subsidy has to be about enabling the greatest possible number of people to experience and enjoy the arts' (ILAM, 1999, p. 3).
- A new organization is being created which will merge the functions of the bodies currently responsible for Museums, Libraries and Archive Council. The new body will have a key role in supporting, representing and notably influencing Lottery funding.
- The essence of the Government's consultation document on the future of museums and arts galleries is that museums must adopt business management practices; for instance: long-term planning, access and quality of services. Thus, new investment in the form of funding will be influenced by efficiency, access and private sponsorship.
- Galleries and museums will increasingly be seen in the local/ regional context rather than as individual operations. 'It must remain a priority to ensure existing collections are well managed and wisely used; bodies seeking support for new museums should demonstrate clearly both the need and the sustainability of their proposals' (MGC, 1998, para 8).

It also emerges from recent developments in this sector that: (i) there will be a greater requirement to update the presentation of exhibits; and (ii) there is a need to employ staff who will provide quality service rather than the staff of old who were basically security attendants.

The latter two factors require financial support and thus add to the problems of funding already in evidence. For example, observations made during the 1997 ATLAS survey in Glasgow noted a general apathy among staff (with the notable exception of St Mungo's and some individuals at other locations) (see Averill *et al.*, 1997). This, it may be argued, is largely due to the cut-backs introduced by the council. Training has been cut back, staffing reduced and morale may be low due to the uncertainty of the future situation. Good management practice and team building exercises may help, but these alone will not resolve the situation and may be difficult to implement in the current climate of uncertainty.

Finally, the local authority could seek to increase its direct funding. However, this would be unlikely given the increased financial constraints on local government witnessed in the past 10 years. For instance, Glasgow museums have had their funding cut annually since 1996. The current budget is 32% less than in 1996 and staffing has decreased by 30%. To put this into perspective; according to Wilson and Simpson (1999) the current budget of approximately £15 million is equivalent to a staffing to visitor ratio of approximately 10 per 100,000 visitors and promotion expenditure of £49 per 1000 visitors; these ratios are well below national averages. In response to this situation, Glasgow is in the process of bidding for metropolitan status which would mean, among other factors, a new and increased funding system for its galleries. In effect, a substantial degree of funding from central government would be gained.

## Conclusion

The successful outcomes of the city's urban regeneration strategy developed in the early 1980s in full recognition of the socio-economic problems and unrivalled (in the UK) negative image are very evident today. In terms of urban regeneration this is perhaps nowhere better illustrated than in the Gorbals – a notorious slum area of the 1970s which has been transformed – '. . . now it is being sought after as an area to live' (Edge, 1999).

The development of tourism has been a major tool in this success albeit limited in terms of its tourism product, particularly in terms of a heritage predating industrialization, and in the potential for new developments (Leslie, 1997). As a tourist destination it is not a 'top ten' European city given the lack of 'real cultural capital' (see Richards, 1996b). In the absence of such Glasgow has gone against the 'norm' in that it has predominantly ignored its 'cultural and symbolic capital' of industrial heritage and developed new cultural attractions.

In effect, the city adopted a proactive tourism strategy which recognized the weaknesses in its tourism portfolio. The strategy was not solely limited to its cultural services, it was and is far more holistic in seeking to develop a foundation based on cultural attractions and events to build on Glasgow's strengths. This strategy commenced with the establishment of the Burrell Collection, hosting of the Garden Festival and opening of the Royal Concert Hall. In combination this approach was instrumental in the city being designated European City of Culture for 1990 – a watershed which marked the change in image and status of the city. But the city has not stood still, recognizing that tourism attractions must be re-created with increasing frequency in order to sustain the novelty value of consumption. 'This [it is argued] is achieved by utilising the cultural and symbolic capital attached to specific places to create new attractions, events and spectacles' (Richards, 1996b, p. 264). In the context of Glasgow this is evident in the seeking of opportunities to expand the image and status of Glasgow – most recently manifest in the designation of Glasgow as the 1999 City of Architecture and Design. A further indication that the council recognizes that it must not stand still is the development of the £32 million (€46 million) National Gallery (an extension to the National Gallery established in Edinburgh in

1859) which, it has been proposed, is to be set-up in a 19th century courthouse in the rapidly developing Merchant City area. The city is also re-developing the SECC and developing the retail sector.

Overall, tourism has contributed substantially to the success of the city's aims in urban regeneration. Furthermore, the collective effects of the main elements of the strategy have had a substantial impact in attracting inward investment and the establishment in the area of new business. Responses to the actual and anticipated growth in business activity are well in evidence (Leslie and Craig, 2000).

It is not surprising therefore that Glasgow is outperforming most other major cities and thus in the context of the UK, many of the '. . . most successful urban sites [which] are the pre-industrial ones; that is even in a European country which had the earliest Industrial Revolution and a more modest pattern of earlier historical architecture' (Townsend, 1992, p. 32 quoted in Richards, 1996b, p. 277). Daiches was indeed prescient when commenting in 1977 on Glasgow's first initiatives to address its economic and social problems and the early signs of attention to the development potential of the arts – 'Glasgow . . . will have a place of rank as an art centre among European Cities' (quoted in Booth and Boyle, 1993, p. 31).

# References

ABSA (1997) *Annual Report.* Association for Business Sponsorship of the Arts, London.

Adams, G. (1994) The pull of cultural assets. In: Fladmark, J.M. (ed.) *Cultural Tourism.* Donhead Publishing, London.

Anon. (1999) Tops for tourists. *The Sunday Post* 2 May.

Averill, F., Giusti, D., Kerrigan, M., Richardson, A. and Walker, L. (1997) *Socio-cultural Tourism in Glasgow.* Glasgow Caledonian University.

Bianchini, F. and Parkinson, M. (eds) (1993) *Cultural Policy and Urban Regeneration: the West European Experience.* Manchester University Press, Manchester.

Booth, P. and Boyle, R. (1993) See Glasgow, see culture. In: Bianchini, F. and Parkinson, M. (eds) *Cultural Policy and Urban Regeneration: the West European Experience.* Manchester University Press, Manchester, pp. 21–47.

Boyle, M. and Hughes, G. (1994) The politics of urban entrepreneurialism in Glasgow. *Geoforum* 25(4), 453–470.

Burrell Inquiry (1997) *The Burrell Collection (Lending) Draft Provisional Order.* Parliamentary Inquiry, Glasgow.

Chang, T.C., Milen, S., Fallon, D. and Pohlmann, C. (1996) Urban heritage-tourism: the global–local nexus. *Annals of Tourism Research* 23(2), 284–305.

Charlton, C. and Essex, S. (1996) The involvement of district councils in tourism in England and Wales. *Geoforum* 27(2),175–192.

Cohen, E. (1993) Investigating tourist arts. *Annals of Tourism Research* 20, 1–8.

Coutts, H. (1986) Profile of a blockbuster. *Museums Journal* 86(1), 23–26.

Crawford, D. (1990) Horizons. BTA London, December, p. 22.

Department of Culture, Media and Sport (1999) *Guidance for Local Authorities on Local Cultural Strategies.* DCMS, London.

DoE (1990) *Tourism and the Inner City: Inner City Research Programme.* HMSO, London.

Dorsey, K. (1998) Open doors for a wider perspective. *The Herald* 12 February.

Edge, S. (1999) A decade later culture boon's Glasgowing on *Scottish Daily Express* p.10.

English Tourist Board (1999) *C&T – Newsletter of the UK Culture and Tourism Group.* No. 1. ETB, London, June.

Evans, G. (1995) Tourism versus education – core functions of museums? In: Leslie, D. (ed.) *Tourism and Leisure – Culture, Heritage and Participation. Tourism and Leisure: Towards the Millennium,* Vol. 1. LSA, Brighton, pp. 145–168.

Fladmark, J.M. (ed.) (1994) *Cultural Tourism.* Donhead Publishing, London.

Glasgow City Council (1994) *Glasgow Museums.* Department of Culture, Glasgow City Council, Glasgow.

Glasgow City Council (1998) *Glasgow Cultural Statistics.* Glasgow City Council, Glasgow.

Glasgow Development Agency (1999) *Glasgow Tourism Statistics.* GDA, Glasgow.

Greater Glasgow Tourist Board (1996) *Glasgow Quick Guide.* GGTB, Glasgow.

Gold, J.R. and Ward, S.V. (eds) (1994) *Place Promotion: the Use of Publicity and Marketing to Sell Towns and Regions.* John Wiley & Sons, Chichester.

Gunn, C.A. (1997) *Vacationscape,* 3rd edn. Taylor and Francis, Washington, DC.

Hall, C. (1996) *Tourism and Politics – Policy, Power and Place.* John Wiley & Sons, Chichester.

Henley Centre (1996) *Tourism Futures.* The Henley Centre, London.

Huber, M., Williams, A. and Shaw, G. (1992) *Culture and Economic Policy: a Survey of the Role of Local Authorities.* Working Paper No. 5, Tourism Research Group, University of Exeter.

ILAM (1999) *Leisure Bulletin.* ILAM, Basildon, 26 August.

Imrie, R. and Thomas, H. (1993) *British Urban Policy and the Urban Development Corporations.* Paul Chapman, London.

Kinchin, P. and Kinchin, J. (1989) *Glasgow's Great Exhibitions.* White Cockade Publishing.

Law, C.M. (1995) *Urban Tourism: Attracting Visitors to Large Cities.* Cassell, London.

Law, C.M. (1998) The role of tourism and recreation in the local economy. Paper presented at 'Urban Tourism – Achievements and Problems'. South Bank University, April.

Leslie, D. (1991) Tourism and Northern Ireland: 1967–1991 – troubled times. Master of Philosophy thesis. University of Ulster.

Leslie, D. (1997) Specialist witness on cultural tourism, 'Burrell Inquiry (1997)'. The Burrell Collection (Lending) Draft Provisional Order. Parliamentary Inquiry, Glasgow, September.

Leslie, D. and Craig, C. (2000) 'All-suite' hotels: a study of the market potential in Scotland. *Journal of Vacation Marketing* 6(3), 221–235.

MGC (1998) *A Policy Framework for Museums in the United Kingdom.* Museums and Galleries Commission, London.

Myerscough, J. (1990) *Glasgow – City of Culture.* PSI, London.

Opperman, M. (1996) Convention cities – images and changing fortunes. *Tourism Studies* 7(1), 10–18.

Page, S. (1995) *Urban Tourism*. Routledge, London.

Pick, J. (1988) *The Arts in a State: a Study of Government Arts Policies from Ancient Greece to the Present*. Bristol Classical Press, Bristol.

Richards, B. (1996) The conference market in the UK. *Insights* March, B-67/82. English Tourist Board, London, UK

Richards, G. (ed.) (1996a) *Cultural Tourism in Europe*. CAB International, Wallingford, UK.

Richards, G. (1996b) Production and consumption of European cultural tourism. *Annals of Tourism Research* 23(2), 261–283.

Richards, G. (1998) Cultural tourism in Europe: recent developments. *ATLAS News* June, 12–15.

Richards, G. and Wilkes, J. (1990) *The Role of Local Authorities in Tourism Development and Promotion*. PNL Press, London.

Richardson, H.W. (1969) *Regional Economics*. Wiedenfeld and Nicolson, London.

Scottish Office (1996) *Scottish Abstract of Statistics*. No. 25. Government Statistical Service, Scottish Office, Edinburgh.

Scottish Tourist Board (1998a) *Cultural Tourism Strategy and Action Plan (1998–2001)*. STB, Edinburgh.

Scottish Tourist Board (1998b) *Scottish Visitor Attractions: Review 1997*. STB, Edinburgh.

Scottish Tourist Board (annual) *Tourism Statistics*. STB, Edinburgh.

Seward, K. (1995) Would you credit it. *Leisure Opportunities* May, 30/31.

Silberberg, T. (1995) Cultural tourism and business opportunities for museum and heritage sites. *Tourism Management* 16(5), 361–365.

Stammage, R. (1990) *Arts and Tourism Tourism* 66 (April/May), 11.

UKTS (Annual) *Tourist Statistics for the UK*. ETB, NITB, STB and WTB.

van der Berg, L., van der Berg, J. and van der Meer, J. (1995) *Urban Tourism Performance and Strategies in Eight European Cities*. Avebury Press, Aldershot.

Vandermey, A. (1984) Assessing the importance of urban tourism: conceptual and measurement issues. *Tourism Management* 3, 123–135.

Vidal-Hall, C. (1996) Competitive spirit. *Conference and Incentive Travel* September, 29–32.

Wilson, I. and Simpson, C. (1999) The decline and fall of Glasgow's Galleries. *The Herald* 16, June, 3.

Zeppel, H. and Hall, C.M. (1992) Arts and heritage tourism. In: Weiler, B. and Hall, C.M. (eds) *Special Interest Tourism*. CAB International, Wallingford, UK, pp. 47–68.

# Clonmacnoise: a Monastic Site, Burial Ground and Tourist Attraction

## Frances McGettigan[1] and Kevin Burns[2]

[1]Athlone Institute of Technology, Athlone, Co. Westmeath;
[2]Dundalk Institute of Technology, Dundalk, Co. Louth, Ireland

## Introduction

Cultural tourism has only recently been recognized as a major phenomenon in Ireland (O'Donnchadha and O'Connor, 1996). Since 1990, however, the Irish Government has expended considerable energy on the development of cultural attractions in the country.

Prior to the 1990s, heritage and culture tended to be subsumed within the realms of general rather than special interest tourism and were indeed an essential part of any destination, helping to convey the intrinsic ethnic, heritage and cultural aspects of the country and to promote its individuality relative to other destinations. Traditionally, while the vast majority of visitors to Ireland may not specifically choose to visit solely because of the historical and cultural attractions, it was probably implicit in their perception of Ireland that such aspects would form an intrinsic part of the holiday experience.

There was a belief in Ireland that the concept of the special interest, historic/cultural tourist might more appropriately be applied to visitors to other destinations which offered 'mega-sights' or 'high culture'. There was also a possible lack of awareness of the fundamental changes in society which have turned culture into a mass market product, or at least into a product for consumption by markets far larger and more varied than the small cultural elite of a generation earlier (Konsola, 1993).

Ancestry and heritage have always had an important appeal for the large Irish Diaspora. This was an important reason for visiting Ireland and becoming acquainted with one's ethnic and ancestral origins and to visit friends/relatives. Both the UK and the North American markets traditionally frequented Ireland in large numbers. However, in the early 1990s there was a new demand from the European market to visit Ireland, and 40% of these visitors had a clear preference for cultural/heritage activities.

In 1992 the then Director General of Bord Fáilte (the Irish Tourist Board), Martin Dully, stated that

> There are people all over the world in search of cultural experience who are eager to enrich their knowledge about other lands and other people's way of life, tradition and customs. Some are interested in archaeology, historic buildings and ruins, others in museums and galleries, concerts, operas or traditional dancing and you will always find people who want to trace their ancestors.

These changes in the marketplace were to some extent met by significant changes in the supply of the product or the creation of cultural manifestations specially for tourist consumption (Cohen, 1988). In the Department of Tourism and Trade's 1989–1993 Operational Programme IR£50 million (€62.5 million) was spent on culture and heritage based attractions. The strategy for developing sustainable tourism (Tourism Development Plan 1993–1997) also contained proposals for new product development.

A number of factors combined to create an emerging realization of the potential relationship between 'cultural tourism' and economic development. Firstly, it was realized that cultural tourism could help the tourism industry in its search for diversified holiday experiences for a market that is growing in sophistication and selectivity, and where cultural diversity offers a wide range of potential tourism products.

Secondly, governments and local authorities become conscious that they possess a rich resource that can be exploited for commercial purposes and potential economic benefits to the local economy.

Thirdly, organizations engaged in the production of cultural performance, the maintenance of the stock of cultural artefacts and buildings and even the shaping and sustaining of local cultural distinctiveness are attracted to a potential source of much needed extra finance, in particular when public subsidies are becoming less certain (Ashworth, 1998).

These developments have ensured that there is now an awareness of 'culture' as an activity and a potential form of tourism, with real economic value.

The emerging significance of 'cultural tourism' in Ireland in the 1990s is reflected by:

- The Operational Programme for tourism 1994–1999 where natural and cultural tourism developments received IR£94 million (€117.5 million) under ERDF funding.
- The creation of a new government department then known as the Department of Arts, Culture and the *Gaeltacht* (Gaelic speaking area of Ireland) with responsibility for administrating funding for natural and cultural tourism projects.

- The formulation of the Heritage Council under the Heritage Act 1995, to propose policies and priorities for the identification, protection, presentation and enhancement of the national heritage.

## What is cultural tourism?

Cultural tourism is a form of tourism built around cultural resources. These range from classic heritage attractions to themed trails to traditional crafts to food and drink and even traditional sports and games (Swarbrooke, 1999, p. 307). MacCannell (1976) refers to 'cultural productions', a term which refers not only to the process of culture, but also to the products which result from that process. In fact, cultural tourism is the consumption of these resources (Richards, 1993).

Bonink (1992) identified two basic approaches to cultural tourism. The first, the 'sites and monuments approach' concentrates on describing the type of attractions visited by cultural tourists and is clearly related to a product based definition of culture which is very useful for quantitative research on cultural tourism.

In Ireland it appears that a 'sites and monument' approach is appropriate to define cultural tourism, when quantifying the market visiting 'fee-paying' attractions. These data are published in a biannual 'Visitor Attraction Survey' since 1991. The types of attraction researched include the following:

- Historic houses/castles
- Interpretative centres/museums
- Parks
- Historic monuments
- Gardens
- Other attractions.

These categories comprise a large part of Ireland's physical heritage (as distinct from its artistic, literary or philosophical heritage). 'Heritage' employed in the cultural arena can be used to describe material forms such as: monuments, historical or architectural remains, and artefacts on display in museums or immaterial forms such as philosophy, tradition and art in all their manifestations; the celebration of great events or personalities in history; distinctive ways of life: and education as expressed, for example through literature and folklore. In the natural arena, heritage can be used to describe gardens, landscapes, national parks, wilderness, mountains, rivers, islands and components such as flora and fauna (Herbert *et al.*, 1989; Zeppel and Hall, 1992).

Built heritage is comprised of man-made, fixed elements (Rapoport, 1984) possessing historical values and meaning which are derived from the settings in which they occur and societal values which ascribe worth to them.

Prentice (1993) reported another typology of built heritage as historic and artistic heritage as opposed to scientific and cultural heritage. The former includes fixed physical elements such as relics (ranging from holy wells to modern religious buildings, forts and modern towns) whereas 'scientific' encompasses elements such as plants, birds, animals, rock and natural habitats; while cultural heritage covers folk and fine arts, customs and languages.

The second approach suggested by Bonink (1992) is the conceptual approach which attempts to describe the motive and meaning attracted to culture tourism activity. One of the motivations for choosing Ireland as a holiday destination is to experience culture and history.

Wood (1984) sees the role of culture as contextual, shaping the tourists' experience of a situation in general without a particular focus on the uniqueness of a specific cultural identity. However, it also warns of a risk of confusion with 'ethnic tourism' which has a direct focus on people possessing a cultural identity whose uniqueness is being marketed for tourists. The term ethnic tourism is appropriate in characterizing people living out an 'Irishness' which is attracting tourists like bees to a honey pot.

Wynne (1992) suggested the disintegration of distinctions between 'high' and 'low' or 'popular' culture, and Hughes and Benn (1994) stated that the distinctions between 'culture', 'tourism' and 'everyday life' were being eroded.

This certainly may be true, but the reality is that the 'attractiveness' of 'culture' as a form of tourism can only fade with the 'Europeanization' and 'globalization' of our everyday lives. At this moment, it allows the tourist to be excited when the experience exceeds the 'expectations' but just as the beauty of sunny beaches was attractive for mass tourism, cultural tourism should be alert to the risk of 'bastardization' of itself as a product.

If we accept the conceptual and technical definitions of cultural tourism by ATLAS (see Chapter 2, this volume) a key factor of both of these definitions is 'cultural attractions' and specific 'attractions'. Attractions may be classified as man-made or natural, nodal or linear in character or may involve a site or an event (Holloway, 1994).

Despite their diversity, these places have in common a 'non-home' appeal (Lew, 1994). All are targeted for purposeful, rather than haphazard trips. Because of the 'pull' they exert on the traveller, all can be classified by the generic term 'attraction', the main power that drives tourism everywhere.

By definition an attraction is magnetic, it draws people. This concept, that an attraction is defined by its pulling power, is antithetical to the beliefs of many for whom an attraction comes into being merely by the owner's declaration and construction.

The concept of attractions has two corollaries of concern to the developer. First, magnetism exists in the eyes of the visitor, and each visitor has unique interests and preferences. Second, magnetism is also a product of the design, development and managerial operation of an attraction.

Designers can create magnetic attractions based on given environmental assets and visitor interests. Emphasis must be placed on the requirement for an attraction to meet the needs of a specific market segment or several segments at one time. When a designer brings market interest and resource potential together to create an attraction, its success is assured.

Another corollary of pulling power is visitor satisfaction. A successful attraction is rewarding to the participants. Of course, attendance figures do not alone reveal the depth of user satisfaction. This is a major challenge in designing and establishing attractions. If a visitor leaves feeling disappointed, uninterested or even defrauded, the attraction may have succeeded in attracting but not in carrying out its complete function. If a developer is to produce successful attractions, his plans and establishments must elicit user satisfaction. To achieve this objective a thorough understanding of market segments is required.

In Ireland, while satisfaction still exists with internal facilities at fee charging visitor attractions, there has been a noticeable drop in visitors claiming to be 'satisfied' with all of the core facilities.

Today Clonmacnoise features as a tourist attraction in the Midland East region, attracting 140,000 visitors in 1997. The site, for statistical records, is classified as a 'fee paying' monument and is one of 19 such attractions in Ireland. This classification of attraction is 6% of the total supply of fee paying attractions while interpretative centres/museums are 40% and historic houses/castles are 26%.

In 1997 5 million visitors came to Ireland and just under 1 million visited monuments. Only 12% of the total visitors came to the 'Midland East' region of Ireland despite the fact that 22% of the 'fee paying' attractions are located here. Clearly, visitor numbers are determined not by attractions but by the overall perception of the region in question.

## Background to the Attraction

### Location

Clonmacnoise is situated close to the centre of the country on a gravel ridge overlooking the River Shannon, the longest river in Ireland. Nowadays, a detour off the main road is necessary to get there, but formerly its location on two major route-ways, the river itself running north/south, and a band of glacial eskers carrying the main east/west route across the country, meant that it was situated literally at the main crossroads of Ireland.

The other major component of the landscape is raised bog, which largely confined overland traffic to the dry sandy eskers. Great variation in river levels between winter and summer alters the scene dramatically through the seasons, in particular the low-lying meadows to the north-east of the site, known as the callows which are submerged by the rising waters of the river each winter. The variety of land types, eskers, callows, raised bogs, remnants of a lake, in the immediate area with their flora and fauna makes the place important ecologically as well as historically.

## History of Clonmacnoise

There is a wealth of history in Clonmacnoise, dating from its humble beginnings in the mid-6th century when St Ciaran first founded a church here. Clonmacnoise ('the meadow of the sons of Nos') evolved over the centuries into a monastery and city of learning of European importance. A centre which boasted many priceless treasures and works of art, it survived frequent raids from native, Viking and Norman plunderers until the 16th century when it was finally despoiled to such an extent that it was eventually abandoned. Today the noble ruins of seven churches, two round towers, grave stones and high crosses stand testimony to the proud history of Clonmacnoise, the most famous of all Irish monasteries.

## Religious significance

Clonmacnoise never lost its religious significance among the local people who have kept its history and folklore alive since the 16th century. It continued to be used as a burial ground, but instead of kings and monks, the right to burial was claimed by local chiefs, and finally the ordinary people, one of whom still survives with the right to be buried in the old monastic burial ground. The feast of St Ciaran is celebrated each year on Pattern Day at Clonmacnoise, when thousands of pilgrims visit the site.

## Early 'tourists' to Clonmacnoise

In the 18th century Clonmacnoise was rediscovered by antiquarians following the visit of the artist Blaymire whose views were reported in an influential book on the *Antiquities of Ireland*. Throughout this period other visitors came to the site and sketched some of the grave slabs or the whole site as did George Petrie in 1818 and called it 'the most interesting place in the British empire'. There was a growing awareness of the importance of the site and during the Victorian times many visitors from Athlone went by boat to Clonmacnoise, for their picnics. The Lawrence collection of photographic records, shows them reclining against the grave slabs while consuming dainty sandwiches (Turbridy, 1987, p. 42).

Clonmacnoise was a popular location for historical societies and in 1886 the Historical and Antiquarian Society organized a field trip attracting 8000 people from all over Ireland to Clonmacnoise. Interest in the site was fuelled by the current political situation and the newly discovered interest in Ireland's past.

During this period the site was under the control of the Church of Ireland and in 1882 the ruins were vested in the Commissioners of Public Works to be preserved as a national monument. One of the churches, Temple Conor, was excluded as it was in use as a Church of Ireland church.

During this period visitors to the site were members of archaeological and historical societies. The first known guiding service that was offered at the site was by Mr Molloy, the son of a local schoolteacher who lived beside the site. *The Midland Tribune, Tipperary Senital and Offaly County Vindicators'* on 5 August 1939 recounted the experiences of Offaly Archaeological and Historical Society. The visitors, better known today as the 'market', included religious and professional people, who were very impressed with the knowledge the guide, Mr Molloy, had about the site. One visitor is noted to have said that when its history would be fully written, Clonmacnoise would loom as large in the world's history as Greece. In 1940 Richard Hayward described in his book *Where The River Shannon Flows* the said Mr Molloy as a wonderful humorous guide to Clonmacnoise. In fact his information was later written up by Heather King as a *Guide to the Ruins.*

The site at Clonmacnoise remained in the hands of the Church of Ireland until 1955 when it was still in use as a public burial ground. It was then taken over by the Commissioners of Public Works.

L.C.T. Rolt in his book *Green and Silver* (Rolt, 1949) describes notices showing how the site is under the charge of the Office of Public Works. He also comments on the state of the site as being overgrown, and that as a burial ground it was submerged beneath a sea of unsightly tombstones of marble or polished granite. The demand for burial space had quite outrun the limited area available. Subsequently, the site was closed as a burial ground, and a new site was opened as a graveyard.

The Commissioners of Public Works carried out work to display grave slabs, and to provide facilities for the visitors to walk around the site (conservation work is ongoing at the site).

The visitor numbers started to increase during the 1960s and 1970s and a formal structure was put in place to handle this.

## Management background

Due to the demand for visits to the site it was necessary to put a formal structure in place to handle day-to-day operations. In 1960 Offaly County Council took on this responsibility by handling queries and selling information on Clonmacnoise. This function was transferred to the Regional Tourism Authority, namely Lakeland Tourism (today known as Midlands East Tourism) in 1973. They introduced a guided information service along with an admission charge at the site. This service operated from two caravans parked at the site until 1976 when the traditional two storey house beside the site became available as a visitor centre.

In 1981 the service operated by the tourism authority reverted back to the Office of Public Works, who took their own admissions, sold publications and extended the opening of the site.

In 1982 the centre was now open all year round, operating with limited facilities, a small car park and increasing visitor numbers. The facilities for the visitors improved with the building of a public toilet close to the site. Throughout this period, extensive conservation work was continuing at the site.

In 1984 the visitor numbers had reached 45,000 and continued to grow. This growth in numbers combined with the concern about the conservation of the 'High Cross' led to the development of a new centre in 1994.

This centre includes a visitor arrival area, an audio-visual presentation area, the conservation area which houses the original High Cross, grave slabs and a coffee shop. In the *Lonely Planet* guide book to Ireland (Smallman and Davenport, 1997) (which is responsible for 34% of visitors finding out about the site) the centre is described as 'three beehives echoing the design of the monastery and which houses the museum'. While the new building may have been controversial, it was put in place prior to a public sector body, namely the Office of Public Works, having to get planning permission or an Environment Impact Statement, before constructing new buildings on a site owned by them.

Now, the site is under the care of a state agency known as *Dúchas*. It is responsible for the protection and conservation of Ireland's natural and built heritage. The word Dúchas has numerous meanings, two of which are 'native place' and 'heritage'.

Dúchas cares for and presents the natural and built heritage of Ireland. This includes responsibility for:

- 80,000 ha of national parks and nature reserves
- 222,500 ha of special protection area for birds
- 700,000 ha of natural heritage areas
- 700 national monuments in state ownership and 150,000 other national monuments are cared for by them
- 19 historic properties and gardens
- 700 km of inland waterways
- Responsibility for archaeology under the National Monuments Act.

An integral element of the management of property in state ownership is not only the provision of access but the encouragement of people to visit heritage sites, provided that the overriding objective of conservation is adhered to. Within Dúchas is the Education and Visitor Service which is organized into four units: Guides and Information, Education and Marketing, Interpretation, and Publication and Media which is responsible for promoting the site.

Dúchas is a new entity in an already crowded and very commercial marketplace of heritage and conservation (Fadden, 1998).

The Heritage Council, established under the Heritage Act 1995, is an independent body which has statutory responsibility to propose policies and priorities for the identification, protection, preservation and enhancement of the national heritage. This includes:

- Monuments
- Archaeological objects
- Heritage objects
- Flora
- Fauna
- Wildlife habitats
- Landscape
- Seascapes
- Wrecks
- Geology
- Heritage gardens and parks
- Inland waterways

The Heritage Council is charged with a duty to undertake specific functions for the conservation of elements of the national heritage in public ownership as well as working with local communities. The philosophy of the council is based on sustainability and the importance of community participation in achieving heritage objectives. The council will work with all interested agencies and individuals to identify, protect, interpret, promote and enhance Ireland's heritage.

In association with the Department of Heritage, Gaeltacht and the Islands, the Heritage Council (1997a) have produced *The Plan 1997–2000* which will guide their activities up to the year 2000. The key three themes, are collecting data, promoting pride in Ireland's heritage, and proposing policy and providing advice.

It is envisaged that the Heritage Council will act as a cohort of all the bodies and individuals involved in the development and implementation of polices affecting Ireland's heritage. These include central and local government, the private sector, non-government organizations, state-sponsored bodies and voluntary agencies. The council seeks cooperation and partnership in carrying out its statutory function from all the bodies who have responsibility, direct or indirect, for our heritage.

Dúchas will work closely with the Heritage Council, implementing policies and strategies regarding all aspects of the site at Clonmacnoise.

## The Cultural Tourism Market

In 1997 the Irish Tourism Industry generated a total of IR£2.8 billion (€3.5 billion) in revenue within the state. It attracted over 5 million overseas visitors whose expenditure represented IR£2.1 billion (€2.7 billion) in foreign earnings. Over a third of these overseas visitors (1.7 million) engaged in some form of heritage or cultural activity. Over 1.3 million visited houses and castles and just under a million visited monuments.

Ireland has a rich supply of cultural and heritage attractions. An audit of the Irish National Heritage in 1985 indicated the existence of 200,000 known archaeological sites and monuments and 60,000 buildings of architectural or historic interest. In 1997 Tourism Development International Ltd produced their fourth biannual visitor attractions survey which revealed that many aspects of our culture, both tangible and intangible, are of significance when it comes to the decision to visit Ireland. In 1997, there were an estimated 10.3 million visits to fee charging attractions in the Republic of Ireland. This represented a growth of 25% since 1995, when the last visitor attraction survey was carried out (see Fig. 7.1).

Of the total increase in visits recorded between 1995 and 1997, an estimated 550,000 visits were made to newly opened attractions and those that had been closed for renovations in 1995. If these additional visits are excluded, the rate of growth between 1995 and 1997 would be 19%. Table 7.1 identifies the five main types of visitor attractions in the Republic of Ireland.

In 1997 more than 3.6 million visitors were attracted to interpretative centres and museums. This growing importance of interpretative centres can be attributed to the sustained (and high) level of investment and development that has taken place throughout the decade. Just over one-quarter (26%) of all visits took place at historic houses/castles (2.7 million visitors) making it the second most significant category. Historic monuments also recorded substantial visitor growth of 18% between 1995 and 1997.

Culture is less important as a motive for domestic tourism in Ireland. The domestic market represents 27% of cultural attraction visits, compared with 73% by foreign visitors. Mainland Europe (38%) is the most significant source market for fee charging attractions in Ireland. The European market is particularly important to attractions in the Southwest and Ireland West

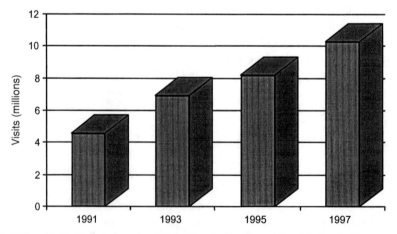

**Fig. 7.1.**   Visits to fee charging attractions in the Republic of Ireland. (From Tourism Development International Ltd, 1997.)

**Table 7.1.**   Visits by type of attraction – Republic of Ireland. (From Tourism Development International Ltd, 1997.)

|  | 1995 | 1996 | 1997 | Growth (%) (1995/1997) |
|---|---|---|---|---|
| Historic house/castles | 2,378,345 | 2,659,464 | 2,711,012 | +14 |
| Interpretative centres/ museums | 2,652,024 | 3,362,047 | 3,620,380 | +36 |
| Parks | 706,241 | 693,663 | 689,912 | –2 |
| Historic monuments | 653,424 | 745,265 | 774,180 | +18 |
| Gardens | 410,369 | 434,635 | 505,533 | +23 |
| Other attractions | 1,360,450 | 1,875,791 | 1,958,892 | +44 |
| Total | 8,160,853 | 9,770,865 | 10,259,909 | +26 |

regions where it accounts for 47% and 49% of attraction visits respectively. All regions in Ireland have seen strong growth in numbers visiting attractions. Dublin has experienced a 41% growth in attraction attendance, for example. This is due to the Dublin region receiving more grant aid for visitor attractions than any other region over the period of the two Operational Programmes 1989–1999. This explains the strong position of attractions like Dublin Zoo, Trinity College, Guinness Hop Store and Powerscourt Gardens being listed among the top ten attractions. Law (1993) suggests that this growth is due to the increase in the number of people taking short breaks for cultural experience in urban areas.

## ATLAS Cultural Visitor Survey

Although the Irish Tourist Board has a wealth of information on attendance at visitor attractions, specific profiles of cultural tourists are less common (Fig. 7.2). In order to analyse cultural tourism demand at Clonmacnoise in more depth, research was conducted in May–August 1997 at Clonmacnoise. An analysis of this research conducted in the framework of the European Association for Tourism and Leisure Education (ATLAS) Cultural Tourism Project, helps to illustrate the current nature of cultural tourism demand in Ireland. The cultural tourism survey at Clonmacnoise covered 176 visitors. It allows us to draw a comparison between cultural consumption in the domestic and foreign tourist markets. The following section summarizes some of the important findings of the survey.

Less than 7% of visitors surveyed came from the local area and just over 18% of visitors came from the rest of Ireland. The remaining visitors came from overseas, with major origin countries being the USA (25%), Germany (22%) France (7%) and the UK (7%).

This high level of overseas visitors explained why only a quarter of visitors indicated they had visited the attraction previously. The respondents generally had a high level of educational attainment, with over 50% having a degree or a post-graduate qualification. Cultural tourists surveyed at the site tended to be from older age groups, with 49% of respondents being over 50 years old, and 27% being retired. The student market only represented 9% of visitors, which is relatively low in comparison to other European cultural tourist destinations. The size of the student market is probably due to poor access to the site from Athlone, while the predominance of older tourists is probably due to the American baby boom and the greying of the European market.

A key question posed in the survey was the extent to which the visitors had travelled specifically to visit Clonmacnoise. When asked how important the site was in their decision to travel, almost 60% said it was 'very important' or 'important' (Fig. 7.3).

The Clonmacnoise research findings also support the distinction between 'specific' and 'general' cultural tourists put forward by the Irish Tourist Board in 1998. A more precise definition of specific cultural tourists could be taken as tourists who identified their visit as being 'cultural', and

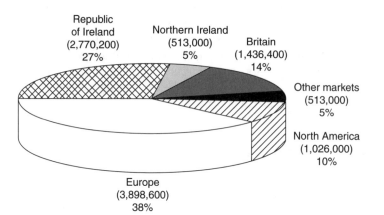

**Fig. 7.2.** Profile of visitors to fee charging attractions in the Republic of Ireland. (From Tourism Development International Ltd, 1997.)

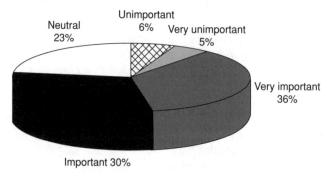

**Fig. 7.3.** Importance of attraction in the decision to visit the area.

who said that the attraction was 'very important' or 'important' as a motivation for their choice of destination. Based on this definition, about 11% of the tourists interviewed could be identified as specific cultural tourists, compared with 8.5% of respondents at other survey sites. Nearly 80% indicated that they were visiting the site to learn new things. The desire of more and more tourists who are willing to learn something new on holidays is positive, and reflects the higher levels of education.

When asked about their total consumption of cultural attractions, 71% of respondents indicated that they had visited other cultural attractions, which included museums (52%), historic monuments (54%) and historic castles at (48%) in the last 12 months, indicating the consumption of cultural attractions both on holidays and when at home. There was a noticeable difference between the level of visits to the usually more accessible heritage sites (museums, historic monuments and castle) and those to performing and visual art attractions. Specific cultural tourists were far more likely to make cultural attraction visits during their stay (65%). This group were not only found to be frequent consumers of cultural attractions but they also have a high level of total tourism consumption, particularly in terms of short holiday breaks. Over 76% of the visitors surveyed had been on holiday in the last 12 months, 45% having taken at least one short holiday and 60% engaging in at least one long holiday in the period (Fig. 7.4). A high frequency of short-break holiday participation is considered by many to be one of the hallmarks of the cultural tourist (e.g. Gratton, 1990).

Cultural consumption in general, and cultural tourism in particular, is likely to be related to employment in the cultural industry. The ATLAS Cultural Tourism Research project indicated that 20% of all cultural tourists interviewed in 1997 had an occupation which was related to the cultural industry, while of those surveyed in Clonmacnoise over 28% indicated that their jobs were connected with the cultural industry.

In spite of the relatively high level of cultural attractiveness of Clonmacnoise, visitors did not tend to stay long. The average stay in the locality is just below two nights and only 20% of visitors stayed more than three nights in the area (Fig. 7.5). Further analysis of the research identifies

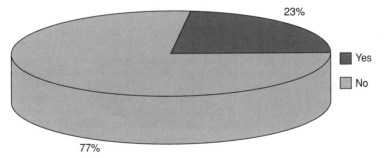

**Fig. 7.4.** Holidays in the last 12 months.

63% made their own holiday arrangements and 22% were on an all-inclusive holiday (Fig. 7.6). Clonmacnoise tends to be a staging point between Dublin and the West of Ireland, and 22% of visitors indicated that they were on a touring holiday. Clonmacnoise therefore tends to act as a stand-alone attraction in a location that does not have a sufficient critical mass of 'real cultural capital' to persuade the majority of visitors to stay in the area. This is just one of the many marketing and management problems which the site faces, and it is a problem that will probably increase as competition from other cultural attractions in Ireland grows.

## Management Issues

### Visitor profile and expectations

The management of Clonmacnoise view this as a dominant issue in their day-to-day activities. They identified some of their customers as having no rapport with the site, lacking appreciation for the product 'built and natural heritage' and being difficult to work with. The impression given by some visitors was that it was a chore to visit the site. In the past this trend had always been found among the North American visitors (24%). However, in more recent years, it is also becoming apparent among the mainland

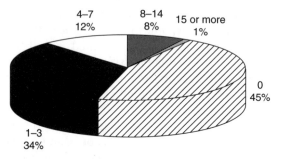

**Fig. 7.5.** Nights spent in the area.

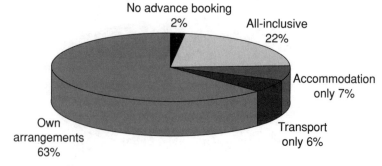

**Fig. 7.6.** Type of booking.

European visitors as well (31%). This is reflected in the ATLAS survey results, which indicated that 22% of visitors were 'neutral' about visiting the site. Part of the explanation for this lies in the fact that Clonmacnoise is used as a 'staging point' between the east and west of Ireland by tour operators.

It appears that Australians (4%), New Zealanders (2%) and South Africans (1%) are the most interested in the site and have the greatest respect for Clonmacnoise.

A large percentage of staff working at Clonmacnoise is from the local area and they have a deep empathy with it. The attitude (apathy, impatience, boredom) of some of the visitors towards the site is inclined to draw a 'negative' response from the staff. While training in 'customer care' will prepare them to deal with this, it is unlikely to overcome the sense of cultural offence felt by the staff.

## Seasonality/congestion

In Clonmacnoise this issue relates to the volume of visitors and the timing of their visits during the peak season, with particular reference to school tours in May and June along with other tours and groups.

It appears to be an issue at the site that the number of school groups visiting at any one time, overlapping with regular visitors to the site, causes some congestion and confusion. To address the peak demand by school tours and to generate new demand the Education and Visitors Services in Dúchas are compiling 'Educational Packs' for the various sites to encourage usage as part of the school curriculum throughout the academic year rather than at the end of the school year. The Heritage Council in association with the Environmental Information Service have published 'Sheer', a *Survey of Heritage and Environmental Educational Resources* which is a database of sites, related to heritage and the environment. This will assist teachers when planning heritage related school visits. Both of these activities will greatly stimulate this market.

In Ireland, the integration of site visits with the school curriculum is underdeveloped. The National Heritage Council has a particular responsibility to work in partnership with other public authorities, educational bodies and individuals in this regard, to 'promote interest, education, knowledge and pride in, and facilitate the appreciation and enjoyment of the national heritage'.

## Control

The manager of Clonmacnoise identifies his role as caretaker and information guide to the site, coupled with being a production line manager, rather than a manager of a 'built heritage' attraction.

The International Committee on Cultural Tourism advocates good management of visitors to cultural tourism attractions. They recognize the fact that the tourist is blamed for eroding cultural sites, trivializing the significance, fostering theatrical reconstructions, obscuring local culture and treating heritage as a consumer good. While there is some truth to all these accusations the culprit is not tourism but cultural site mismanagement or wholesale lack of management. Good management of cultural tourism is central to the mission of conservation.

Heritage managers have traditionally been cast in the role of balancing the demands of sympathetic resource management with demands from the marketplace, while also meeting the stringent requirements of being 'guardians' of a nation's heritage. The task of site management in this situation is made difficult by the historic and sensitive nature of the site and the growth in visitor numbers along with the challenge of representing the wishes of the local community in managing the site.

## Marketing Issues

The process of marketing Ireland as a tourist destination is now firmly based on partnership between the state sector and the industry. The state sector, comprising the Government Department of Tourism and Bord Fáilte, is now receiving considerable financial support from the European Union (EU) as well as working closely with the commercial sector. Increased emphasis and funding has been given to marketing Ireland abroad under the *1994–1999 Operational Programme for Tourism*. The Overseas Tourism Marketing Initiative, a 'consortium' of state and industry interests, is working to promote Ireland as a destination, leveraging funds from the exchequer and the EU based on seed investment from the tourism sector. This effort contributed some IR£6.7 million (€8.5 million) to marketing Ireland as a destination in 1998.

In addition, four heritage marketing groups have been assisted with heritage focused funding from the European Regional Development Fund marketing board over the past few years. These groups include Heritage Island, Great Houses, Castles and Gardens of Ireland, Heritage Towns and Culture Ireland. The government division responsible for the marketing of national monuments comes under the heritage service, Dúchas.

### Dúchas – marketing strategy

Marketing is a new activity for Dúchas, hitherto they were strictly conservationists. For Dúchas the three main issues for the future will relate to site protection and sustainability, capital investment over the next 5–7 years and more effective marketing. They are presently preparing marketing plans for heritage in Ireland.

## Clonmacnoise marketing to date

Attractions in general, and heritage attractions especially have tended to underinvest in marketing. Prior to the formation of Dúchas, Clonmacnoise practised its marketing initiatives at local level. Cooperative marketing of heritage and tourism attractions was undertaken with consortia of local authorities including Midlands East Tourism, Athlone and District Tourism, and local organizations including Elly O'Carroll and the Tourism Society. Cultural and heritage itineraries were created and joint ticketing agreements were made with other local attractions such as Kilbeggan Distillery and West Offaly Bog Train. All such marketing was carried out with local input and implemented at national level.

A recent report *Tourism 2000*, commissioned by the Irish Tourism Industry Confederation, stressed that serious consideration should be given to the creation of a Tourism Development Authority (TDA). Its role would be to coordinate the multiplicity of organizations involved in tourism. A key element would include coordinated marketing which would hopefully lead to a courtship forming between TDA and cultural tourism. The objectives of such a relationship should be to develop planning and partnership marketing, national tourism policies relating to our cultural heritage, methods of collecting data on economic impact and tourist profiles. The main issues that need to be addressed in relation to marketing included:

- Standardized marketing
- Marketing incorporating the host community
- Preserving cultural identity and integrity
- Recording market profiles
- Educating the tourist and host community.

## Standardized marketing

Cultural tourism to heritage attractions is a form of special interest tourism. It is characterized by two seemingly contradictory phenomena: the unique and the universal. Therefore it is difficult to generalize about the marketing of visitor attractions as it is such a heterogeneous field, due to the variations in sites/attractions, products and markets, and the ownership structure of attractions. Dúchas proposes the adoption of a standardized marketing strategy for heritage attractions in Ireland, but this may lead to further commodification of culture as a tourist product, and to culture being 'invented, trivialized and commercialized' for financial reasons at the expense of 'true' culture. The continuous fossilization of culture in the promotion and marketing of different attractions at national level may lead to a decline in the numbers of specific cultural tourists due to this artificial approach. Dúchas is adopting a branding approach for its heritage attractions in Ireland which may create a standard brand image for such a varied product.

## Partnership with the host community

Cultural tourism is often promoted for political and economic reasons which have little connection to the 'way of life' of local residents. It is acceptable that the stimulus and funding for development comes from outside the local area, but the form of development should be locally controlled. To date government bodies have developed existing and new facilities, derelict buildings have been developed, foreign tour operators have created cultural tourism package holidays for the non-cultural tourist, with local people having little or no say in the process. This is entirely at odds with the concept of sustainable tourism. The history of the community is told to tourists by outside professionals and local people who still work at the site. The manager/caretaker is a local individual who appears to have reduced control and empowerment at site level, and this may lead to lack of interest by local people and therefore a loss of authenticity.

The recognition of local identity and interests of the host community must at all times play a central role in the formulation of marketing.

## De-marketing

One potential solution to making Clonmacnoise a sustainable tourism product is to adopt the concept of de-marketing. The problem with this idea is who decides to de-market the attraction and how will it be implemented. It is believed that once carrying capacity is reached, strategies to prevent tourist attendance should be implemented. Therefore, task forces and steering committees and programmes of workshops at local and regional level need to be established. Such committees should have an input on the marketing and future direction of the heritage site, therefore placing responsibility on the host community to protect their heritage and maximize local benefits. Maintenance marketing is also a concept that Clonmacnoise could adopt once a desirable market segment is reached – this is when the current level of demand on the site equals the host community desired tourist profile. The task now is to sustain the level of visitor interest by keeping the quality of services at the predetermined level.

## Market profiles

The future integrity of the site should be a priority when marketing it. In the market analysis it was identified that cultural tourists do not constitute a uniform market segment, but also have separate needs. Cultural tourism marketing will need to pay more attention to the division between cultural and specific cultural tourist, between repeat and first time visitors and between cultural tourists from different countries if they are to achieve a sustainable cultural tourism market. The Heritage Council of Ireland has expressed the need for more accurate forms of data collection in order to make decisions from an informed background. Dúchas should consider implementing a method of monitoring at each site in order to produce accurate data.


## Competition

Ireland will increasingly face global competition from new emerging cultural tourism destinations. As the cultural markets become increasingly globalized, so competition between attractions at local, national and international level will increase. In view of the fact that cultural tourism is seen as a lucrative market, it is not surprising that many countries are seeking to promote it.


## Education

Another possible strategy that Clonmacnoise could adopt is educating visitors about the history of the site and linking this to the present and to the future. This should include educating the tourist and the host community about the negative impacts of over-use of sites and places – particularly with sensitive forms of cultural and heritage tourism. Clonmacnoise is encountering too many consumers visiting at the same time, and a percentage of tourists who do not want to be at the site. Clonmacnoise could adopt the strategy of educating more visitors towards being cultural tourists. The Visitor Attraction Survey 1997 identified that the family market represented 19% of those visiting monuments/historic houses, therefore targeting the child as a consumer is a possible niche market that Clonmacnoise should consider. The creation of education packs would make a visit more meaningful for the child and for the adult. The future success of cultural tourism in Ireland will depend on partnership between all segments who have a vested interest in cultural tourism, which must include the local communities, government bodies, the tourism industry and professionals. Finally, quoting John Swarbrooke (1999): 'in the increasing globalised tourism industry, this may mean having to modify the well known marketing cliché of "think globally, act locally", so, instead, for cultural tourism we will talk about "thinking locally, acting globally"'.


# Cultural Issues

The physical layout of the site, as it has been developed recently, does not constitute a particularly enlightened response to the magnificent resources of this ancient monastic site. While the development provides necessary reception, information and interpretative facilities, the overall endeavour is compromised by the following aspects of the development:

**1.** The scale, layout and location of the car park is such that it seriously intrudes on the quietness of the monastic site.

**2.** The size and architectural treatment of the visitor centre subverts the order of the site, making the monastic ruins appear secondary to the information centre when the reverse ought be the case. Indeed many visitors would have difficulty deciding where the 'interpreted' stops and the 'interpretation' begins!

The net effect of these aspects is a general loss of the mystery, power and meaning which the site previously held and this must count as a serious deficit from the visitors' point of view, which is likely to have a negative impact in the medium to long term.

To better assess these conflicts, it is instructive to analyse them in terms of the spatial zones of a site suggested by Gunn (1997). This theory holds that at the core of each attraction is a nucleus – the main event – surrounded by an inviolate belt and the zone of closure.

## Nucleus

The prime element of an attraction, the *raison d'être*, is the nucleus. For an area rich in historic significance, it is the landscape or building. In the design of an attraction the nucleus must authentically represent its foundation and be of a type and quality to match or surpass the images held by tourists. If the nucleus is a fragile or rare resource extreme care must be taken in planning for visitors especially for large numbers.

## Inviolate belt

The function of attractions depends equally on the setting, or inviolate belt. The visitor can reach a feature (nucleus) only by passing through some buffer space which may be small or large, of brief or extended duration.

A person's mindset or anticipation of an attraction has much to do with their reception and approval when the nucleus is reached. It is unfortunately the case in Clonmacnoise that the inviolate belt has been eroded by the inappropriate proximity of both the visitor centre and its car park to the ancient monastic site itself.

## Zone of closure

This is the surrounding area within which must be found one or more service centres as well as transportation linkage between the service centre and the attraction. No matter how remote the attraction, some service centre must be available and accessible for the attraction to function.

Good examples exist elsewhere of attractions which have been sensitively developed to the greater satisfaction of the visitor and true to the uniqueness (and frequently the fragility) of the attraction concerned (e.g. Glenveagh Castle, Co. Donegal).

While many of the visitors to Clonmacnoise may not be aware of these drawbacks, anyone familiar with the history and character of Clonmacnoise will feel that the site has suffered a loss of authenticity, mystery and simplicity. This must be considered a very high price to pay for increased exposure and visitor numbers.

Indeed, this issue brings us face to face with the broader cultural issue of the balance between commercial exploitation of cultural resources and the preservation of their innate, fragile, time bound form and meaning. We are forced to confront the further realization that the entire nature of Clonmacnoise has undergone a fundamental change arising from its development as a tourist attraction and the 'jury is still out' on whether this change will be seen as positive or negative.

Clonmacnoise has, throughout its long history, undergone countless changes including its virtual destruction and yet it has survived into modern times as a provocative icon of Early Christian Ireland.

We can only hope that the changes wrought in the recent past do not contribute to the cultural plunder of this extraordinary site.

## Conclusion

Cultural tourism is now establishing itself as an economic activity in Ireland. The targets set by the government and other agencies to exploit the cultural tourism resources assisted by incentives from the EU, have been vindicated by the growth in visitor numbers and the volume of economic activity generated.

However, concerns must be expressed regarding the vast increase in the number of products offered under the label of cultural tourism, even though this has yet to lead to any noticeable decline in product quality. In the future it may be advisable to distinguish 'qualitatively' between the products on offer and market them under appropriate labels. The relevant bodies need to be alert to changes and possible falls in demand in the marketplace, and to put strategies in place to deal with these.

There is now a wealth of experience which should allow more informed judgements to be made in relation to the future development of cultural tourism. These lessons are already being reflected in legislative changes in Ireland, e.g. The Heritage Act 1995 and changes made to the Planning Laws 1994–1998. Furthermore, the 'partnership' ethos, of the public, private and voluntary sectors should be to the fore. Clonmacnoise as a visitor attraction has developed over the years into a significant attraction in the region. Yet the economic benefits have not rippled out to the wider locality to date due to 34% 'excursionists' and 46% short-day (one to three nights) visitors coming to Clonmacnoise.

There is now an opportunity for a reversal of this situation by the recent introduction of new amenities and improved access to the region. The Midlands area of Ireland is also emerging as an important commercial and industrial centre, and it is in the interest of all agencies, operators and organizations that the 'image' and profile of the region is improved both culturally and economically. The evidence on the ground is that this process has already begun.

Another potentially exciting horizon is opening up for sites such as Clonmacnoise arising out of the recent evidence of a renewal of interest in spiritual matters. These stirrings are not finding expression in the traditional sphere of religion, but are being manifested more in a reaction to the frenetic pace of modern life, of materialism and a perceived loss of spirituality and connection to nature.

This phenomenon may hold exciting possibilities for Clonmacnoise in conjunction with similarly provocative sites in the Shannon basin to perhaps become a contemporary source of spiritual inspiration. The precise form this would take is as yet unclear but this phenomenon merits investigation in the context of the other possibilities listed here.

Considering the trends identified in the research into the pattern of use and the profile of the visitor, Clonmacnoise is likely to see changes. Already there is a hint of this with a renewed interest in the old medieval pilgrim paths. The route from 'Ard Keenan' to Clonmacnoise was retraced for the first time in 700 years in September 1998.

Clonmacnoise may be set to regain some of its original meaning through the development now likely to take place in its next phase as a 'cultural tourism attraction'.

## Acknowledgements

We would like to acknowledge the following students, Miriam Bergin, Dympna Scanlon, Marie Keane, Charlotte Pusche, Susan Balfe, who carried out the questionnaires at the site.

# References

Ashworth, G.J. (1998) Managing the cultural tourist. In: Ashworth, G.J. and Dietvorst, A.D.J. (eds) *Tourism and Spatial Transformations – Implications for Policy and Planning.* CAB International, Wallingford, UK, pp. 265–283.

Bonink, C. (1992) Cultural tourism development and government policy. MA dissertation, Rizksuniversiteit, Utrecht.

Cohen, E. (1988) Authenticity and commoditization in tourism. *Annals of Tourism Research* 15, 467–486.

Fadden, D. (1998) Dúchas, The Heritage Service. Paper presented at 'Visitor Attraction Conference', National Art Gallery, 1998.

Gratton, C. (1990) Consumer behaviour in tourism: a psycho-economic approach. Paper presented at the Tourism Research into the 1990s Conference, Durham, UK. December, 1990.

Gunn, C. (1997) *Vacationscape: Developing Tourist Areas.* Taylor and Francis.

Herbert, D.T., Prentice, R.C. and Thomas, C.J. (eds) (1989) *Heritage Sites: Strategies for Marketing and Development.* Aldershot, Avebury.

Heritage Council (1997a) *The Plan 1997–2000.* Heritage Council, Kilkenny.

Heritage Council (1997b) *Annual Report 1996.* Heritage Council, Kilkenny.

Holloway, C. (1994) *The Business of Tourism,* 4th edn. Pitman, London.

Hughes, H.L. and Benn, D. (1994) Entertainment: its role in the tourist industry. Paper presented at the Leisure Studies Association Annual Conference, Glasgow.

Konsola, D. (1993) Culture tourism and regional development: some proposals for cultural itineraries. In: Konsola, D. (ed.) *Culture, Environment and Regional Development.* Regional Development Institute, University of Athens, Athens, pp. 18–43.

Law, C.M. (1993) *Urban Tourism: Attracting Visitors to Large Cities.* Mansell, London.

Lew, A.A. (1994) A framework of tourist attraction research. In: Ritchie, J.R.B. and Goeldner, C.R. (eds) *Travel, Tourism and Hospitality Research,* 2nd edn. John Wiley & Sons, New York, pp. 291–304.

MacCannell, D. (1976) *The Tourist: a New Theory of the Leisure Class.* Macmillan, London.

O'Donnchadha, G. and O'Connor, B. (1996) Cultural Tourism in Ireland. In: Richards, G. (ed.) *Cultural Tourism in Europe.* CAB International, Wallingford, UK, pp. 197–215.

Prentice, R. (1993) *Tourism and Heritage Attractions.* Routledge, London.

Rapoport, A. (1984) *The Meaning of the Built Environment: a Non-verbal Communication Approach.* Chapman & Hall, London.

Richards, G. (1993) Cultural Tourism in Europe. In: Cooper, C.P. and Lockwood, A. (eds) *Progress in Tourism, Recreation and Hospitality Management.* Vol. 5, pp. 99–115.

Rolt, L.C.T. (1949) *Green and Silver.* G. Allen & Unwin Ltd, London.

Smallman, T. and Davenport, F. (1997) *Lonely Planet Ireland.* Lonely Planet Publications, Australia, pp. 420–423.

Swarbrooke, J. (1999) *Sustainable Tourism Management.* CAB International, Wallingford, UK.

Tourism Development International Ltd (1997) *Visitor Attractions Survey.* TDI, Dublin.

Tubridy, M. (1987) *The Heritage of Clonmacnoise.* Environmental Science Unit, Trinity College.

Wood, R.E. (1984) Ethnic tourism, the state and cultural change in Southeast Asia. *Annals of Tourism Research* 11, 186–197.

Wynne, D. (1992) *The Culture Industry.* Aldershot, Avebury.

Zeppel, H. and Hall, M.L. (1992) Arts and heritage tourism. In: Weiler, B. and Hall, M.C. (eds) *Special Interest Tourism.* Belhaven Press, London.

# Cultural Heritage Sites and Their Visitors: Too Many for Too Few?

**8**

## Sue Berry* and Graham Shephard

*School of Service Management, Faculty of Business, University of Brighton, Eastbourne, UK*

## Introduction

Cultural heritage sites play a significant role in tourism but heritage managers must remain in touch with their market in order to optimize the use of the site. The heritage market has three dimensions: current visitors to the specific sites, potential visitors that are attracted to cultural heritage sites and finally the residents of principal catchment area(s). The need for better information about actual and potential visitors is especially important now because the market for cultural tourism attractions such as country houses, historic landscape parks and museums appears to be saturated in some parts of the UK.

Understanding how tourism markets in the different types of destination region function is becoming of major importance for the development and promotion of cultural heritage attraction sites. The South-East of England is a significant tourist destination but it is also a major market for the cultural heritage sites within it. This segment of the market is not growing, however. In such regions cultural heritage sites now have to fight for survival, not only against other categories of attraction but also against each other. This is principally because the supply of cultural heritage sites has outgrown demand (see Chapter 1, this volume). To maintain the interests of a local market, cultural heritage sites need to be able to offer reasons for regular visits and they have problems with achieving this because there are limits to what can be done without losing the uniqueness of the site.

* Present address: 4 Juggs Close, Lewes, BN7 1QP, UK.

© CAB *International* 2001. *Cultural Attractions and European Tourism*
(ed. G. Richards)

## Definition of a Tourism Region

A mature destination region such as the south-east of England can be defined in many ways and no matter which definition is chosen someone will disagree with it. Defining the boundaries of any tourism region in England for the purposes of research or for planning is also not easy because none of the agencies that are greatly involved with tourism share common boundaries (Jones and MacLeod, 1999). The new Regional Development Agencies and the Tourist Boards have different boundaries and yet the government set up both, albeit at different times (Holloway, 1994; South-East Development Agency, 1998). Most of the published official data use either England as their region or are broken down to the boundaries of the regional tourism board (StarUK, 1999).

The region covered by the South-East England Tourist Board includes Kent, East and West Sussex and Surrey and this area will be used as being the most convenient for this case study (Fig. 8.1). It is also useful because of the long historical associations between all four of the counties. Surrey and Kent had some early spas that attracted leisure-seeking Londoners from the late 1600s (White and Harte, 1994; Savidge and Bell, 1995). Their populations became the major customers of the seaside resorts along the coast to which the routines of the spas were taken from the 1740s (Farrant, 1983). By the mid-19th century, seaside resorts sprawled along the coastlines of Sussex and Kent (Farrant, 1983; Walton, 1983; Whyman, 1985).

Describing the characteristics and the spatial distribution of facilities, resources and tourists within any region is a challenge (Smith, 1996; Human, 1999). A major characteristic of this destination region is that it is

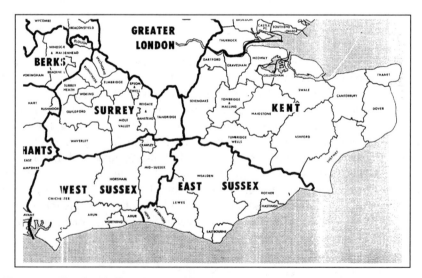

**Fig. 8.1.**   The South-East England Tourist Board Region. (From Berry, 1999.)

the warmest region of the UK and one of the driest. For historic gardens that are located in rural areas, the relatively dry climate is an advantage because the number of days when visitors are likely to be able to enjoy the site is higher than in most other parts of the UK. The region's dry climate is also one reason why there were so many seaside resorts (Granville, 1841). The South-East is one of the most highly populated regions in Europe and is due to have more houses constructed within it, partly to accommodate immigration from the north and west of the UK (DTER, 1998; Whitehead *et al.*, 1999). Due to its complex topography and long coastline, it is regarded by inbound visitors as one of the most attractive regions of England that is easily accessible to south London and to the European littoral (Berry, 1994). It is a compact region that is increasingly cut off from the North and the Midlands by the expansion of London (SEETB, 1998).

The South-East is a gateway region, 60% of the people that travel by air in the UK pass through Gatwick and Heathrow (just on the western boundary of this region). Dover is the major passenger port for the UK (South-East Development Agency, 1998) and the Channel Tunnel is accessed from near Ashford. The region's transport infrastructure is weak and poor access to many parts of it is now recognized as an issue (South-East Development Agency, 1998). Connectivity is poor. The issue is compounded by the travel pattern of the region's residents, 78% of whom travel by car to work, many travelling further than they did because of changes in the location of jobs (South-East Development Agency, 1998). Leisure travel adds to the strain on the road and rail infrastructure.

The congestion on the roads is reducing the distances that people can travel within a given period of time. The South-East lacks a good east–west road or rail route. Poor connectivity by road or by rail is making some areas relatively more inaccessible than they were and is reducing the catchment areas of some cultural heritage sites (Berry and Standeven, 1993; Burley,1995; Smith, 1996; South-East Development Agency, 1998).

The development of both road and railway may be fraught with political problems. The advantage of the roads is that they give greater flexibility for all users than railways. The lack of investment has meant that the seaside resorts of the South-East have been allowed to decline to the point where Hastings in East Sussex suffers from high unemployment, social problems and physical decay, all of which have made this isolated town into one of the most dysfunctional in Britain (South-East Development Agency, 1998). In 1999, a conference about resort regeneration revealed that the gross domestic product for the resorts of East Sussex is only 70–75% of the national average (Whitehead *et al.*, 1999). The cultural heritage sites outside the resorts have become major attractions and yet many of the resorts have a major role to play as cultural heritage attractions in their own right. They are part of the cultural history of the country and some, such as Brighton, have areas of outstanding architectural interest along their fronts (Farrant, 1989).

Within this region, cultural heritage attractions have three distribution patterns. Most of the urban ones are in the seaside resorts, all of which were investing in them by the mid-1800s when Brighton purchased the Royal Pavilion (Morley, 1984). The rural ones are in clusters such as those in the vicinity of Tunbridge Wells and Guildford, around which a number of country houses are now open to the public. There is also a line of country houses under the lee of the South Downs, mainly on the Greensand from Firle Place in East Sussex along to Stansted, most of which are now open to the public (Hudson, 1998; Berry, 1999a).

Recent research for the SEETB indicates that the region's lack of a clear modern identity within the UK makes marketing the region difficult (SEETB, 1998). However, this region has strong interrelationships within it. The northern part, which includes some of south London, provides many day-tripper visitors for the attractions within it (SEETB, 1998).

## Definitions of Cultural Heritage Sites

Cultural heritage sites include heritage sites, arts and drama events and exhibitions. Most cultural heritage sites fall into one or more of the following categories that cover all of the sites that are included in this discussion. They are sites with:

- Associations with people or events of national standing, e.g. Battle Abbey (Battle of Hastings) and Chartwell (Churchill's home in Kent).
- Outstanding architectural or landscape merit, e.g. outstanding gardens such as Sissinghurst in Kent or Bodiam Castle in East Sussex.
- Collections of artefacts or art, mostly begun by enthusiasts and now largely in public museums and art galleries, e.g. Brighton Museum and Art Gallery.
- Small historic houses that may be regarded as worthy of saving because they are of vernacular interest, such as The Clergy House in Alfriston, East Sussex.
- Part of the cultural heritage of the region, including seaside heritage.

The emphasis of this chapter is on heritage sites. Most cultural heritage sites have a product life cycle, some purely because of the impact of wear and tear. Others decline in popularity simply because people, places and periods fall out of fashion. Cultural heritage sites have a very limited ability to adapt without losing their identity. Most have very severe limitations on the capacity that are imposed by the scale and layout. Charleston Farmhouse (East Sussex) has a capacity of no more than 19,000 visitors a year within its current opening hours and visitor patterns (Berry, 1998b). It is the limitations placed by the nature of cultural heritage sites that mean that the majority cannot and never will pay their own bills (Berry, 1996; Leask and Yeoman, 1999).

Cultural tourism in this instance means all movements of people to cultural heritage sites away from their usual place of residence. Thus a day trip to a museum in a hometown is not included in cultural tourism but one to an adjacent town is. The reason is that a local trip does not transfer resources from one place to another, a trip from one place to another does. If the trip is an intra-regional one, then the economic impact may be hard to measure. This is a particular problem in the South-East where so much cultural travel is within the region (Burley, 1995; Piggott, 1995; Lewes District Council, 1998).

Cultural heritage sites in this region are owned by public, private and charitable bodies. Brighton and Hove own most of the buildings that are open to the public in the town, such as the Royal Pavilion and Preston Manor. The National Trust, which is a national conservation charity that owns properties all over the region, attracts the largest numbers of visitors, 1.1 million to properties in Kent and East Sussex alone (National Trust Annual Reports). Many country homes that are still privately owned, such as Glynde Place, or managed by trustees, such as Stansted, are opened every summer (Hudson, 1998). A few small museums and houses are privately owned. All share the problem of balancing the need to earn income from a site and keeping its character (Berry, 1993–1999).

If the owner of the site is a charity, such as the National Trust, whose main objective is conservation, the need to attract visitors to pay the bills for a site has to be carefully balanced against negative impacts. Charities have to consider whether the investment will pay because such trusts cannot subsidize commercial activities such as shops. These activities must contribute to the work of the charity (Berry, 1999b). Other owners are also aware of the need to balance care and cash flows in order to keep the uniqueness of their products (*Historic House*, 1999; Leask and Yeoman, 1999).

## The Development of Cultural Tourism in the South-East

The South-East has a combination of cultural attractions in the form of sites (such as historic buildings) and localities (for example, historic towns and seaside resorts with a heritage of historic buildings); together they are a major part of the attractiveness of the region to visitors. The majority of the cultural heritage sites cannot be described as reflecting the region's history. Most are connected with: (i) national events such as the Battle of Hastings which happened to take place in the region; or (ii) national fashions in gardening and architecture (Sissinghurst, Bodiam Castle); or (iii) the many people of national standing who have lived in the region (Quebec House). Some of the cultural heritage sites do indeed reflect local culture such as the Weald and Downland Museum and the seaside heritage such as the piers and the de la. Warr Pavilion in Bexhill. The majority located in the region because of accidents of landownership or access to London (Farrant, 1989).

Cultural tourism has been a mainstay for the tourism of the region for a long time. The region attracted a wealthy clientele to its spas and seaside resorts from about 1660 to around 1930 (Berry, 1999a). The spas of Epsom and Tunbridge Wells (which had theatres and other cultural facilities) lost their hegemony to the seaside resorts in the late 18th century (Farrant, 1981). These had good theatres and other urban cultural attractions by 1850 (Dale, 1967; Farrant, 1981). The first seaside resort to invest in the ownership of cultural tourism facilities was Brighton which purchased the Royal Pavilion from Queen Victoria to prevent it being demolished and opened it to the public. The local authority eventually restored the building (Morley, 1984).

From the late 19th century, when the clientele for the resorts included lower middle class and working class people from London, many of the visitors began to explore the surrounding area on bikes, in charabancs and then by coach. Penshurst Place in Kent was one of the first country houses that opened to the public. Thus this was an area where the interdependency of holiday resorts and cultural attractions was established quite early (Tinniswood, 1998).

Since the 1950s, the role of the South-East as a tourism region has changed. It is no longer largely a destination region that serves other parts of the country as well as London. Now most of its attractions are heavily dependent on the local market. If communications are not improved, that intra-regional dependency will continue to rise (SEETB, 1998; StarUK, 1999).

Although some cultural heritage sites had opened before 1970, most of them have followed the national pattern and opened since 1970 (English Tourist Board, 1998). By 1998 there were clear signs of saturation (Berry, 1998a). The volume of visitors was not rising as quickly as the number of attractions and their total visitor capacity. Visitor capacity has been increased in many larger cultural heritage sites such as Sissinghurst (a garden) by the addition of an interpretative centre, a large restaurant, plant sales and walks around the periphery of the site (National Trust, 1993–1999).

## The Tourism Market in the South-East

The South-East has many major attractions that range from theme parks such as Chessington that attract around 1.7 million visitors annually to major seaside heritage features such as the Palace Pier in Brighton which was visited by 3.5 million people in 1997 (Anon., 1998a). Canterbury Cathedral is the most popular cultural and religious attraction with 1.6 million visitors and Leeds Castle the most visited historic house attracting more than half a million visitors, followed by the Royal Pavilion (Brighton) with 394,000 visitors (SEETB, 1999). The majority attract fewer than 50,000 visitors each and many require heavy subsidies, e.g. from the taxpayer (Preston Manor in

Brighton) or endowments (National Trust properties such as Knole). The attractions also have to compete with historic towns such as Lewes and Guildford with attractive architecture that acts as a backdrop (Berry, 1996). Guildford is thought to attract between 60,000 and 90,000 staying visitors (*English Heritage Monitor*, 1996).

In spite of the long tradition of dependency on tourism, the majority of the visitors to attractions and destinations in the South-East live either within the region or in London, which has always been the major source of visitors (Farrant, 1981; Berry, 1999a). As more people use cars to travel so the proportion of staying visitors has declined. Most of the visitors to attractions and destinations are now day-trippers. Thus the region is now more dependent upon leisure day trips than it is on overnight stays (StarUK, 1999). Of the remainder, the biggest group is domestic visitors from elsewhere in the UK. The international travellers are the smallest group but spend more per head than the others.

For many years the South-East was the second most successful tourism region in the UK, after London. However, that dominance in terms of earnings and of volume of visitors is now being lost, as the relative decline in the number of inbound visitors indicates. The South-East still comes second in the league of earnings by all UK tourism regions from international visitors. However there was a significant drop in the South-East's share of the tourism cake between 1987 and 1997, from 11.7% to 9.6% (Anon., 1999a). Other regions are catching up. At the same time, while the volume of domestic tourism is increasing, the role of the South-East in that market is also declining (Anon., 1998b, 1999b).

The research on visitor trends and the views of visitors are patchy. Few attractions have either a regular research programme or access to information gained from others. Information sharing would be invaluable and would not jeopardize those who did so because the responsibility for what to do would still remain with the individual attractions. The weakness of the organization of data is underlined by the problems of the organizers of the Rodin Exhibition in Lewes (East Sussex). This highly successful venture attracted more than 65,000 visitors. When the organizers were seeking to establish how to pitch their planning, they had difficulty obtaining data and that made projecting the financial requirements difficult. The Rodin Exhibition was built around the fact that E.P. Warren, a wealthy American art collector and dealer who lived in Lewes between 1892 and 1902, commissioned The Kiss from the sculptor. Twenty-eight pieces of sculpture by Rodin were exhibited in the Town Hall from late May until the end of October 1999. SculptureCo consists of local people from the private and public sectors (Myles, personal communication, 1999).

The lack of a regional database that included all of the cultural attractions and exhibitions was one of the handicaps that the exhibition organizers faced when they sought data. The organizers based their estimate of about 30,000 visitors upon local data that had been assembled for a project by the tourism team at the University of Brighton and consultations with some art galleries that run temporary exhibitions (Myles, personal communication, 1999). Highly effective marketing pushed the numbers well over the projections.

## The Pattern of Visiting and Visitor Management

The following section is a summary of the results of several recent visitor surveys, including the European Association for Tourism and Leisure Education (ATLAS) Cultural Tourism Project. The questionnaires for the ATLAS research were distributed at Scotney Castle, a garden in Kent and at Batemans, the country home of Rudyard Kipling, an author who wrote during the early 20th century. In all, 273 questionnaires were collected and analysed. All the surveys undertaken generated similar results.

The lifeblood of the South-East is the day visitor drawn dominantly from socio-economic groups ABC1, and aged between 40 and 60, of whom 60% are female. More than 70% are from the region and visit the sites for leisure rather than for educational reasons. The majority has been in further or higher education (90%) and regard themselves as professional or skilled workers. Most travel as pairs and drive less than an hour to visit an attraction. As traffic densities continue to increase in the South-East so the distance that is covered is declining. Most visit either because there has been a recommendation or because one of the party has been there before. Typically, direct promotion attracts less than 40% of all visitors; it is the way in which the sites are managed that is the most important means of attracting visitors. The majority of successful sites such as Scotney and Batemans where the ATLAS survey was based, have a strong identity that makes them memorable, a good ambience and are well managed. It is the genius loci rather than any associations with people that matter most. So in the instance of Charleston Farmhouse, it is the atmosphere created by the Bloomsbury set rather than the fact that members of it lived there that matters (Burley, 1995; Berry,1998b; Chrysalis, 1998).

Those who run cultural attractions have to look carefully at how visitors think, because enough income must be generated to cover both operating and capital costs. Both are rising because of the demands of legislation and the expectations of visitors. Effective management aims to generate income from visitors in two ways: by increasing the numbers and by enticing more expenditure out of each one. The majority of the cultural attractions that have managed to increase or to maintain their numbers and to increase their income from visitors are working hard to improve their marketing and they are also investing heavily. As the ATLAS research shows, visitors are principally looking for a pleasant environment in which they can relax (average score 4.48 on a 5 point scale, compared with 3.80 for other ATLAS survey sites), and learning new things and new experiences come second. To respond to visitors' expectations, larger cultural heritage sites are investing in more facilities by utilizing more buildings (Sissinghurst) or building service buildings if planning permits (Bodiam) and expanding the areas that the public can use (Scotney and Batemans). In some instances there has been a dramatic improvement in numbers as at Borde Hill where the visitor numbers have risen from 10,000 to 75,000 a year in the last decade (*Historic House*, 1999). Most owners of larger attractions, or of groups of attractions such as Brighton Council and the National Trust (Scotney and Batemans), are investing more in training of staff so that they can handle visitors more effectively.

The smaller cultural heritage sites of 40,000 visitors or less, many of which are losing visitors, normally lack the space (e.g. Alfriston Clergy House) or the money (e.g. the Sussex Archaeological Society) to make improvements (National Trust, 1989–1998; *Sussex Archaeological Society Accounts*, 1989–1998). There is also the risk that they will lose their genius loci or that more visitors will do a lot of damage because of the limited carrying capacity of small buildings and sites. Indeed it would probably be better conservation practice to close and let or sell them as in the case of Wilmington Priory, a small rural agricultural museum which is now managed by the Landmark Trust as a holiday let. The overall trend has been that the bigger attractions have retained or increased their numbers at the expense of both the smaller ones and rivals of a similar size that have not invested (Anon., 1997; Figs 8.2 and 8.3). The visitor numbers for the National Trust's properties in Kent and East Sussex reveal the dilemma that faces such a conservation body. Investment in their larger properties where there is the potential has maintained the total visitor numbers at 1.1 million and ensured that expenditure by visitors has increased (Berry, 1996–1999; National Trust Annual Reports, 1989–1998).

No matter how much money is spent on keeping the retail and other facilities attractive, the cultural heritage sites cannot change much or they will lose their identity which is, as the ATLAS survey shows, of major

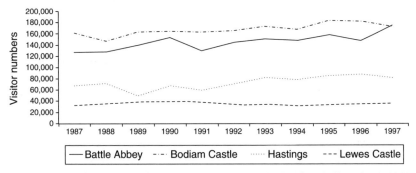

**Fig. 8.2.** Visitor trends to larger historic properties in the South-East from 1987 to 1997. (From G. Shephard and *English Heritage Monitor*.)

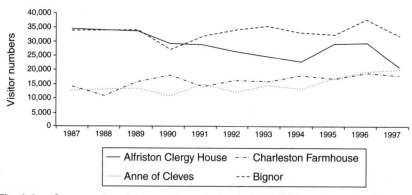

**Fig. 8.3.** Comparative visitor numbers to 4 small South-East properties from 1987 to 1997. (From G. Shephard and *English Heritage Monitor*.)

importance. Indeed it could lose the very thing that people come to see. Scheduling and other planning controls also limit what may be done to most of the sites (PPG 15, 1995). The frozen nature of such attractions poses a problem in the South-East because of the need to attract repeat visitors. This region is not a tourist region in the sense that the South-West is (National Trust, 1999). There, most attractions can assume that they have visitors that are staying a week or more. In the South-East, the repeat visitor from the locality is far more important than in the South-West. The strategy therefore may have to be very different.

As the ATLAS survey showed at Scotney and at Batemans, the majority of the repeat visitors are not regular visitors and this is one of the issues that cultural sites in the South-East have to cope with. The majority of visitors do not return within the same season. When the market is based on a fairly small catchment area, repeat visits matter.

Events, changes in interpretation, opening up parts of the building while conservation is in process, longer hours, innovative shops (Charleston Farmhouse) and opening up parts of the site for walks (Scotney Castle), art courses and exhibitions are among the many activities that are used to try to attract people. All of this costs money and these costs have to be recouped from visitors (Berry, 1996–1999).

The managers of some cultural heritage sites in the South-East have recognized that they need to understand their localities better and are trying to establish why local people do not visit. In 1994 the Sussex Archaeological Society discovered that a considerable proportion of the people that were asked why they had not visited Lewes Castle and other sites had never heard of them and said that they might visit now that they knew of them. Thus sites cannot assume that visitors do not go because they do not want to. In this instance, leaflets and other traditional marketing literature were not reaching the people for whom they were intended, neither locals nor visitors (Berry, 1994). Ensuring that local people are contacted and encouraged to visit is an important facet of marketing that most sites seem to underplay, perhaps too fixated on the belief that the visitor comes from further afield (Bloch, 1997; Grant *et al.*, 1997). The Sussex Archaeological Society's research project was among many that revealed that random distribution of leaflets is not effective but that group marketing and especially carefully targeted group marketing is. The membership book that members of the National Trust receive is a powerful group-marketing tool. The research by the Sussex Archaelogical Society also established a link between local knowledge and a good local reputation and recommendation. The National Trust is now seeking to broaden its market to appeal to sectors that simply do not visit even if they know of the Trust's sites (Taylor, personal communication, 1999).

While large organizations such as the National Trust are developing visitor research programmes that will consist of a mixture of questionnaires and interviews, the majority of the research is limited and small scale (Pontini, personal communication, 1999). Few attractions are looking at the patterns of travel and the impact of changes in the regional economy and infrastructure. The most effective approach would be to share research and research costs and meet and discuss the results. With the development of modern research techniques that extract ever more information from smaller samples, the costs would not be prohibitive (Ryan, 1995; Cramer, 1997). The survival of the majority of cultural heritage sites in this region is dependent on such coherent and well planned group action. As more houses are built in the region in line with recent government proposals, the need to be able to utilize the local market will become more important. Projects such as the ATLAS Cultural Tourism Project, which enables comparisons to be made between different sites and regions in a changing market, will be of ever greater value.

## Conclusion

Cultural heritage sites in the South-East have to contend with many adverse factors. These include: environmental decline in the resorts, congested transportation systems, the threat of yet more housing developments that may jeopardize the landscapes that surround rural sites and a decline in the tourism visits because of poor accessibility from traditional markets in the London region. A new challenge that did not live up to the expectations of adverse impacts on the attractions of the South-East was the Millennium Dome, the impact of which was a cause of great concern before it opened at the start of 2000 (Cubbage, 1999). The majority of cultural heritage sites are becoming more businesslike in their approach to attracting and managing visitors and that is reflected in the assessment of the better managed ones such as Scotney and Batemans where the ATLAS research was undertaken. Not until managers understand the visitors who come and the latent demand will they cope with the fact that they now appear to be in a saturated market for the product as it is at the moment (Bloch, 1997; Grant *et al.*, 1997). A more proactive approach to understanding and to explaining themselves to visitors from their locality must be a major part of managers' approach in the next millennium.

# References

Anon. (1997) Visitor trends at attractions in 1996. *Insights* F7–F10.

Anon. (1998a) Holiday taking by the British in 1997. *Insights* F1–F7.

Anon. (1998b) Tourism by UK residents in 1997. *Insights* F21–F26.

Anon. (1999a) Overseas Tourists to the UK. *Insights* F27–F33.

Anon. (1999b) Regional distribution of overseas and domestic tourism in 1997. *Insights* F35–F42.

Berry, S. (1994) Conservation, capacity and cashflows; tourism and historic building management. In: Seaton, A.V. *et al.* (eds) *Tourism: the State of the Art.* John Wiley & Sons, Chichester, pp. 712–718.

Berry, S. (1996) The changing economics of heritage tourism; who pays and who benefits? In: Robinson, M. (ed.) *Tourism and Cultural Change.* British Educational Publishers, Newcastle, pp. 39–52.

Berry, S. (1996–1999) Chairman of Regional Finance Committee, Kent and East Sussex Region of the National Trust.

Berry, S. (1998a) Compilation of data from all heritage attractions in East and West Sussex from 1987 to 1997 from SEETB data, annual reports and personal contact.

Berry, S. (1998b) *Charleston Farmhouse Visitor Survey.* University of Brighton, Eastbourne.

Berry, S. (1999a) Brighton in the early 19th century. In: Leslie, K. and Short, B. (eds) *An Historical Atlas of Sussex.* Phillimore, Chichester, pp. 94–95.

Berry, S. (1999b) Charities and heritage tourism. *Tourism Recreation Research* 24(2), 31–36.

Berry, S. and Standeven, J. (1993) *Inbound Tourism – Location Report.* Tourism Officers of East Sussex Group, Eastbourne.

Bloch, S. (1997) The future of museums. *Insights* September, D7–D12.

Burley, A. (1995) The National Trust: an investigation into visitor types with a consideration as to possible methods of increasing income at individual properties. Thesis, University of Brighton, Eastbourne.

Chrysalis (1998) Batemans visitor survey Lamberhurst. National Trust. October.

Cramer, D. (1997) *Basic Statistics for Social Research.* Routledge, London.

Cubbage, F. (1999) The millennium opportunity – political posturing or practical advantage? *Tourism* spring, 14–15.

Dale, A. (1967) *Fashionable Brighton.* Oriel, Newcastle.

DTER (1998) *Where Shall We Live?* Consultative Paper 1998.

*English Heritage Monitor* (1996) English Heritage, London.

English Tourism Board (1998) Sightseeing trends in 1997. *Insights* A92.

Farrant, S. (1981) *Georgian Brighton.* University of Sussex.

Farrant, S. (1983) The development of seaside resorts in Sussex 1740 to 1840. In Geography Editorial Board (eds) *Sussex Environment Landscape and Society.* Sutton, Gloucester.

Farrant, S. (1989) The development of landscape parks in eastern Sussex 1700–1720. *Journal of Garden History* 17, 166–180.

Grant, M. *et al.* (1997) Seasonality. *Insights* A5–A9.

Granville, A.B. (1841) *Spas of England: Bath.* Adams and Dart reprint 1971.

*Historic House* (1999) Historic Houses Association.

Holloway, J.C. (1994) *The Business of Tourism.* Pitman, London, pp. 216–225.

Hudson, N. (1998) *Historic Houses and Gardens.* Hudsons, Banbury.

Human, B. (1999) Sustainable tourism management: the lifecycle. *Insights* A143–A148.

Jones, M. and MacLeod, T. (1999) Towards a regional renaissance. Reconfiguring and rescaling England's economic governance. *Transactions of the Institute of British Geographers* NS24, 295–313.

Leask, A. and Yeoman, I. (1999) *Heritage Visitor Attractions.* Cassell, London, pp. 39–53.

Lewes District Council (1998) *Visitor Survey.* Lewes District Council, Lewes.

Morley, J. (1984) *The Making of the Royal Pavilion.* Sotheby, London.

National Trust (1989–1999) *Annual Accounts.* National Trust, London.

National Trust (1999) *Valuing our Environment.* Study produced by Tourism Associates. National Trust and Tourism Associates, Exeter, pp. 5–6.

Piggott, S. (1995) Visitors to National Trust Properties in Kent and East Sussex: analysis of a visitor survey. Thesis, University of Brighton, Eastbourne.

PPG 15 (1995) *Department of the Environment Planning Guide Number 15.* HMSO, London.

Ryan, C. (1995) *Research Tourist Satisfaction.* Routledge, London.

Savidge, A. and Bell, C. (1995) *Royal Tunbridge Wells.* Midas, Tunbridge Wells.

SEETB (1998) *Images of the Southeast.* Tunbridge Wells, SEETB.

SEETB (1999) *Regional Tourism Fact Sheets: Southeast England.* English Tourism Council, London.

Smith, S.J. (1996) *Tourism Analysis: a Handbook.* Longman, Harlow, pp. 204–248.

South-East Development Agency (1998) *State of the Region.* SEEDA, Guildford, pp. 19–25.

StarUK (1999) Web site of the English Tourist Board. http://www.staruk.org.uk/mapse.htm

*Sussex Archaeological Society Accounts* (1989–1998) Sussex Archaeological Society, Lewes.

Tinniswood, A. (1998) *The Polite Tourist.* National Trust, London, pp. 159–180.

Walton, J. (1983) *The English Seaside Resort.* Leicester University Press, Leicester.

White, T. and Harte, J. (1994) *Epsom: a Pictorial History.* Phillimore, Chichester.

Whitehead, C., Holmans, A. and Marshall, D. (1999) *Housing Needs in the Southeast: a Research Report.* Enterprise LSE and Property Research Unit London LSE.

Whyman, J. (1985) *The Early English Seaside.* Sutton, Gloucester.

# Urban Heritage Tourism: Globalization and Localization

## Michael Green

*Department of Physical Education, Sports Science and Recreation Management, Loughborough University, UK*

## Introduction

This chapter aims to provide some insights into the significance of both 'global' and 'local' factors in the shaping and mediating of urban heritage tourism development – one element of the broader category of 'cultural tourism' (Richards, 1996a). 'Representations of heritage', or 'attractions of culture', in three European cities are used as case studies: The Dutch Textile Museum in Tilburg in The Netherlands; the Basque Archaeological, Ethnography and Historical Museum in Bilbao, Spain; and the National Space Science Centre (NSSC) development in Leicester, UK.

At the global level, the conceptual debates surrounding the globalization-localization discourse provide the underlying theoretical framework of the chapter – e.g. see Harvey (1989); Giddens (1990, 1991); McGrew (1992); Robertson (1992); Friedman (1994); Featherstone (1995); Waters (1995); Öncü and Weyland (1997). At the local (city) level, the focus is on the potential for disparity between local actors involved in the development of urban heritage tourism *vis-à-vis* the attractions of culture cited above. Interviews conducted during 1997–1998 in Tilburg, Bilbao and Leicester across municipal/provincial authorities, tourism promotion agencies, museum associations and the attractions of culture in the three cities, provide instructive insights into the processes underlying the development of urban heritage tourism at the local (city) level.

It is acknowledged that the selection of material here is necessarily subjective and an in-depth analysis of *all* the recent globalization theory is beyond the scope of this chapter. However, an attempt is made to illustrate the relationship between the latter and the development of cultural attractions in three European cities. Essentially, the ensuing discussion reflects Richards' observation that:

> The dialectical opposition between the forces of globalization and localization will play an even more crucial role in the development of cultural tourism in the future. On the one hand, the spread of a global culture will make elements of European culture accessible to a wider audience, both through the development of tourism and the media. On the other hand, resistance to the erosion of local identities implied by globalization will stimulate increasing use of culture as a means of local differentiation, and thus as a means of tourism development and marketing.
>
> (Richards, 1996b, p. 326)

Thus the aim here is to contribute to a clearer focus, and a framework for further research into the ways in which local factors interrelate with global processes of change *vis-à-vis* the development of cultural attractions in Tilburg, Bilbao and Leicester.

## The Global–Local Dialectic

It has been argued that, although the terminology might be new, the concept of globalization is not a recent phenomenon (Hall, 1991a; Robertson, 1992; Cantelon and Murray, 1993). Hall (1991a), for example, suggests that globalization in the present context, is about new forms, new rhythms and new impetuses in the globalizing process. Hall also suggests that what is unique about these new forms of globalization is the notion of 'harmony in diversity'. Here, the 'global' is far from being something which, in a systematic fashion, envelops everything, creating similarity: the global 'works through particularity, negotiates particular spaces, particular ethnicities, works through mobilizing particular identities . . . thus there is always a dialectic, a continuous dialectic, between the global and the local' (Hall, 1991b, p. 62).

Cantelon and Murray have interpreted Hall's 'harmony in diversity' to mean that, at one level, localized national culture continues to operate 'but beyond the national boundaries is the synchronous transnational culture with its different cultural flow' (1993, p. 278). This flow has been cultivated and propagated by numerous international agencies and institutions, for example, the European Union (EU) and the World Tourism Organization.

Friedman (1994), for example, suggests that global relations have been most easily identifiable in terms of visible institutions or organizations, constructed within already existing global fields, e.g. colonial administrations, the media corporations and transnational and multinational corporations. Friedman goes on to argue that multinationals, for example, are a historically generated product of a given phase of global relations and, significantly, cites the tourism industry as an instructive example of the latter.

According to Giddens (1991), the concept of globalization is best understood as expressing fundamental aspects of 'time–space distanciation' – related to the intersection of 'presence' and 'absence' and the interlinking of social events and social relations 'at distance' with local contextualities. Thus, for Giddens, globalization has to be understood as '. . . a dialectical phenomenon, in which events at one pole of a distanciated relation often produce divergent or even contrary occurrences at another' (1991, p. 22). As Giddens explicitly acknowledges, globalization is a dialectical process because it does not result in '. . . a generalized set of changes acting in a uniform direction but consists in mutually opposed tendencies' (1990, p. 64).

McGrew (1992) takes Giddens' work a stage further and questions the substantive form of these 'opposed tendencies', highlighting several 'binary oppositions' or 'dualities' within the globalization discourse. A brief consideration of two of these dualities in relation to cultural tourism development in Europe follows.

## Homogenization versus differentiation

Herbert suggests that tourism plays a part in the mixing of Europeans and, as it grows, there are more points of contact and opportunities for interaction and, significantly, that 'tourism is influential within this role in contradictory ways. It standardizes but also differentiates . . .' (1995, p. 15). Moreover, Richards argues that 'in an increasingly globalized and homogenized cultural landscape, the need to establish local difference through the ownership of customs, rituals, art works, buildings and even whole landscapes becomes even more acute' (1996c, p. 64). Thus, although all urban areas are tourism–historic destinations to differing degrees, they are heterogeneous in structure and function (Ashworth and Tunbridge, 1990).

## Integration versus fragmentation

Globalization creates new forms of global, regional and transnational communities or organizations which unite people across territorial boundaries, e.g. the transnational corporation or bodies such as the World Tourism Organization. At the same time, it also divides and fragments communities both within and across traditional nation-state boundaries (McGrew, 1992). For example, racial and ethnic divisions become more profound where the development of a more economically orientated city development policy style, aimed at the revitalization of the city, has led to social polarization. Such polarization is manifest in scenarios where '. . . projects, developed in public–private partnerships, [which] are meant not for the integration of disadvantaged groups within society, but for servicing the pleasures of the "well-to-do"' (Mommaas and van der Poel, 1989, p. 263).

To summarize, the cultural impact of globalized tourism is multiple and complex, however, Waters (1995) identifies some key dimensions which can be outlined here in order to better inform the ensuing discussion of the Tilburg, Bilbao and Leicester case studies. Firstly, the extent of globalized tourism indicates the degree to which tourists themselves conceptualize the world as a single place which is without internal geographical boundaries. Secondly, globalization exposes tourists to cultural differences thereby confirming the validity of local cultures and their distinctiveness. Thirdly, 'tourism extends consumer culture by redefining both human practices and the physical environment as commodities' (Waters, 1995, p. 155).

The argument being developed here is that it is the complex interconnections or interrelatedness between *both* global and local processes which account for the particular ways in which an area's local history and culture are utilized 'as a resource for local economic and social development within a globally evolving economy and society' (Urry, 1995, p. 152).


## Global Cultural Flows

Waters (1995) suggests that the notion of 'cultural interrelatedness' highlighted earlier is linked to a continuous flow of ideas, information, values and tastes mediated through mobile individuals, symbolic tokens and electronic simulations. Reference can be made here to Appadurai's (1990) approach to the 'global cultural economy' which incorporates several of the important fields in which these developments or flows occur. For Appadurai, the new global cultural economy has to be understood as 'a complex, overlapping, disjunctive order, which cannot be understood in terms of existing centre-periphery models . . .' (1990, p. 296). Five dimensions of global cultural flow have been identified: (i) *ethnoscapes*, the distribution of mobile individuals, e.g. tourists and migrants; (ii) *mediascapes*, the distribution of information; (iii) *technoscapes*, the distribution of technology; (iv) *finanscapes*, the distribution of capital; and (v) *ideoscapes*, the distribution of political ideas and values, e.g. freedom and democracy (Appadurai, 1990).

Of significance here, is Appadurai's (1990) observation that these 'scapes' are inflected by the historical, linguistic and political contexts of disparate actors: nation-states, multinationals, diasporic communities and even face-to-face groups. The significance of the role of the nation-state is considered below (and in more depth later in the chapter) and the relevance of diasporic communities is subsequently examined in more depth with regard to the NSSC in the multicultural city of Leicester. Appadurai cites the individual actor as the 'last locus' of this set of perspective landscapes and suggests that the latter are 'eventually navigated by agents who both experience and constitute larger formations, in part by their own sense of what these landscapes offer' (1990, p. 296). It is here that the perspectives of key local actors in Tilburg, Bilbao and Leicester are instructive. These 'local perspectives' will subsequently be shown to inform the shaping and mediating of global factors in the development of cultural attractions at the local (city) level.

The critical point for Appadurai (1990) is that the global relationship between these landscapes is deeply disjunctive and variable, since each landscape is subject to its own constraints and impetuses. At the same time, each acts as a constraint and a parameter for movements in the other – thus substantiating the dialectical relationship between the global and the local.

One further point which has relevance here, is Appadurai's conception of the nation-state: '. . . the relationship between states and nations is everywhere an embattled one' (1990, p. 303). Moreover, Appadurai goes on to suggest that national and international 'mediascapes' are exploited by nation-states to ameliorate, for example, 'the potential fissiparousness of all ideas of difference' (1990, p. 304). With specific regard to the nation-state and cultural (heritage) attractions, Appadurai (1990, p. 304) argues that:

> States . . . are everywhere seeking to monopolize the moral resources of community, either by flatly claiming perfect coevality between nation and state, or by systematically museumizing and representing all the groups within them in a variety of heritage politics that seems remarkably uniform throughout the world.

In order to avoid the danger of a bland homogenizing culture, implicit in the above observation, Walsh suggests that there has to be a role for educative facilities which allow 'people to come to terms with the richness and variety that can be found in different places' (1992, p. 146). It is beyond the scope of this chapter to analyse the relationship between education and museums here, however, it is an area that may warrant further study (Boylan, 1992; Walsh, 1992; Moore, 1997; MacDonald, 1998).

Having provided an overview of the theoretical linkages surrounding the global–local discourse and cultural and tourism development in Europe, we can now turn our attention to a more specific consideration of the key theoretical debates underlying the development of cultural attractions in European cities.

## Global Economic Restructuring

Cities or urban conglomerations in Europe are diverse in the way that they are affected by recent economic and political changes. As Bramham *et al.* (1989, p. 278) note:

> . . . urban processes are specific to certain periods and certain places, depending on the relation between the local economic and political infrastructure to transformations of a global and national scale. Cities and urban conglomerations are positioned differently within historical time and global space.

With regard to Bilbao, for example, Gonzalez (1993) suggests that the city is undergoing a comparatively late transformation of its economic base in relation to many other western European cities. As Gómez observes, within a comparative study of de-industrialization in Glasgow and Bilbao: 'While Glasgow provides a severe example of de-industrialization in terms of both scope and speed, given the dominance of heavy industry, Bilbao followed a similar pattern some years later' (1998, p. 107).

Moreover, Gonzalez (1993) goes on to note that a pivotal feature of Bilbao's economic fabric is the change in the pattern of employment from manufacturing to services and in the increasing use of culture and tourism policy to revitalize and regenerate the city, not least in the creation of employment. The latter can also be related to the growth of multinational enterprises which have wide-ranging perspectives when considering new locations. This has led to rivalry among different locations to attract inward investment of mobile 'footloose' capital (Harvey, 1989; Jessop, 1997; Gómez, 1998). The promotion of unique events, cultural policies, promotion of tourism or image improvement are all different versions of the same approach: the attempt to regenerate or to further develop the economic base of the urban area (Gómez, 1998). Elements of such processes are also evident in the cities of Tilburg and Leicester, as revealed below *vis-à-vis* Harvey's (1989) approach to globalization, economic restructuring and postmodernity.

Harvey examines Marx's thesis of the annihilation of space by time and *inter alia* attempts to demonstrate how this explains the complex shift from 'Fordism' to the flexible accumulation of 'post-Fordism'. Evidence of this 'complex shift' is manifest in Tilburg, Bilbao and Leicester. In Bilbao, for example:

> There is also clear evidence of the emergence of self-contained, relatively autonomous work groups organized around particular problems, and characterized by flexible patterns of part-time employment. All these signs correspond to a process of change from a Fordist to a post-Fordist economy.
>
> (Gonzalez, 1993, p. 81)

Indeed, Richards (1996a) is one of a number of authors (e.g. see also Featherstone, 1991; Corijn and Mommaas, 1995; Urry, 1995) to suggest that postmodern tourism is related to a fragmentation of class structures/cultures, a concern for image, for authenticity, with differentiated markets and post-Fordist, flexible patterns of production. Moreover, Harvey (1989) also suggests that the latter involves a new 'spatial fix' and, most significantly, new ways in which time and space are represented. Central to Harvey's analysis is the concept of 'time–space compression':

> Space appears to shrink to a 'global village' of telecommunications and a 'spaceship earth' of economic and ecological interdependencies . . . and as time horizons shatter to the point where the present is all there is . . . so we

have to learn how to cope with an overwhelming sense of *compression* of our spatial and temporal worlds.

(Harvey, 1989, p. 240, original emphasis)

For Harvey (1989), this intensification of globalization has been most pronounced in the spheres of manufacturing production and finance, e.g. the decline of the textile industry in Leicester and Tilburg. Moreover, Corijn and Mommaas (1995) suggest that, from the perspective of European urban development, certain trends can be identified relating to globalization. Two pertinent examples are provided here: first, the growth of South-East Asian economies as a result of these countries' increasing role as sites of transnational production. A clear example of the latter, in the field of urban heritage tourism, is evident in Chang *et al.*'s analysis of Montreal and Singapore – and one which can be related to the decline of the textile industry in Tilburg and Leicester and thus the subsequent development of cultural attractions in the two cities:

> Equally significant to Montreal's changing economic fortunes was the new international division of labour that was taking hold at this time. Many of the city's traditional industries, such as textile and clothing manufacture, faced heightened levels of competition from low labour-cost countries in Asia and Latin America.

(Chang *et al.*, 1996, p. 290)

The second trend highlighted by Corijn and Mommaas (1995) is the fundamental change in the relationship between nation-states and the economy and the ongoing 'de-localization' of the economy. National governments are increasingly involved in a global/regional competition for transnational investments and, as a result of the changes related to the global economic restructuring processes highlighted earlier, feel forced to adapt to market-orientated strategies, thereby liberating economic conditions and financial resources. Paradoxically, this further reduces nation-states' controlling and correcting capacities. In an attempt to compensate for this loss of autonomy, governments increasingly make use of both higher levels of supranational organization, such as the EU, and lower levels of economic integration – e.g. urban regions – for the creation of more adaptive international economic policies. Thus, at this point, it is worth while to examine in more depth the current debates surrounding the 'problematic' role of the nation-state and the implications of the latter for the development of cultural attractions in European cities.

## Declining Role of the Nation-state?

It could be argued that what is emerging in Europe today is a model of 'overlapping and pluralistic authority structures' (cf. McGrew, 1992; Hirst and Thompson, 1996). The latter has been likened to medieval political practice and organization. Bull (1977), for example, refers to a form of 'new medievalism', which suggests a re-formulating of political community, no longer identified with the territorial nation-state. Indeed, McGrew argues that, 'as in medieval times, we are forced to think in terms of overlapping global, regional, transnational, national and local political communities' (1992, p. 96). Moreover, McGrew goes on to suggest that it is in this sense that globalization can be said to be 'dissolving, rather than contributing to, the transcendence of the sovereign nation-state . . . sovereignty, and with it the nature of the "political community", is being reconstituted by the forces of globalization' (1992, p. 96).

The concept of new medievalism and overlapping and pluralistic authority structures is instructive here. Jessop (1997) suggests that cities and regions in Europe now engage in their own forms of foreign economic policy in such diverse fields as industrial policy, tourism development and labour markets. Jessop also notes that: 'In Europe the authorities and agencies involved operate supranationally at the EU level as well as transnationally and often bypass their national state when doing so . . .' (1997, p. 36). The 'Europe of the Regions' strategy is an example of the latter in so far as the EU is currently cooperating with sub-national regions in identifying potential economic and political spaces for a new political settlement premised on subsidiarity rather than sovereignty (Jessop, 1997).

Featherstone (1995, p. 111) observes that the interactions occurring between nation-states, particularly those which involve increasing competition and conflict, can have an integrative effect, *vis-à-vis* 'the self-image of the nation: the image or national face presented to the other'. He goes on to argue that the increasing intensity of contacts nation-states have with regional contexts compounds the pressures 'to present a coherent and distinctive identity' (1995, p. 111). However, Featherstone also notes that, apart from the external presentation of the national face, the internal dimension of power resources particular groups possess in order to suit their own particular interests must be considered. As Maguire observes, it is the 'dominant groups' within society which promote the discourses that come to represent identities via producing meanings about the 'nation' (1993, p. 295). This leads to questions at national and local level: for example, does a 'national' project, such as the NSSC in the multicultural city of Leicester, suggest a unified and homogeneous representation of identity? As Walsh (1992; p. 128) notes:

> The provision of such cultural services has not been designed to enhance
> or highlight differences within societies, or to promote a critique and
> questioning of representations of the past. Most cases have successfully
> denied difference. . . . Such a heritage is endorsed through the promotion
> of a homogeneous communal identity. . . .

The issues of representation/identity outlined here are considered in more depth in the discussion of the city case studies. Attention will now turn, more specifically, to a consideration of some of the key issues underlying the prevalence of the development of cultural (heritage) attractions in disparate European urban contexts.

## The Prevalence of Cultural Attractions in European Cities

The explanations advanced for the prevalence of cultural and heritage tourism are various and diverse. However, they tend to converge *inter alia* around notions that tourists want more cultural and heritage experiences, whether these be meaningful and 'authentic' (MacCannell, 1976) or as an opportunity to produce their own meanings from the tourism experience (Urry, 1990, 1995). These explanations can be related to the earlier discussion on global processes and the collapse of boundaries between the 'cultural' and the 'economic' – a key feature of postmodernity (Harvey, 1989; Urry, 1990; Featherstone, 1991; Walsh, 1992). As Urry notes: 'There is a de-differentiation of the "cultural economy . . ." and an aspect of the latter, for example, ". . . is the dissolving of the boundaries of what is artistic production and what is commercial"' (Urry, 1990, p. 85).

The notion of the 'heritagization of space' (Walsh, 1992) is instructive here and can be related to the earlier discussion on globalization and de-industrialization which has resulted in the fragmentation and weakening of certain social/cultural hierarchies. Harvey (1989), for example, argues that the economic restructuring that has taken place in many western European cities has led to the increasing abstraction of the characteristics of certain spaces. This abstraction has become more refined and intense to the point where 'the active production of places with special qualities becomes an important stake in spatial competition between localities, cities, regions and nations' (Harvey, 1989, p. 295). For example, with regard to the city of Leicester, the City Council, and its attendant agencies and partners, are actively pursuing a vision which positions the city in a European dimension (Leicester City Council, 1998). This vision will necessarily involve competition with other places through the strategy of place promotion (Harvey, 1989; Walsh, 1992; Ball and Stobart, 1996; Chang *et al.*, 1996). Walsh notes some implications of such a strategy: 'As spaces compete with one another, they must attempt to promote an image, an attractive marketing surface, which will lure the multinational to their place' (1992, p. 136).

The critical argument underlying the concept of the heritagization of space, especially in the urban environment, suggests that: 'Heritage space . . . is one constituted by a mixture of misquoted styles which serve to destroy the identity of a place' (Walsh, 1992, p. 137). The opposing argument is that heritage spaces can help maintain an identity of place, through emphasis on historical characteristics which stand as a metaphor for that place. However, there is a danger that only safe and selected images will be preserved or constructed and that over time the image of a place will be based only on superficialities (Walsh, 1992; Maguire, 1993; Featherstone, 1995). This is not to suggest that, for example, this is the case with regard to the NSSC in Leicester: the aim here is to provide some preliminary insights into the underlying processes within which the development of the NSSC is proceeding and to provide a framework within which further research can be undertaken into the NSSC's role as a cultural attraction in Leicester's city strategy.

Having considered some of the underlying theoretical debates surrounding the globalization–localization discourse and the implications of the latter for the development of cultural attractions in Europe, we can now turn our attention, more specifically, to the case studies of Tilburg, Bilbao and Leicester.

## Case Studies: Tilburg, Bilbao and Leicester

Firstly, a brief overview of Tilburg, Bilbao and Leicester is provided in order to situate these cities in 'historical time and global space' (Bramham *et al.*, 1989, p. 286) – thus enabling the ensuing analysis to incorporate '. . . not only local circumstances but perhaps through these . . . more national, global or historical processes' (Bramham *et al.*, 1989, p. 286). The overview helps to synthesize the theoretical debates outlined earlier in the chapter and suggests that all three cities could be categorized as 'declining cities' (Bianchini, 1993), where policies have been used to support strategies for the diversification of the local economic base and the reconstruction of the city's image. Moreover, with regard to the latter, Gratton and Richards observe that: 'These cities have suffered decline due to the disappearance of their old manufacturing base' (1996, p. 80) – pertinent to all three of the cities discussed below.

### Tilburg

Tilburg is situated in the North Brabant region of The Netherlands, where economic growth is high. The city is expanding and it is estimated that by 2015 the population will be approximately 200,000 (Gemeentearchief Tilburg, 1998). Tilburg had undergone a decline in its major industry during the 1960s: 'The monoculture of Tilburg's textile industry has been replaced by variety and modern industry is represented in the city' (Gemeentearchief Tilburg, 1998). Thus the city is currently promoted as a 'Modern Industrial City', an issue that proved contentious with the local actors involved in the development of tourism in the city.

The following observation reflects the impact of the globalizing trends discussed earlier, the relationship between the city's industrial policy and employment and the decline of Tilburg's textile industry:

The progressing globalization and the concurring increasing competition have put a pressure on employment. Until the 1960s the textile industry was of vital importance to Tilburg. This industry has almost completely disappeared and has been replaced by a wide range of industrial companies, including multinationals such as Fuji, Philips and DAF.

(Gemeentearchief Tilburg, 1998)

It is clear, therefore, that the city of Tilburg reflects many of the globalizing trends related to the processes of economic restructuring discussed earlier.

## Bilbao

Bilbao is the capital of Vizcaya, one of three provinces constituting the Basque Country in the north-west of Spain and is at the core of a metro-politan area of over 1 million people (Gonzalez, 1993; Gómez, 1998). The 'first industrialization' of the city was based around mining, metallurgy and shipbuilding. From 1950 until the mid-1970s there was a continuous increase in industrial employment in Vizcaya and low unemployment, generally. However, during the mid-1970s, the city's industrial base began to decline (Gómez, 1998).

Bilbao is currently experiencing a transformation of its economic base, with a shift away from mass production towards a pattern of more flexible production and the use of cultural policy as part of an urban regeneration plan (Gonzalez, 1993; Goytia Prat *et al.*, 1995). In terms of employment trends, the industrial sector experienced a 34% decrease between 1975 and 1992, whereas the tertiary sector achieved a 40% increase (Uribarri, 1993). As noted earlier, Gonzalez (1993) suggests that all these signs correspond to a process of change from a Fordist to a post-Fordist economy (Henry, 1993). Thus the city of Bilbao can be seen to reflect many of the global trends highlighted earlier.

One further point to note with regard to Bilbao is the environment within which the public sector's cultural and tourism policy makers operate. The public sector in Bilbao consists of a complex set of institutions (Gonza-lez, 1993; Maiztegui-Oñate, 1996). There are three levels of local govern-ment: the Basque autonomous community, the Diputación (provincial authority) and the municipality. Thus, as Gonzalez notes: 'Co-ordination between these three levels is, therefore, a crucial task' (1993, p. 75).

## Leicester

Leicester is situated in the East Midlands region of England, with a population of 270,000 (Nash and Reeder, 1993). Leicester is a multicultural city manifest in the migrations, post-Second World War, from Europe, the

Caribbean, Asia and Africa. Indeed, the Asian population is estimated to be over 90,000 (Nash and Reeder, 1993).

Nash and Reeder also note that the local historian, W.G. Hoskins, described Leicester as 'at first sight a wholly uninteresting city' (quoted in Nash and Reeder, 1993, p. vii). Whereas, today, Leicester is promoted as 'A City Full of Surprises' (Leicester City Council/Leicester Promotions, 1997; see also Ball and Stobart, 1996). Moreover, Nash and Reeder observe that the '. . . apparent economic success of Leicester disguised fundamental underlying structural problems that a change in the economic climate during the 1970s . . . exposed' (1993, p. xii). The latter relates to the decline of the city's manufacturing base, particularly the local footwear and textile industries. In 1991, the city's Environment and Development Department noted that the recession of the 1970s and early 1980s resulted in 'a dramatic shift in employment nationally from manufacturing into service industries' (Leicester City Council, 1991, p. 1). While Leicester still maintains an above average manufacturing presence, it is the service sector which has grown during the late 1980s, e.g. 'Personal, Cultural and Recreational Services' experienced a growth in employees between 1984 and 1987 of 30% (Leicester City Council, 1991, p. 2).

Thus some analogies are evident with the city of Tilburg which, as noted earlier, has also experienced a decline in its textile industry, e.g. in the underlying causes of the decline in the cities' manufacturing base. In Tilburg it was, in part, due to the pressure of imports from abroad (Gemeentearchief Tilburg, 1998). This is reflected in Leicester: 'The substantial closures within some of Leicester's traditional industries, in particular, textiles and footwear . . . has been caused by competition from imported goods . . .' (Leicester City Council, 1991, p. 2).

Finally, and significantly for this discussion, in 1991 Leicester's Environment and Development Department concluded that: 'The local economy in Leicester is affected by both local and national factors. The creation of a Single European Market in 1992 will test the ability of Leicester's businesses to compete in a wider arena' (Leicester City Council, 1991, p. 7).

The final section of the chapter provides some insights into the development of cultural heritage attractions in Tilburg, Bilbao and Leicester *vis-à-vis* the significance of global, national and local factors outlined above. The potential for disparity among local actors involved in such development in Tilburg, Bilbao and Leicester is also discussed.

## Global and local influences in the development of cultural heritage attractions in Tilburg, Bilbao and Leicester

At the global scale, widespread economic re-structuring and de-industrialization have stimulated the growth of urban heritage tourism in both developed and developing nations. These broader processes are, in turn, mediated by influences (economic, political, sociocultural and environmental) that emanate from the local level.

(Chang *et al.*, 1996, p. 284)

Reflecting the earlier discussion on global–local perspectives, Richards (1996d) suggests that the increased interest in local cultures may well be due to the alienation and uncertainty caused by globalization and time–space compression as conceived by Harvey (1989). However, Richards goes on to note that culture and tourism are resources that can be operationalized at the local level to give cities a competitive advantage in an increasingly competitive European and global tourism market. The following section provides evidence of the role that both global and local factors play in the development of cultural (heritage) attractions in Tilburg, Bilbao and Leicester.

At the Textile Museum in Tilburg a senior source suggested that: 'The city council became more interested in cultural areas about ten years ago and is now trying to present Tilburg as a cultural city'. However, the city's local authority is currently promoting the city as 'Tilburg: A Modern Industrial City' (Gemeentearchief Tilburg, 1998). Significantly, tensions are apparent with regard to this imagery, reflected by the city's (regional) tourism promotion office (hereinafter VVV): 'The local authority uses the slogan, "a modern industrial city". We don't think that this is a good idea. The word "industrial" does not portray a positive image for tourism purposes'. The potential for disparity, alluded to here, is considered in more depth later.

An officer from Tilburg's local authority Cultural Department highlighted the value of tourism, while reflecting on the decline of the textile industry and the city's response to global changes related to economic restructuring:

> The first step following the decline of the textile industry was to establish the education sector. The second was a combination of logistics, transport and the shift to a more modern city. Then . . . we realised that culture was important for Tilburg and how important it was to attract visitors and to make Tilburg more attractive for its own inhabitants. We were fortunate that we had old industrial buildings to develop into cultural centres, like the Textile Museum.

With regard to Bilbao, there is the question of whose culture is being represented. Although the Archaeological, Ethnography and Historical Museum *is* representing local Basque culture, ambivalence is evident elsewhere. Goytia Prat *et al.* (1995) suggest that global or 'centrality infrastructures', such as the Guggenheim Museum, Bilbao, have been promoted ahead of more traditional/local cultural initiatives. Moreover, with reference to industrial heritage, which can arguably be conceived of as 'local traditional culture', a senior manager from the Cultural Projects Department of the Diputación (Provincial Authority) suggested that: 'Industrial heritage is not utilised as a tourism resource at present, more important, are prestige projects such as the Guggenheim or the Music Hall'. Reflecting the earlier point regarding Bilbao's current cultural regeneration strategy, it was also noted that: 'We see the Guggenheim more for the city's image and a way of attracting tourists to spend money. The Basque Government decided that it needed an international project to raise the city's profile. We need to attract tourists, not local people'.

In Leicester, the development of the NSSC also evokes questions concerning who/what is to be represented via this cultural attraction. With reference to the earlier observations on globalization, identity and 'harmony in diversity' (Hall, 1991a, b), it is clear that there *is* an emphasis on cultural diversity in the City Council's strategy (Leicester City Council, 1998). However, a senior source in the city's Arts and Leisure Department commented that '. . . diversity can also alienate people'.

Given the earlier discussion on global economic restructuring processes, postmodernity and the fragmentation of social/cultural hierarchies, the argument being developed here is that the consumption of certain heritage or museum products serves to enhance the identity and cultural capital (Bourdieu, 1984) of certain individuals and groups. Such issues are increasingly the subject of debate (Moore, 1997; MacDonald, 1998). As MacDonald (1998, p. 14) observes, within a wider discussion on *Museums, Science* and *Culture*:

> While there has undoubtedly been a proliferation of different, particularly minority, 'voices' speaking in the public arena, the old political and cultural high ground has not simply been relinquished. On the contrary, what we have seen is an escalation of intellectual battles over the legitimacy of different kinds of representation.

This is a complex debate in which only key points can be dealt with here. For example, Moore suggests that the fostering of a strong local identity, through a museum or any other agency '. . . could create an "us" and "them" hostility against the rest of the world. Some communities perhaps need to lose a little of their closed identity!' (1997, p. 18). Moore's view is reflected in the Museums Association's position on the social role of museums: 'Museums foster a sense of identity with, and pride in, the community. They also help to develop cross-cultural understanding and appreciation of other people's customs and history' (Museums Association, 1991, p. 7). The latter observations have some resonance with Leicester City Council's view that a 'shared heritage should be developed' – articulated in the Council's *Regeneration* theme:

> Regeneration gives a sense of local identity by making Leicester more attractive and accessible, promoting and preserving its heritage and living cultures. Valuing diversity is an essential part of this, as is the need to unite communities through pride in a shared heritage; everyone should be able to enjoy the City and appreciate its history.
>
> (Leicester City Council, 1998, p. 11)

Thus it is argued here that, while the acknowledgement of local factors in shaping and mediating urban heritage tourism development is vital, greater attention needs to be focused on the ways in which these factors interrelate with global processes of change. The chapter concludes with a consideration of the potential for disparity between local actors involved in the collective goal of developing cultural heritage attractions in Tilburg, Bilbao and Leicester.

## The potential for disparity in the development of cultural (heritage) attractions

> Cities differ in their inheritance of urban forms and undertake heritage conservation for varied reasons. Local political and economic aspirations also differ, ensuring that the heritage theme adopted by planning authorities varies from place to place. Thus, although heritage tourism may be the chosen strategy, different destinations tend to accentuate themes particular to their culture and location . . .
>
> (Chang *et al.*, 1996, p. 286)

The potential for disparity in the development of cultural (heritage) attractions in Tilburg, Bilbao and Leicester arises due to a number of different issues. The issues considered here include: (i) the lack of coordination and/or integration between the organizations involved in managing cultural and tourism products (horizontally and vertically); (ii) the increasing significance of the economic imperative in cultural and tourism development; (iii) who/what is to be represented via the development of cultural and tourism attractions.

In Tilburg, the potential for disparity arises from a certain lack of coordination horizontally, i.e. between the semi-autonomous bodies managing cultural and tourism products in the city. For example, the suggestion from the Textile Museum was that: 'Due to the high cost and protracted levels of bureaucracy in dealing with the VVV, it is easier for us to do the work ourselves and not use them as a go-between'. However, this comment does not concur with the view of a senior manager from the VVV: 'I am not aware of any instance when they [the Textile Museum] have said that we are too costly'. This lack of coordination between cultural and tourism organizations in Tilburg was also reflected by an officer from the city's local authority Cultural Department, which is responsible for elements of cultural and tourism products in the city: 'The local authority has no direct relationship with the VVV, in fact they are an autonomous company'.

With regard to Leicester, the potential for disparity can also be seen at a horizontal level. The City Council's 'Strategic Direction' is currently focusing on a vision for Leicester as 'a quality European city' (Leicester City Council, 1998, p. 4). However, there is some ambiguity regarding this strategy within the City Council. This is clear in the following comment from the City Council's Arts and Leisure Department: 'It is certainly the image that the senior politicians responsible for services in Leicester strive to achieve . . . whether it is achievable and the most appropriate image to project, for a number of reasons, is debatable'.

As in Tilburg, there is also evidence of potential disparity between the City Council and Leicester Promotions, the city's tourism promotion agency: 'Leicester Promotions did a lot of research and came up with the slogan, "A City Full of Surprises". . . . I've yet to meet anyone who likes it, apart from the people who work for Leicester Promotions. We find it very hard to see its value' (Arts and Leisure Department Officer) Arguably, these observations suggest that, despite the articulation of a coherent vision for Leicester, (Leicester City Council, 1998) some ambivalence remains between the various actors involved in cultural and tourism development in the city. It is further argued that these comments may be indicating a 'lack of identity' in Leicester: thus can the development of the NSSC ameliorate this incipient identity crisis? It would appear not, given the following comment from a senior source in Leicester's Museums Service:

> I don't think that the Science Centre will necessarily create an identity. The only way that they could do it is by having huge community projects that make people have to interrelate to it, but at the moment it won't. There is no reason why people should go to it, apart from once, because it is a permanent display.

With regard to the representation of ethnic minorities in the multicultural city of Leicester, the suggestion from the city's Museums Service is that these groups have not been considered in the development of the NSSC:

> I don't think that the project has been developed with any reference whatso- ever to ethnic minorities. . . . The project has been developed without any reference to expert opinion and knowledge and what communities are, and how they work with museums and heritage centres, etc.

However, this does not concur with the city's Arts and Leisure Department's identification of 'Cultural Diversity' as one of its four corporate priorities (Leicester City Council, 1998, p. 4); nor indeed with official literature produced by Leicester City Museums Service. For example: 'We will explore cultural diversity whilst at the same time presenting Leicester's wider heritage in a way that is welcoming and accessible to all cultural groups' (1998, p. ii). Moreover, the NSSC is cited by the Museums Service as 'a major visitor attraction' which will play 'a major role in the regeneration of the city' and contribute to 'its identity as a tourist destination' (Leicester City Museums Service, 1998, p. 27). It would appear, therefore, that although the NSSC is currently conceived of as playing a major role in Leicester's positioning strategy as 'a quality European city' (Leicester City Council, 1998, p. 4), ambivalence remains as to who/what is represented *vis-à-vis* the NSSC as a cultural attraction in the city.

With regard to Bilbao, the issue can be seen as one of 'vertical disparity', i.e. the complex relationship alluded to earlier (Gonzalez, 1993; Maiztegui-Oñate, 1996) between the Basque Government, the Diputación and the City Council. For example, in general, due to their relative fiscal autonomy, the Diputación and City Councils in Vizcaya enjoy virtual independence from Basque Government intervention. However, it appears that there *is* a relationship between these levels and, significantly, this is usually manifest where budget shortfalls appear:

> The city council can ask for shortfalls in budget from the provincial authority and, likewise, the provincial authority can ask the Basque Government for funding if required. This means that higher levels of the hierarchy can influence what the lower levels do with the funding (Cultural Projects Department Officer, Diputación).

Moreover, a local issue regarding 'heritage', which can also be related to the different political levels of administration in the Basque Country, was highlighted by a senior source from the Basque Archaeological, Ethnography and Historical Museum: 'We have heritage laws governing which level has competency in a particular area of heritage. For example, we cannot do anything with the national level as they have different competencies than us'. Thus it is argued that, despite ostensible fiscal autonomy, the relationship between the different levels of administration in the Basque Country is a key factor in the development of cultural and tourism policy in Bilbao.

The degree of coordination and/or integration *between* policy departments within the cities' local authorities, e.g. between the economic, social, cultural, and tourism spheres, is an important aspect of local level processes relating to the development of cultural (heritage) attractions. In Tilburg, 'tourism' is not located within a specific department as outlined by an officer from the city's local authority Cultural Department:

> It is quite complicated here in Tilburg. There is some integration, but it is not complete. For large cultural events, the Cultural Department interacts directly with the Sports/Leisure department, for instance, but there is no Tourism Department, as such. Tourism issues are spread across many departments.

Tilburg's Cultural Department also highlighted the significance of the economic imperative in many of their activities, thereby reflecting Jansen-Verbeke, who suggests that in The Netherlands: 'The current interest in urban tourism resources is largely inspired by the economic benefits from tourism' (1989, p. 233). Arguably, the latter point is reflected in the following view from the VVV in Tilburg: 'If the local authority wants to use the services of the tourism office, then we will do it . . . but if the (financial) input does not cover the output, we do not get involved'.

At a wider level, the increasing significance of the economic imperative for urban cultural and tourism development is clear within an analysis of the growth of the 'heritage industry' in Manchester in the 1980s. Mellor (1997, p. 62) highlights some of the negative aspects of such developments:

> Heightening the city's profile in the global marketplace . . . has become a criterion of successful local management. Of necessity the 'back-stage'

neighbourhoods of the city have been relegated on the policy agenda in return for uncertain long-term benefits to that abstract value – the city's image.

Mellor's observations regarding Manchester can be related, in part, to the increasing commodification of culture. As Richards (1996b, p. 103) observes: 'Although the commodification of culture implied by cultural tourism development may be distasteful to some, the increasing convergence of economic and cultural policies at all administrative levels in Europe make it increasingly difficult to ignore'.

Economic justifications can also be related to the increasing demands from conservative national governments and economic rationalists for greater industry self-sufficiency in tourism marketing and promotion, often through the privatization or corporatization of tourism agencies or boards. With reference to Tilburg and Leicester, examples of such restructuring is evident in The Netherlands and Britain, where the commercialization of tourism services is now apparent (Richards, 1995).

In Bilbao, an officer from the Diputación's Cultural Department acknowledged that: 'There is no tourism department, as such, in Bilbao. The Diputación has departments in Heritage, Sport/Youth and Cultural Action . . . and cultural policy here is more related to the arts in general rather than tourism; for example, music, dance, museums and also sports'. It is interesting to note that museums are envisaged as part of the arts and the link to tourism is not made. The latter may be related to the following observation from the city's Archaeological, Ethnography and Historical Museum: 'Until recently it has been mainly local people visiting the museum as it relates to the Basque Country but now, with the Guggenheim Museum opening, we are attracting more tourists'.

Thus, reflecting the earlier consideration of global economic restructuring and the implications of this restructuring for the development of cultural (heritage) attractions at the local level, Richards suggests that: '. . . the new economic focus of cultural tourism development at local level is also reflected at national and European levels, as concerns about unemployment have pushed other issues further down the agenda' (1996d, p. 89). Of particular interest is the trend towards convergence of the economic and cultural spheres and how this convergence may lead to the potential for disparity in the development of cultural (heritage) attractions in European urban areas as revealed in Tilburg and Bilbao, between municipal/ provincial authorities, tourism promotion agencies, museum associations and cultural (heritage) attractions.

One further issue to consider in Bilbao is that of differing aspirations among local actors as to what resources should be promoted as cultural and tourism attractions. The issue in Bilbao is the lack of support for the city's industrial heritage. It is (tentatively) argued that this may relate to the point made earlier, i.e. the city's relatively late transformation from an industrial to a post-industrial city (Gonzalez, 1993; Gómez, 1998). As an officer from the Diputación's Historical Heritage Services Department commented:

'Industrial heritage has only been thought worth conserving over the past ten years'. Moreover, a senior source in the Basque Archaeological, Ethnography and Historical Museum suggested that 'the lack of interest' in industrial heritage is a complex matter: 'It is related to the fact that "industry" is not covered under the heritage laws, and also to do with people's mentality and cultural values . . . many still see industry as dirty, and not something to be seen as a tourism product'.

Thus, Bilbao provides an instructive example of a 'de-industrializing city' not yet fully embracing industrial heritage tourism to the extent, for example, revealed in Tilburg. However, the realization that industrial heritage is worth conserving, and utilizing as a tourism resource, is beginning to evolve in the city. This is highlighted by the emergence of the *Association for the Defence of Industrial Heritage* (ADIH), a private association working closely with the Diputación and the Basque Government. Promotional brochures have been produced, entitled *Patrimonio Industrial de Vizcaya* (Industrial Heritage of Vizcaya), for four embryonic industrial heritage sites. Arguably, an excerpt from one of these brochures, *La Carola* – an open framework electric Gantry crane – is signposting the future for Bilbao and its as yet largely undiscovered industrial heritage as a cultural attraction and tourism resource:

> La Carola continues to tower, tall and serene, over the centre of an area which is now being developed for leisure pursuits. It is a witness of an era when there was work on the river beyond the most optimistic expectations, and the echoes of our past still reverberate through its girders.
>
> (Diputación Foral de Vizcaya, 1995)

The establishment of the ADIH, and the higher profile its promotional brochures are now providing for industrial heritage sites, suggests that the local actors involved in the development of cultural attractions in Bilbao may yet incorporate industrial heritage projects, such as the Textile Museum in Tilburg, into their overall tourism portfolio.

It would appear then that there is not a coordinated approach between the local actors involved in cultural and tourism development in Tilburg, Bilbao and Leicester. Decisions appear to be the province of disparate organizations (either horizontally or vertically) involved in various aspects of cultural and tourism development in the three cities.

## Conclusions

With regard to the significance of global and local factors in the development of cultural (heritage) attractions in European cities it is clear, from the evidence presented in this chapter, that global economic trends are implicated in the pervasiveness of heritage tourism in cities throughout the world. However, the argument developed throughout is that *both* global and local factors are significant in the development of cultural tourism attractions in Tilburg, Bilbao and Leicester. This supports Chang *et al.*'s conclusion – within a study of the 'global–local nexus' and urban heritage tourism in Montreal and Singapore: 'The global and the local should . . . be enmeshed in any future theoretical frameworks that are developed to help understand the processes and outcomes of urban heritage tourism' (1996, p. 285).

While it can be argued that certain *global* macro-level trends have resulted in the cities of Tilburg, Bilbao and Leicester embracing cultural attractions within their respective urban heritage tourism strategies, albeit to varying degrees, it is clear that *local* developments should also be taken into account. This is clear, for example, in the different ways in which local actors conflict/negotiate in their approach to the development of cultural (heritage) attractions – and thereby also revealing the potential for disparity in such development.

The potential for disparity is evident, for example, in Tilburg, highlighted by the lack of coordination and interaction between the Textile Museum, the (regional) tourism promotion office and the local authority. Moreover, the local authority is currently promoting the city as a 'Modern Industrial City' (Gemeentearchief Tilburg, 1998). This imagery does not concur with the view of Tilburg's (regional) tourism promotion office: 'The word "industrial" does not portray a positive image for tourism purposes'. Similar discord is apparent in Tilburg and Leicester with regard to city imagery, between the City Council and Leicester Promotions – the city's tourism promotion agency – over the use of the latter's slogan for promoting Leicester as 'A City Full of Surprises'.

With regard to Bilbao, further ambiguities have been revealed surrounding the issue of whose culture is being represented *vis-à-vis* cultural (heritage) attractions in the city. For example, Goytia Prat *et al.* (1995) suggest that 'centrality infrastructures', such as the recently opened Guggenheim Museum, have been promoted ahead of more traditional cultural/tourism projects. Arguably, the suggestion that the Basque Archaeological, Ethnography and Historical Museum has only recently attracted more tourists following the promotion and opening of the Guggenheim, reflects the latter observation.

Two further points can be noted with regard to Bilbao, which also relate to the chapter's global–local theme. Firstly, the suggestion that prestige projects such as the Guggenheim are currently more important for the city's image as it moves from an industrial to a post-industrial city (Gonzalez, 1993; Gómez, 1998) can also be seen to reflect the discussion of the increasing economic imperative in cultural tourism development (Jansen-Verbeke, 1989; Gratton and Richards, 1996; Richards, 1996d).

Secondly, it is evident that local actors involved in the development of cultural (heritage) attractions in Bilbao have yet to formulate a coherent strategy for the city. This may be related to the complex (vertical) relationship alluded to earlier between the Basque Government, the Diputación and the City Council (Gonzalez, 1993; Maitzegui Oñate, 1996) where, despite ostensible fiscal autonomy between the different levels of administration, it was suggested that funding issues *are* influential in cultural and tourism development in the city.

With regard to the multicultural city of Leicester, there are ambiguities surrounding the development of the NSSC and local identity. For example, within the City Council's *Regeneration* theme, there is significant emphasis placed on valuing cultural diversity (Leicester City Council, 1998). However, in Leicester, the Museums Service revealed 'that the project has been developed without any reference whatsoever to ethnic minorities'. Moreover, the City Council currently conceives the NSSC as playing a role in the image of Leicester as 'a quality European city' (Leicester City Council, 1998, p. 4), while Leicester City Museums Service regards the NSSC as contributing to 'its identity as a tourist attraction' (1998, p. 27). However, despite this being the image senior politicians aspire to in Leicester, ambivalence remains elsewhere.

Relationships between global and local cultures is of particular significance in Leicester, with regard to the diverse ethnic groups in the city. Clearly, this is an important area for Leicester decision makers generally and, more specifically, for those involved with the NSSC development. It is also an area that is conspicuous by its lack of research. As Ghannam observes: 'The role of ordinary people as active agents in negotiating religious and global discourses in their daily life and the formation of their local identities is largely neglected' (1997, p. 132).

It is suggested here that the local actors involved in the NSSC development – Leicester's Millennium Project – might benefit from evaluating Greenwich's experience in developing the Millennium Dome. Greenwich Borough published a document in 1996 entitled *The Cultural Plan for the Millennium*, in which the Deputy Leader of the Borough expressed a 'local sense of place' on behalf of the local community:

> It is essential to have a Cultural Plan in place for the millennium celebrations to ensure that the benefits of such a celebration are maximised for local people, and that possible threats are identified and measures taken to minimise their effect . . . failure to undertake such an exercise could lead to the Exhibition being regarded as an unwelcome visitor who called in uninvited, and left without a thought for the future.
>
> (Harris quoted in Hall, 1998, p. 13)

Underlying the comments of the Deputy Leader is the recognition that an ambiguous and temporary perspective to projects such as the Millennium Dome (and the NSSC in Leicester?) will not lead to a sustainable future for local people. It remains to be seen whether Leicester's city strategy will embrace the issues raised here relating to the development of the NSSC as a cultural (heritage) attraction for the city.

Thus, within the process of cultural tourism development in Europe – of which urban heritage tourism is just one element – the forces of globalization cannot be viewed as developments unrelated to those agents and actors operating at the local (city) level. Within a broader discussion on culture and globalization, the latter argument can also be seen to reflect Featherstone (1995, p. 103), who suggests that:

> What does seem clear is that it is not helpful to regard the global and local as dichotomies separated in space or time; it would seem that the processes of globalization and localization are inextricably bound together in the current phase.

It is also clear that national borders have become increasingly permeable in the contemporary world (Öncü and Weyland, 1997). However, it does not necessarily follow that the national/local policy context has been rendered meaningless. On the contrary, the rapid integration of national economies into global markets may set limits upon the viability of cultural (heritage) tourism policies that national state governments may initiate, but the capacity of local actors to develop or implement such policies in their own temporal–spatial contexts, should not be underestimated. Therefore, any attempt to make practical and political sense of cultural (heritage) tourism policy developments in European cities should acknowledge that processes of globalization and localization interrelate, to produce place-based 'political' struggles.

Finally, it is suggested that the insights gained from studying the global–local dialectic, *vis-à-vis* an analysis of comparative case studies involving the development of cultural (heritage) attractions in three European cities, supports the argument that similarities *and* differences do exist between urban heritage destinations. Moreover, it is clear that the implications of global processes, such as the de-industrialization manifest in Tilburg, Bilbao and Leicester, and the increasing significance of the service sector, should be incorporated into future attempts to theorize cultural (heritage) tourism development in European cities. However, such theories will be incomplete unless they embody an analysis of the role that local factors play in shaping and mediating such global processes.

## References

Appadurai, A. (1990) Disjuncture and difference in the global economy. In: Featherstone, M. (ed.) *Global Culture: Nationalism, Globalisation and Modernity.* Sage, London, pp. 295–310.

Ashworth, G.J. and Tunbridge, J.E. (1990) *The Tourist–Historic City.* Belhaven, London.

Ball, R. and Stobart, J. (1996) Promoting the industrial heritage dimension in Midlands tourism: a critical analysis of local policy attitudes and approaches.

In: Robinson, M. *et al.* (eds) *Managing Cultural Resources for the Tourist.* Centre for Travel and Tourism, Sunderland, pp. 21–38.

Bianchini, F. (1993) Remaking European cities: the role of cultural policies. In: Bianchini, F. and Parkinson, M. (eds) *Cultural Policy and Urban Regeneration: the Western European Experience.* Manchester University Press, Manchester, pp. 1–20.

Bourdieu, P. (1984) *Distinction.* Routledge, London.

Boylan, P. (ed.) (1992) *Museums 2000 – Politics, People, Professionals and Profit.* Routledge, London and New York.

Bramham, P., Henry, I., Mommaas, H. and van der Poel, H. (eds) (1989) Leisure and urban processes: conclusion. In: Bramham P. *et al.* (eds) *Leisure and Urban Processes: Critical Studies of Leisure Policy in Western European Cities.* Routledge, London, pp. 277–301.

Bull, H. (1977) *The Anarchical Society.* Macmillan, London.

Cantelon, H. and Murray, S. (1993) Globalisation and sport, structure and agency: the need for greater clarity. *Society and Leisure* 16(2), autumn, 275–292.

Chang, T.C., Milne, S., Fallon, D. and Pohlman, C. (1996) Urban heritage tourism: the global–local nexus. *Annals of Tourism Research* 23(2), 284–305.

Corijn, E. and Mommaas, H. (1995) *Urban Cultural Policy Developments in Europe.* Council of Europe, Strasbourg.

Diputación Foral de Vizcaya (1995) *Patrimonio Industrial de Vizcaya: La Carola.* Departamento de Cultura Servicio de Patrimonio Histórico, Bilbao.

Featherstone, M. (1991) *Consumer Culture and Postmodernism.* Sage, London.

Featherstone, M. (1995) *Undoing Culture: Globalisation, Postmodernism and Identity.* Sage, London.

Friedman, J. (1994) *Cultural Identity and Global Process.* Sage, London.

Gemeentearchief Tilburg (1998) Tilburg Home Page. http://www.tilburg.nl

Ghannam, F. (1997) Re-imaging the global: relocation and local identities in Cairo. In: Öncü, A. and Weyland, P. (eds) *Space, Culture and Power: New Identities in Globalising Cities.* Zed Books Ltd, London and New Jersey, pp. 1–20.

Giddens, A. (1990) *The Consequences of Modernity.* Polity, Cambridge.

Giddens, A. (1991) *Modernity and Self-Identity.* Polity, Cambridge.

Gómez, M.V. (1998) Reflective images: the case of urban regeneration in Glasgow and Bilbao. *International Journal of Urban and Regional Research* 22(1), 106–121.

Gonzalez, J.M. (1993) Bilbao: culture, citizenship and quality of life. In: Bianchini, F. and Parkinson, M. (eds) *Cultural Policy and Urban Regeneration: the Western European Experience.* Manchester University Press, Manchester, pp. 73–89.

Goytia Prat, A., Larrauri, M.C. and San Salvador del Valle Doistua, R. (1995) *Culture and Neighbourhoods: the City of Bilbao.* Interdisciplinary Institute of Leisure Studies of the University of Deusto, Bilbao.

Gratton, C. and Richards, G. (1996) The economic context of cultural tourism. In: Richards, G. (ed.) *Cultural Tourism in Europe.* CAB International, Wallingford, UK, pp. 71–86.

Hall, S. (1991a) The local and the global: globalisation and ethnicity. In: King, A.D. (ed.) *Culture, Globalisation and the World-System.* Macmillan, London, pp. 19–39.

Hall, S. (1991b) Old and new identities: old and new ethnicities. In: King, A.D. (ed.) *Culture, Globalisation and the World-System.* Macmillan, London, pp. 41–68.

Hall, V. (1998) UK focus: from the inside looking out. *Tourism Concern* No. 28, 12–14.

Harvey, D. (1989) *The Condition of Postmodernity.* Basil Blackwell, Oxford.

Henry, I.P. (1993) *The Politics of Leisure Policy.* Macmillan, Basingstoke and London.

Herbert, D.T. (1995) Heritage places, leisure and tourism. In: Herbert, D.T. (ed.) *Heritage, Tourism and Society.* Mansell, London, pp. 1–20.

Hirst, P. and Thompson, G. (1996) *Globalisation in Question: the International Economy and the Possibilities of Governance.* Polity, Cambridge.

Jansen-Verbeke, M. (1989) Inner cities and urban tourism in the Netherlands: new challenges for local authorities. In: Bramham, P. *et al.* (eds) *Leisure and Urban Processes: Critical Studies of Leisure Policy in Western European Cities.* Routledge, London, pp. 233–253.

Jessop, B. (1997) The entrepreneurial city: re-imaging localities, redesigning economic governance, or restructuring capital? In: Jewson, N. and MacGregor, S. (eds) *Transforming Cities: Contested Governance and New Spatial Divisions.* Routledge, London, pp. 28–41.

Leicester City Council (1991) *Environment and Development Department: Key Facts About Leicester, No. 3: The Economy.* Leicester City Council, Leicester.

Leicester City Council (1998) *Arts and Leisure Department Service Plan.* Leicester City Council, Leicester.

Leicester City Council/Leicester Promotions (1997) *City Barometer.* Leicester City Council, Leicester.

Leicester City Museums Service (1998) *(Draft) Statement of Purpose/Key Aims, 1998–2002.* Leicester City Council, Leicester.

MacCannell, D. (1976) *The Tourist: a New Theory of the Leisure Class.* Macmillan, London.

MacDonald, S. (1998) Exhibitions of power and powers of exhibition: an introduction to the politics of display. In: MacDonald, S. (ed.) *The Politics of Display: Museums, Science, Culture.* Routledge, London and New York.

Maguire, J. (1993) Globalisation, sport and national identities: 'the empires strike back'? *Society and Leisure* 16, 293–322.

Maiztegui-Oñate, C. (1996) Cultural tourism: new uses for cultural heritage. *World Leisure and Recreation* No. 1, 26–28.

McGrew, A. (1992) A global society. In: Hall, S. *et al.* (eds) *Modernity and its Futures.* Polity Press/OU, Cambridge, pp. 60–102.

Mellor, R. (1997) Cool times for a changing city. In: Jewson, N. and MacGregor, S. (eds) *Transforming Cities: Contested Governance and New Spatial Divisions.* Routledge, London, pp. 28–41.

Mommaas, H. and van der Poel, H. (1989) Changes in economy, politics and lifestyles: an essay on the restructuring of urban leisure. In: Bramham, P. *et al.* (eds) *Leisure and Urban Processes: Critical Studies of Leisure Policy in Western European Cities.* Routledge, London, pp. 254–276.

Moore, K. (1997) *Museums and Popular Culture.* Cassell, London and Washington.

Museums Association (1991) *A National Strategy for Museums.* Museums Association.

Nash, D. and Reeder, D. (eds) (1993) *Leicester in the Twentieth Century.* Alan Sutton in association with Leicester City Council, Phoenix Mill, Far Thrupp, Stroud, Gloucestershire.

Öncü, A. and Weyland, P. (1997) Introduction: struggles over *lebensraum* and social identity in globalising cities. In: Öncü, A. and Weyland, P. (eds) *Space, Culture and Power: New Identities in Globalising Cities.* Zed Books Ltd, London and New Jersey, pp. 1–20.

Richards, G. (1995) Politics of national tourism policy in Britain. *Leisure Studies* 14, 153–173.

Richards, G. (1996a) Production and consumption of European cultural tourism. *Annals of Tourism Research* 23(2), 262–283.

Richards, G. (1996b) European cultural tourism: trends and future prospects. In: Richards, G. (ed.) *Cultural Tourism in Europe.* CAB International, Wallingford, UK, pp. 311–333.

Richards, G. (1996c) The social context of cultural tourism. In: Richards, G. (ed.) *Cultural Tourism in Europe.* CAB International, Wallingford, UK, pp. 47–70.

Richards, G. (1996d) The policy context of cultural tourism. In: Richards, G. (ed.) *Cultural Tourism in Europe.* CAB International, Wallingford, UK, pp. 87–105.

Robertson, R. (1992) *Globalisation: Social Theory and Global Culture.* Sage, London.

Uribarri, I. (1993) Desindustrialización. Unpublished paper presented at the Conference on Bilbao Peatonal, Jornados de Zutik, 28 April.

Urry, J. (1990) *The Tourist Gaze: Leisure and Travel in Contemporary Societies.* Sage, London.

Urry, J. (1995) *Consuming Places.* Routledge, London and New York.

Walsh, K. (1992) *The Representation of the Past: Museums and Heritage in the Post-Modern World.* Routledge, London.

Waters, M. (1995) *Globalisation.* Routledge, London.

# The Budapest Spring Festival: a Festival for Hungarians?

## László Puczkó and Tamara Rátz

*Tourism Research Centre, Budapest, Hungary*

## Introduction

Cultural tourism is one of the fastest growing segments of tourism. The popularity of mass tourism destinations is shrinking as the visiting clientele changes. Especially in the developed world, more and more people are visiting cultural attractions, such as festivals, museums, concerts and traditional events. As the ninth most visited country in the world in 1997, Hungary has made some attempts to attract these travellers by providing special events or festivals for them. In many cases, the events already exist, but the tourists or the potential visitors do not know about them. Hungarian incoming tourism is heavily affected by seasonality as some 35–40% of visitors arrive during the 3 month summer season (Hungarian National Tourist Office, 1998). An attempt at extending the season is to offer special attractions before or after the main season, focusing on themes that meet the demand of well-defined visitor segments. In this chapter we briefly introduce the history and development of the Budapest Spring Festival (BSF) and we analyse the visitor market of the BSF as a cultural attraction. The BSF was chosen because it is a very important cultural festival which has not been analysed before.

## The Budapest Spring Festival

Cultural programmes, events and festivals are supported by national tourism organizations throughout the world because of their favourable impacts on tourist services, such as diversification of supply and decreasing seasonality.

Festivals can have an extra appeal for potential visitors because they are organized to show something unique or special that represents the culture (art, dance, music, history, etc.) of a destination and its community (Getz, 1991; Hall, 1992). Cultural events can extend the tourist season or can launch a mini-season, such as the Budapest Spring Festival has done.

## The early years

The BSF was first staged in March 1981. The contents and the structure of the Festival were developed in 1979 by a group of young professionals and artists who founded the festival concept on three major elements (Lengyel, 1997; Turisták apostola, 1997):

- The main idea was to be the first European cultural festival of the year. Festival organizers generally tend to place their events during the main summer tourist season, as an additional programme for existing visitors or in order to attract new audiences. With the timing right before Easter, the BSF would become the first international cultural event in the European festival season.
- The Hungarian organizing team created an eclectic programme including different arts, sport and gastronomic events and congresses. While it was a very complex programme, they placed classical music as the central theme of the BSF. The organizers wanted to attract as many international tourists as possible, since in the early 1980s, the country was desperately lacking foreign currency.
- The third element was to bring Hungarian culture (mainly music) into the limelight. Hungarian culture had not been well known outside Hungary, although many artists (composers, actors, etc.) of Hungarian origin have enjoyed international success. So the organizers wanted to introduce the many different facets of Hungarian culture to an international audience.

The financial support in the first year was provided from the Hungarian Tourism Office's central budget. Since the second year (1982) it has been drawn from different sources, such as the Tourism Industry Development Fund, ministerial budgets, contributions by hotel and travel companies and more recently sponsorship.

To provide a programme appealing enough to draw tourists to Hungary, the festival was designed to be unique, genuine and aimed to have world stars on stage. The budget of the BSF was rather limited so the organizers decided to invite world famous Hungarian artists to participate and to help to launch the event. Many of these artists had not been living in Hungary but they were pleased to be invited and came voluntarily to perform. We should name some of them:

- The pianist György Cziffra – who created a competition for young Hungarian artists and provided scholarships for the winners, supporting their first years for better international recognition.
- Amerigo Tot, who created the first logo of BSF.
- Éva Marton, opera singer.
- André Kertész and Juan Gyenes, photographers.
- Zoltán Kocsis, András Schiff and György Ránki, pianists.

The festival organizers have tended to invite one leading artist or group (i.e. composers, conductors orchestras, and opera singers) each year since, as their appearances have been considered as the key factor for international success. Their 'name' could provide the basis for international marketing activities.

In the first year, Béla Bartók was chosen as the theme, as that year was the 100th anniversary of Béla Bartók's birth. As he is a well-known composer, this timing made a favourable contribution to the marketing activities. The name of Bartók led to better international recognition of the BSF.

Leading names alone are not enough to gain international recognition and success in the festival business (Getz, 1991). Another success factor of events can be the duration of the programme. The organizing team decided to limit the programme to 10 days, long enough to provide a large variety of programmes, but still short enough for tourist packages. The slogan of BSF was: '10 Days – 100 Venues – 1000 Events'.

The Festival was really successful during the first few years leading to full hotels and restaurants in Budapest. Unfortunately after the political changes in 1989–1990, the whole organizational structure of the Festival was changed. The initial contents and aims were diminished, only the early spring timing of the Festival has remained. Because of the continuous financial problems and organizing mistakes by the new staff, the Festival started to lose its initial advantages. The original focus was lost, the programme was extended to 4 weeks and other provincial towns became involved. The festival became a 'run-of-the-mill' event.

## Rejuvenation

Some tourism experts and the Hungarian Society of Tourism raised their concerns about the BSF at the 'Prime Minister's Conference and Open Day at the Parliament for Tourism' in May 1996. This conference resulted in some favourable changes. In 1996, as part of the 1100th anniversary of the Hungarian state, a year-long cultural and tourist programme series, the 'Hungary '96' was arranged. A new team has been set up by the Ministry of Industry, Trade and Tourism, the Ministry of Culture, and Education and the Municipality of Budapest to organize the festival and to run the managing company. The duration of BSF has again been shortened to an 18 day period in mid-March.

The BSF has been re-established as the most important series of artistic events in Hungary, and is helping to develop the cultural and touristic image of the country. The aims of the Festival have been the following as established by the new organizers (Lengyel, 1997):

- Introducing many facets of Hungarian cultural life, creating interest in domestic tourist sites and quality artistic events both in Hungary and abroad.
- Stimulating new performances and products/works by organizing events (such as dance, music, folklore, film and theatre) and exhibitions (such as applied arts, photo and fine arts).
- In harmony with the Hungarian character of BSF, making domestic people and foreigners (both possible visitors and those who are already here) aware of as many famous international and Hungarian artists as possible.
- To increase the hotel occupancy rates before the main season.
- To generate more foreign exchange by selling tourist services and cultural programmes.
- To enhance the cultural-touristic image of Hungary.

## The management company

The company that runs the whole organization process from inviting artists, through marketing to evaluation is the Budapest Festival Centre Non-profit Company (BFC). This company has been responsible for all the three festivals that are held in Budapest every year:

- Budapest Spring Festival.
- Budapest Autumn Festival (programmes introducing contemporary arts, held in October).
- Budapest Farewell (held in June celebrating the withdrawal of Russian troops from Hungary).

The BFC staff consists of ten permanent employees. During the Festival they also hire many university/college students as guides, hostesses/hosts, translators, etc.

The majority of financial resources covering all the costs of the BSF (such as marketing, wages, costs of inviting special guests, etc.) have recently been provided by three institutions: the Ministry of Culture and Education (now Ministry of National Cultural Heritage), the Municipality of Budapest and the Ministry of Trade, Industry and Tourism (since 1998 known as the Ministry of Economy). The budget was US$1.28 million (€1.1 million) in 1997, out of which only 10% came from companies sponsoring BSF. The main sponsor of the BSF '97 was the TVK Rt. (Tisza Chemical Works Ltd), one of the largest chemical companies in the country.

## The BSF programme

Initially, the detailed contents of the programme are suggested by the BFC to the Festival Art Council (a supervisory body of artists and representatives of ministries). Then the Council discusses the proposal (such as the main theme and most important guest(s) of the Festival, concerts, available sites, and joint programmes with other organizers, etc.). This negotiating process results in the final programme (Box 10.1). In 1997, 173 different programmes, exhibitions, plays, concerts, parades, etc., were offered at 53 sites. In that year altogether 274 art groups and artists participated in the performances, including 23 foreigners. Apart from the BSF, other bodies organized several other events, contests, etc. These also were marketed in the official brochure but under the title 'Other events during the Festival'.

## Development plans

In recent years the BSF has enlisted eight other Hungarian cities to join and organize their own festival programme during the BSF.

These eight cities have been planning, organizing and managing their programmes independently from BSF during the BSF. The so-called 'special

---

**Box 10.1.** Budapest Spring Festival programmes.

- Orchestral concerts
- Chamber concerts
- Musica Sacra – religious (organ and chorus) music
- Operetta festival – including a contest during 6 consecutive days between Hungarian theatre companies playing operetta
- Opera and ballet performances
- Folk music
- Conferences – symposia (on arts, cooking, etc.)
- Open-air events – to create festival-feeling in Budapest (such as Easter Festival – egg-painting, etc.)

- Folk dance (Meeting of 'Dance Houses' and Fair)
- Hungarian Dance Panorama (17 contemporary dance performances)
- Theatre plays (in Hungarian and some in German or English)
- Film programmes (most important pieces of Hungarian movie production)
- Exhibitions
- Other events in Budapest during the Festival (including exhibitions, plays, dance performances, fashion shows, contests organized by other companies)
- 'Our guest city' scheme (one city for one day)
- Other events (such as exclusive concerts)

guest city' status of the BSF has been rotated among the eight cities. The official programme leaflets promote these events but other forms of support have not been provided by the BFC. In 1997, Debrecen (eastern Hungary) was the guest of the festival in Budapest for one day. There are other towns that would like to be involved but the Festival Art Council has rejected all the candidates.

In 1997, the BFC revitalized the tradition of organizing a special evening for young, talented artists where representatives of artist agents, impresarios, leading newspapers are invited. With this so-called 'Miniforum', they would like to help these young artists to start their international career.

To provide better information, the BSF employed 240 young people in 1997, who were out on the streets providing information and brochures for the passers-by. Two hundred thousand copies of the official brochure were published in three languages (Hungarian, German, English). Apart from these forms of information, one could find some information through the Internet, TV coverage, billboards, articles and programme reviews in daily and weekly papers, or by calling an information hotline run by a phone company.

The new strategy states that the BSF should cater to wider market needs while maintaining the artistic quality and image of the festival. Almost all visitor segments are targeted in this new strategy, but we still can identify some main segment groups such as:

- People who live and/or work in Budapest (both Hungarians and foreigners).
- Foreigners who come to Budapest anyway, and are in town during the festivities.
- Foreigners who come to see the events of BSF as their main motivation (mainly Germans, Americans and, in increasing numbers, British and Italians).
- Domestic visitors who come to see the events only (Budapesti Tavaszi Fesztivál '97, 1997).

The BSF attracted about 150,000 visitors in 1997 during the 18 days (14–31 March); 20% of the tickets had been purchased by travel agencies in advance which might indicate, without having more detailed data on the distribution of visitors, that at least every fifth visitor was a foreigner. (The organizers do not know the possible distribution of Hungarian visitors by their place of residence.)

## Visitor research

In order to obtain a reliable sample for the European Association for Tourism and Leisure Education (ATLAS) surveys in Budapest, the following research criteria were employed:

- A random sample of events and sites was selected from the programme (three each every day, for 10 days). That meant 108 sites and programmes altogether.
- Visitors were interviewed before plays, during breaks or after a visit.
- Every third visitor passing by the interviewer had to be interviewed.
- The target number of interviews per site was set at ten.

Altogether 1042 questionnaires were filled in during the BSF. Apart from the standard data analysis, at the end of the chapter a competitive analysis of Budapest, Prague and Vienna is provided, because these capitals are in competitive situation in the international cultural tourism market. We pay special attention to the distribution and motivation of BSF visitors.

## Research results

Less than 10% of the survey respondents came from abroad. The largest number of foreign visitors came, not surprisingly, from Germany (Fig. 10.1). All other countries, with the exception of the UK, play marginal roles. These figures seem to contradict the estimate of 35% foreign visitors by the BFC, but it should be noted that while the ATLAS sample covered all the events and sites of the Festival, the BFC had only collected information at the major events where foreign visitation is well over the average. The estimate of 10% foreign attendance therefore seems to be realistic.

Table 10.1 indicates that most BSF visitors live in and around Budapest (67.9%). They attend the Festival mainly for recreational or leisure purposes. Of visitors to Budapest, 16.3% identified themselves as being on holiday, i.e. being leisure tourists in the city. About half of this group was from abroad (drawn from 17 different countries), and the other 50% came from Hungary.

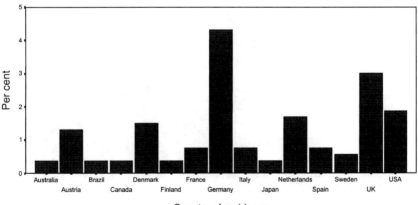

Country of residence

**Fig. 10.1.** Foreign visitors to the Budapest Spring Festival.

The remaining visitors (14.2%) were either on business or students studying in Budapest. One reason for the high proportion of young people between 20 and 30 could be that younger people have become very active in their lifestyle. University and college students and young professionals are looking for cultural attraction programmes in their leisure times. The cultural life of Budapest has been very lively and bustling with about 100 dance and music performances every week. The average ticket prices are moderate, even by Hungarian standards, so there is nothing to stop people going out regularly.

We should also note that in spite of the strict research rules, some sampling bias could not be avoided, as the student interviewers might have asked visitors closer to their age. This may be why we have a relatively high share of young people in the sample (Fig. 10.2). The share of students in the sample was 28.4%, being the second largest group after the employees (42.8%). This high proportion of students is however consistent with a number of other arts attractions covered in the ATLAS research, for example in Poland (see Chapter 11, this volume).

A large number of visitors in the sample were expected to come to Budapest only for the Festival. Altogether, 28.8% of the respondents did not live in the area and 18.3% of them had come to Budapest to see the Festival

**Table 10.1.** Distribution of respondents by place of residence.

| Respondents | Local residents (%) | Visitors (%) | Total (%) |
|---|---|---|---|
| On holiday | N/A | 16.3 | 16.3 |
| Not on holiday | 67.9 | 14.2 | 82.1 |
| Total | 67.9 | 30.5 | |

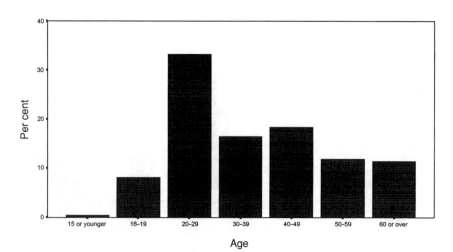

**Fig. 10.2.** Age distribution of respondents.

as their primary motivation. Additionally, for 7.5% of the respondents the BSF (or one of the Festival's events) had been an important decision making factor. Almost 8% of the respondents in the sample had arrived in Budapest with a different motivation than attending the BSF, but were attracted by the Festival programmes. The cultural motivation of respondents was very strong, as 75.6% of the visitors had visited other cultural attraction(s) during their stay, apart from the one where they were interviewed. The sample showed rather high loyalty to the Festival, as 65.5% of residents and 36.2% of visitors had visited the BSF at least once before 1997.

In the survey, we tried to identify the main motivation factors of BSF. In Table 10.2, we can see that BSF-goers were looking for new experiences and they expected a relaxing visit. It can also be assumed that the respondents had very sound cultural motivation while they were on holiday, as many of them reported regularly visiting museums (with a mean score of 3.76 on a five point scale). Participation in a cultural event seems to be an activity (preferably) done in groups, as 57% of respondents agreed with the statement 'I am visiting this attraction to accompany other people'.

It seems that an interest in cultural tourism is not limited by occupational background, since 73% of the respondents did not have any culture-related job connection.

Special emphasis was put in the research on the leisure patterns of non-Budapest residents (Table 10.3). Visitors to the BSF showed sound cultural interest as they had planned to visit many different cultural sites of the Hungarian capital. Festivals got the lowest mean, but that is easy to understand, as besides the BSF there was no other festival in town. The majority of visitors (52.4%) spent a week in Budapest, one-third of them (31.2%) paid a shorter visit (a city break). They spent their time together with their partners (40.7%) or in small groups. Only about 15% of them came alone.

In Table 10.4, we can see the average visitation data of the whole sample. These figures show that performing art events have the highest level of visitation and festivals have the lowest. Of course, in their nature, festivals

**Table 10.2.** Motivations of visitors.

|  | Mean[a] | Standard deviation[a] |
|---|---|---|
| 1. I am visiting this attraction to experience new things | 4.13 | 1.15 |
| 2. I am visiting this attraction to relax | 4.11 | 1.21 |
| 3. When I go on holiday, I always visit a museum | 3.76 | 1.32 |
| 4. I am visiting this attraction to learn new things | 3.61 | 1.33 |
| 5. My friends often visit this attraction | 3.2 | 1.37 |
| 6. I am visiting this attraction to accompany other people | 2.43 | 1.51 |
| 7. This visit is connected with my work | 1.78 | 1.43 |

[a]1, disagree; 5, agree.

are organized for special occasions and only a few times of the year, in comparison with performing arts, where there may be performances every day.

Those on holiday described their trip mainly as a cultural holiday (40.6%), a city break (35.9%), or part of a touring holiday (11.2%). Visitors not from the area stayed in hotels (42%) or with friends or relatives (37.2%). This latter accommodation type was typical for the Hungarian visitors only.

In terms of occupation (Fig. 10.3), the professionals (i.e. doctors, lawyers, teachers, etc.) were the largest group in the sample (57.1% out of the 576 employed respondents).

The educational qualifications of BSF visitors were dominated by two main levels, i.e. secondary school (36.2%) and higher education (51%) (Fig. 10.4).

The majority (64%) of the self-employed, and the retired visitors (52.8%) also had some kind of higher degree. The majority of the students (62.8%) were studying in secondary schools. In the Hungarian educational system post-secondary education is not too developed, this is the reason why this category was not really represented.

Along with the educational and occupational data, it is interesting to analyse the answers for annual gross incomes (Fig. 10.5).

**Table 10.3.** Visits to cultural attractions during stay in Budapest.

| Attractions | Visitors during their stay in Budapest | |
| --- | --- | --- |
|  | Mean | Standard deviation |
| Museums | 2.47 | 1.86 |
| Monuments | 3.09 | 3.43 |
| Art galleries | 1.95 | 2.05 |
| Historic houses | 2.57 | 2.91 |
| Performing arts | 2.95 | 3.26 |
| Festivals | 1.13 | 1.38 |

Figures show frequency of visits.

**Table 10.4.** Visits to cultural attractions during leisure time.

| Attractions | All respondents as leisure activity during the last 12 months | |
| --- | --- | --- |
|  | Mean | Standard deviation |
| Museums | 6.97 | 10.06 |
| Monuments | 8.31 | 24.42 |
| Art galleries | 5.46 | 11.34 |
| Historic houses | 7.39 | 17.16 |
| Performing arts | 11.88 | 19.61 |
| Festivals | 1.38 | 1.76 |

Figures show frequency of visits.

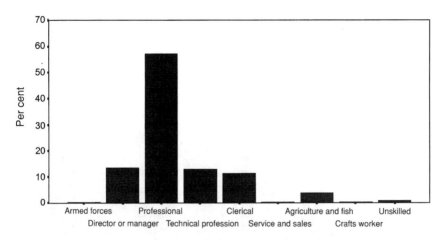

**Fig. 10.3.** Occupational groups of employees (per cent of all respondents).

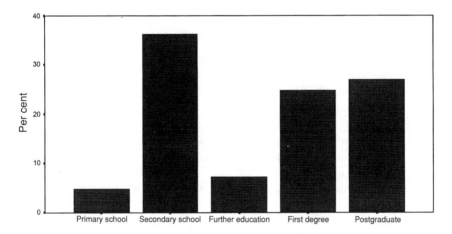

**Fig. 10.4.** Highest educational qualifications (per cent of all respondents).

In the original questionnaire, there was a different scale for indicating income groups, but we had to adapt the categories to the national circumstances. Not surprisingly, the foreign visitors belonged to the higher categories while the domestic visitors showed a relatively balanced distribution among the categories.

## The Budapest–Vienna–Prague Triangle

One of the most interesting aspects of this research project is the comparison of the attractiveness of European cities as cultural destinations (Figs 10.6 and 10.7). Among the 18 cities listed as potential destinations for a cultural

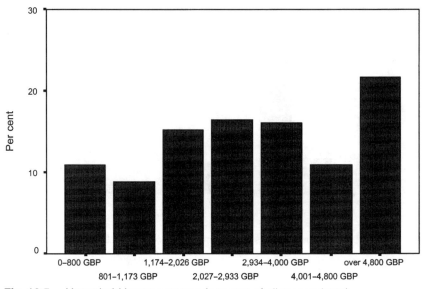

**Fig. 10.5.** Household income groups (per cent of all respondents).

holiday, we hoped to see Budapest in a very good position, but this turned out to be too optimistic.

If we filter out those respondents who did not mention Budapest at all, the result of the comparison would be favourable. Favourable, but we should remind the reader of the fact that the vast majority of the respondents were Hungarians. The picture was not that bright if we consider the ranks given for each city. Budapest, in this filtered sample (Fig. 10.7), only received an average rank (3.02 out of 5), while its most important competitors, i.e. Vienna and Prague, received far better rankings (Vienna: 3.4; Prague: 3.36). (In comparison with the total Hungarian sample, Budapest, Vienna and Prague had 3.0, 2.6 and 3.4 rank scores, respectively.)

Vienna and Prague have been seen as the major competitors of the Hungarian capital in various fields. In tourism, competition is the strongest in cultural and city tourism, due to the similar characteristics of the three capitals. The lack of cooperation in tourism marketing among the cities cannot be considered either a clever or a successful strategic approach, it is rather tactical and short sighted (Budapesti Turisztikai Hivatal, 1998). The fight for foreign tourists is a serious question almost everywhere in the world, not just in Central and Eastern Europe. Given their favourable geographic situation and somewhat different cultural profiles, these cities should coordinate their tourism marketing activities. Both Prague and Budapest are about 3–4 h away from Vienna, i.e. geographically they are situated very close to each other, particularly from an American, Australian or Japanese perspective. Coordinated tourism marketing should thus be especially beneficial in the overseas markets.

We decided to break the sample into two groups, i.e. first we analysed the answers of visitors to Budapest, then the opinions of those living in and around Budapest. It is assumed that responses of the two groups will differ as group members have different perceptions of the destinations. Figure 10.8 presents the ranking of visitors (the figures in brackets after the cities indicate the number of respondents mentioning the place). As the interviews were held in Budapest during a cultural event, it might be expected that those

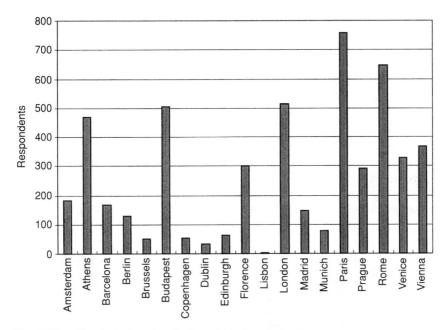

**Fig. 10.6.** Number of respondents mentioning each city.

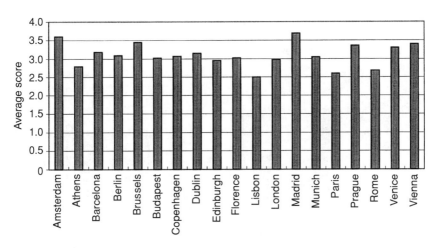

**Fig. 10.7.** City rankings (respondents mentioning Budapest only).

visiting the city would naturally tend to give Budapest a high ranking. In spite of this, however, all three cities achieved almost the same share in the lower section of the scale, while in the upper part (positions one and two), the differences were very high. As these data show, Budapest was considered as a relatively good destination for a cultural holiday. The better ranking of Prague in the second and third position should highlight the fierce competition. The position of Vienna was somewhat surprising as in terms of overall visitor numbers it has been dominating the region (Budapesti Turisztikai Hivatal, 1998).

The responses of people living in the area (Fig. 10.9) indicated a more balanced picture, putting Prague in a better position in spite of the fact that Prague was mentioned by the lowest number of respondents, in comparison to the other two cities. That can mean that Prague was very tempting for people living in Budapest. Another reason could be that Vienna has been a much better known and more frequently visited place than Prague, for historical and political reasons. Historically, Budapest belonged to the Austro-Hungarian Monarchy (as did Prague) for about 230 years, so the links have become very close. After 1989, the first Western destination of Hungarians was Vienna (mainly for shopping). During the socialist era, Prague was one of the socialist capitals, but since the political changes its popularity has been growing much faster than that of the other capitals.

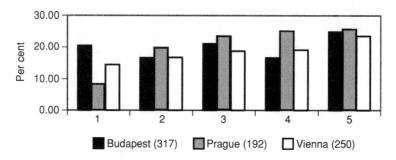

**Fig. 10.8.**   Ranking of cities by visitors.

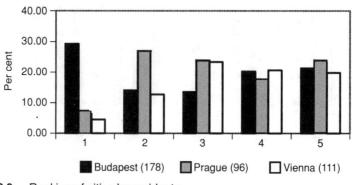

**Fig. 10.9.**   Ranking of cities by residents.

It would be far more practical to form a cooperation between these three capitals, making the most of the synergy effects by attractions in tourism, in order to reach international generating markets and try to attract tourists together into the region. Only when tourists have become familiar with Central and Eastern European attractions, should these capitals differentiate their products.

## Conclusions

The BSF is predominantly visited by local people, as a leisure activity. The number of tourists, especially of foreign tourists, is rather low, considering the international aspirations of the event.

The BSF has a long tradition and is a well-established cultural event with very good timing. Many Hungarian artists and art groups are celebrated all around the world, their artistic capabilities being appreciated on international level. The site of the Festival in the Hungarian capital gives it one of the most picturesque locations in Europe and the quality of tourist facilities has become similar to that of other European capitals. The average price level of cultural events, in spite of the continuously high, but now decreasing inflation level, is still moderate, especially for foreign visitors.

It seems that the current low levels of foreign visitation and the relatively low ranking of Budapest as a cultural destination relate to a lack of cultural capital relative to the city and Hungarian culture on the part of potential visitors. Hopefully the results of the ATLAS research will help the BSF to improve its marketing abroad and ultimately to attract more foreign tourists.

## Acknowledgements

The authors wish to thank the following individuals for the provision of data relating to the BSF: Dr Márton Lengyel, Budapest University of Economic Sciences/Tourism Research Centre and Ms Andrea Koch, Budapest Festival Centre, NpC.

## References

Budapesti Tavaszi Fesztivál '97 (1997) *Budapesti Fesztiválközpont Kht,* Internal Company Report, Budapest.
Budapesti Turisztikai Hivatal (1998) *Statisztikai adatok (Statistical data).* BTH, Budapest.
Getz, D. (1991) *Festivals, Special Events, and Tourism.* Van Nostrand Reinhold, New York.
Hall, C.M. (1992) *Hallmark Tourist Events. Impacts, Management & Planning.* Belhaven Press, London.

Hungarian National Tourist Office (1998) *Tourism in Hungary 1997*. HNTO, Budapest.

Lengyel, M. (1997) European Tourist Premier in March, *Hungarian Travel Magazine* No. 1, 8–14.

Turisták apostola (1997) *Cash Flow 1995*. VI(3), 124–126.

# The Consumption of Cultural Tourism in Poland

## Barbara Marciszewska

*Department of Tourism and Recreation, University School of Physical Education, Wiejska, Gdańsk, Poland*

## Introduction

This chapter reflects a long-standing desire of the author to combine integrated research techniques with the individual Polish perspective which can contribute to the transnational research adopted by the European Association for Tourism and Leisure Education (ATLAS) Cultural Tourism Project. Fladmark (1994, p. 6) points out that:

> . . . cultural identity is, of course, a product not of isolation but of interrelation, and therefore has to be regarded as a continuing process. It would be even more important for the countries which have recently rejoined the large family of Europe to create the framework for co-operation and integration.

Our national approach to cultural tourism in Poland has not been merely to cover an individual cultural tourism market but has aimed to bring meaningful information for the comparative international analysis of cultural tourism developments and trends across Europe. Such work would seem to be important for the development of the ATLAS Cultural Tourism Project as previous research did not cover Eastern Europe (Richards, 1996). It is true that 'cultural consumption has grown, and tourism is an increasingly important form of cultural consumption' (Richards, 1996, p. 3) but there is a distinction between socio-economic conditions and, consequently, patterns of cultural consumption in postmodern capitalist countries and in economies in transition (Eastern and Central Europe). The thesis that consumption drives production does not apply to Poland as much as to developed European countries because the real incomes of population limit the level and structure of consumption, particularly leisure consumption, such as cultural tourism. 'It can be argued that new shopping developments in the high street are mainly for luxury consumption and for the leisure of the new *nouveau riches* and foreigners, with over nine-tenths of the population being reduced to the role of window-shopping' (Jung, 1994, p. 266). It seems to be a common feature of Eastern and Central European countries that some parts of their societies live below the official poverty level. They have often different and distinctive needs and expectations other than leisure.

The role of culture in post-communist Poland has been shaped by a sharp polarization of wealth within Polish society.

> Between 1989 and 1993 there was a rapid production of an embryonic capitalist strata (many with ties to the former communistic nomenclatura) and the concomitant service classes (finance, consultancy, marketing, advertising). These groups replaced the intelligentsia as role models. Their consumption patterns and lifestyles have become ostentatious signs and criteria of success.
>
> (Jung, 1994, p. 265)

On the other hand the changes in patterns of free-time activities in Poland in the 1980s were related to the economic decline and political difficulties. Leisure was concentrated on low-cost, passive and home centred activities (Marciszewska, 1998, p. 183). 'Changes in the use of free time between 1976–1984 coincide with patterns observed among the unemployed in industrialized market economies' (Jung, 1990, p. 98). As a consequence, a decline in many areas of free-time activities was observed in the early 1980s and a new role for leisure was created during the process of political and economic reforms in the 1990s. 'Through its quick opening to the West and massive imports of products, services, values and lifestyles [imported] culture and recreation became part of a "modernisation" or "Westernisation" project' (Jung, 1994, p. 273). This process has created room for the postmodern shift to figural forms of culture in Poland.

The meaning of the term 'cultural tourism' should perhaps be established at the outset. As ATLAS has defined this term and subsequently refined the definition in the light of research findings, we will base the conceptual definition of cultural tourism in this chapter: (i) on that of ATLAS: 'The movement of persons to cultural attractions away from their normal place of residence, with the intention to gather new information and experiences to satisfy their cultural needs' (Richards, 1996, p. 24); and (ii) on Fladmark's definition as a starting point: 'Cultural tourism may be defined as that activity which enables people to explore or experience the different way of life of other people, reflecting social customs, religious traditions and the intellectual ideas of a cultural heritage which may be unfamiliar' (Fladmark, 1994, p. 4).

The second definition, in our opinion, highlights the wider sense of cultural tourism in a rapidly changing Europe, because it includes the 'learning element' and concerns any activity undertaken by people in the tourist destination not only during their movement to cultural attractions. As Fladmark's definition is not clearly compatible with the World Tourism Organization definition of tourism I would like to suggest the following as appropriate for the analysis of consumption of cultural tourism (it includes elements derived from both the ATLAS and Fladmark definitions):

> Cultural tourism may be defined as that activity of persons in their tourist destination and during their travel from their normal place of residence which enables them to explore or experience the different way of life of other people, reflecting the social customs, religious traditions and intellectual ideas of a cultural heritage in such a way as to fulfil their cultural needs, desires and wants.

Cultural desires and wants are very important elements in the definition as they constitute the sense of postmodern consumption.

> Consumption is founded on a lack – a desire always for something not there. Modern/postmodern consumption consumers, therefore, will never be satisfied. . . . This desire to consume could persist, therefore, through economic recession, if not through economic depression. One day it will all change. But until then, people living under the influence of postmodern capitalism's consumer culture will continue to desire the unattainable – that is the satiation of all their desires.
>
> (Bocock, 1993, p. 69)

To analyse consumption as concerned with desires and the social construction of identities in postmodernity it is necessary to provide a means of conceptualizing desires and their links with the social processes within the framework of developed capitalism. However, as desires should be seen rather as being in part the consequence of the social and cultural practices of society, they must also be taken into account in an analysis of consumption in transforming European economies.

Cultural tourism development in Poland faces a number of barriers similar to those which have been known in Central and Eastern European countries (CEEC) in the context of sustainable tourism development (Hall, 1998, p. 429):

**1.** There is often a need for governmental intervention and/or public–private partnership ventures to assist longer-term sustainability.

**2.** There are increasing opportunities in CEEC for cultural attractions to act as a basic resource for tourism, organized and sustained through locally owned small enterprises; cultural attractions can become a meaningful factor of economic development in order to be able to raise incomes, stabilize the labour market and sustain cultural heritage.

**3.** Many conflicts have been raised by the necessity for the parallel development of mass tourism and of cultural tourism products for Western European tourists looking for 'special' experiences.

The concept of consumption has a variety of meanings, depending upon the major theoretical framework of which it is a component part. 'Consumption in late twentieth-century economies may be seen as a social and cultural process involving cultural signs and symbols, not simply as an economic, utilitarian process' (Bocock, 1993, p. 3). It is seen in this study as being based increasingly upon desires and wants, not simply upon needs. But this does not mean that this approach is to be understood as a substitute for an economic one – but rather as the complement of the latter. Futhermore, Ryan (1991) considers the implications of changing work patterns for tourism in the future. He points out that a tourism based on the needs of post-industrial societies needs to be more considerate of social impacts and shows how marketing is being incorporated into tourist planning, shaping lifestyle and perception of place. A cultural tourism product is not only a cultural attraction, it is also the experience of places visited and what happens there. All the activities and processes involved are connected by a series of internal and external interactions. Values, images, impressions, stereotypes and even needs and desires can be changed or confirmed. It is therefore necessary to take them into account in an analysis of consumption of cultural tourism as well.

## Poland's Cultural Tourism

Poland's overall tourism product is based upon natural and man-made resources as well as an experience which is conditioned by the social and cultural environment (i.e. Poland's history, heritage, landscape and culture). The ATLAS research in Poland in 1997 was undertaken in the Gdańsk region on the Baltic coast. The Gdańsk District's natural and built environment reflects the aesthetic qualities of the Kashubian Lakes and the scenic coast line of the Gulf of Gdańsk. The heritage of Gdańsk itself ranks highly on the cultural map of European cities. Its architecture and 1000-year tradition, as well as its importance in Polish and European history, has meant it has benefited substantially for many years as a tourist destination for both Polish citizens and foreign tourists. Many cultural attractions situated in the Old City and in Sopot have become main visitor activities. In this way cultural and historical attractions form an important component of the Gdańsk District's tourism product with the potential to develop heritage sites in conservation zones.

Religious sites, historical properties and museums are constant elements of the tourist package but they are particularly significant factors influencing tourism demand among young scholars and foreign tourists, mainly from Germany. Much recent research demonstrates a renewed interest in heritage tourism in Gdańsk. But tourists come to Gdańsk mainly to rest – they visit famous historical monuments while being in the city for other purposes, for example on business (*Tourism Market Research in the Province of Gdańsk*, 1994). There are many attractions both with and without admission charges which are subjects of interest for both tourists and the local community.

The image of the Gdańsk District as a tourism destination is based on two major assets. The first is the image of the Old City of Gdańsk as a rich ensemble of architecture supported by entertainment facilities. The second is the current image of the Kashubian Region with its numerous lakes. This image has been formed during the last three decades and is based upon the beautiful landscapes, forests and clean lakes.

Heritage is not a new element in Poland's appeal as a tourism destination, although there is a growing recognition by the public and private sector tourism industry and central and local tourism administration of the potential for promoting and implementing improvements to the nation's culture in a systematic manner. This is partly an implication of the European and worldwide growth in heritage tourism associated with 'new tourism' (Poon, 1993) as tourism markets become more segmented, flexible and require a more individual approach to the consumer's needs, expectations and desires. Cultural tourism may expand interest in tourist destinations like Gdańsk and similar cities in Poland which contain cultural amenities, heritage sites, centres for the arts, ancient monuments and natural resources if they combine both the cultural attractiveness and leisure facilities expected by a variety of tourist groups. Yet there is no ongoing debate on the way in which heritage resources can be used in a sustainable approach to tourism recreation development; rather, in general, heritage sites, historical monuments and museums are separated from potential leisure activities. It would appear that they are not packaged in an attractive enough manner to give tourists an opportunity to combine them with active leisure activities (e.g. sport activities, fishing) during their stay in the Gdańsk District. At the present time heritage and cultural tourism are influencing the socio-economic and cultural development of the city. On the other hand it is necessary to take into account that 'the benefits derived from the heritage and tourism industries will be greatest if development proceeds with the active maintenance of the cultural resources as a prime consideration' (Moulin, 1991, p. 51). The development and promotion of heritage and cultural resources may therefore build upon the district's strength as a tourist destination since a significant proportion of overseas visitors are attracted by these forms of tourism product. But will this situation continue if a larger number of visitors, both domestic and foreign, are in search of a product? It may then be necessary to create rich tourism packages with leisure alternatives. However, this will need to be accompanied by detailed market research so that visitor perceptions and expectations are matched by the tourist experience they provide (Page, 1994, p. 86).

We should welcome the fact that heritage and cultural tourism have featured prominently in tourism development in Europe as consumers search for new types of visitor experience focused on the value of cultural heritage. However, over the last decade the public and private sector in Poland have identified niches in the market for new recreational tourism products which should not be separated from cultural tourism products. The

complementary nature of touristic products can be seen as a new opportunity for flexibility of tourism supply and higher quality of service. If we take
into account the satisfaction of foreign tourists we have to agree with
Devereux (1998, p. 39) 'that cross cultural aspects of service require cross
cultural understanding. A national perspective is not enough'. In this context
cross-national market research and cultural encounters can be seen as
important factors of cultural tourism development.

## Attractions as a Component of the Tourism Product

Tourist attractions can be grouped into those which are natural and those
which have been constructed. Built attractions are principally the products
of history and culture, but also include artificially created entertainment
complexes such as theme parks.

In the late 1960s three groups of artificial features were defined:

- Cultural – religious sites, modern culture, museums, art galleries,
  buildings, archaeological sites
- Traditions – folklore, animated culture, festivals
- Events – sports, cultural events.

A number of attempts have been made during the last three decades to
classify attractions. Some authors have suggested dividing them into
'resource-based' and 'user-based' or 'reproducible' and 'non-reproducible'.
For the purposes of this chapter we have adopted the classification of attractions drawn up by Wanhill (1993, p. 26). Here attractions are distinguished
as natural resources: landscapes, lakes and forests in the Kashubian Region
and the coast of the Gulf of Gdańsk and built products. The latter are most
commonly the results of Polish history, culture and tradition, which have
a legacy of historical monuments and buildings but they also include
artificially created entertainment complexes, e.g. theatrical performances,
cinema, etc. According to this approach we can classify the cultural places
and events as indicated in Table 11.1.

## Research Method

The ATLAS research was carried out using the standard questionnaire
translated into Polish: 2195 respondents visiting 13 types of cultural tourism
attractions in five towns situated in the north of Poland were interviewed.
Respondents were interviewed before and after the cultural event. A purpos-
ive sampling procedure was adopted for the cultural institution in which
the survey was undertaken. Only valid answers were taken into account in
reduction and analysis of the data. The characteristics of respondents are
illustrated in Tables 11.2–11.6.

The occupational profile of the 2195 respondents was similar to that of the entire labour force. Only 48.3% of the respondents surveyed were employed. This is somewhat less than the employment rate in Poland, which was 51.5% in 1997 (*Rocznik Statystyczny*, 1998, p. 121). More than 10% of cultural visitors were unemployed. This rate is similar to the registered

**Table 11.1.** Classification of attractions surveyed in northern Poland, 1997.

| Type of resources | Site | Event |
|---|---|---|
| Natural resources | Landscapes, lakes and forests in the Kashubian region (examined in a separate project) | Outdoor recreational activities (not surveyed) |
| Artificial resources | Historic monuments and buildings in the north of Poland<br>Museum of Warmia and Mazurk, Olsztyn | Theatrical performances (Gdañsk and Gdyniya)<br>Cinemas (Gdañsk, Gdynia, Torua, Elblag)<br>Art galleries (Sopot and Elblag)<br>Planetarium (Olsztyn)<br>Exhibitions<br>Football match |

**Table 11.2.** Age profile of respondents.

| Age group | Per cent |
|---|---|
| 15 or younger | 3.8 |
| 16–19 | 12.5 |
| 20–29 | 39.4 |
| 30–39 | 22.6 |
| 40–49 | 14.9 |
| 50–59 | 5.2 |
| 60 or over | 1.6 |

**Table 11.3.** Highest educational qualification.

| Qualification | Per cent |
|---|---|
| Primary school | 9.2 |
| Secondary school | 35.4 |
| Further education | 23.1 |
| First degree | 13.8 |
| Postgraduate | 18.5 |
| Total | 100.0 |

unemployment rate in the fourth quarter of 1997 (*Rocznik Statystyczny,*
1998, p. 136). A majority of the respondents were of working age (about
90%). People employed in culture, recreation and sport comprise only 1.0%
of the entire labour force in Poland (Rocznik, 1998, p. 125). In contrast,
about 7% of the visitors surveyed during the ATLAS research were employed
in culture. Almost 52% of the cultural visitors are in the same household
income bracket (€0–5000) which is typical for an average Polish family.
An average monthly disposable income of households is about €400 and
the average monthly salary is around €280 (Rocznik, 1998, pp. 150, 174,
454). In all, the respondents give quite a good picture of an average Polish
citizen.

**Table 11.4.** Occupational group.

| Occupational group | Per cent |
|---|---|
| Armed forces | 2.3 |
| Director or manager | 8.6 |
| Professional | 27.1 |
| Technical professions | 16.7 |
| Clerical | 17.6 |
| Service and sales | 11.6 |
| Crafts worker | 6.9 |
| Others | 9.3 |

**Table 11.5.** Occupation type.

| Occupation type | Per cent |
|---|---|
| Employee | 48.3 |
| Self-employed | 12.8 |
| Retired | 3.1 |
| Homemaker | 3.0 |
| Student | 21.3 |
| Unemployed | 10.4 |
| Others | 1.1 |
| Total | 100.0 |

**Table 11.6.** Normal occupation connected with culture (per cent).

| Answers | Type of culture | | |
|---|---|---|---|
| | Monuments or museums | Performing arts | Visual arts |
| Yes | 3.3 | 3.1 | 6.9 |
| No | 96.7 | 96.9 | 93.1 |

## Results and Discussion

As the main purpose of this chapter is to examine factors influencing the consumption of a cultural tourism product we begin with an explanation of the reasons for visiting cultural attractions.

Table 11.7 indicates that respondents visit cultural attractions mainly to experience and learn new things or to relax. These data confirm the findings of earlier studies that participation in cultural tourism is often connected with the aspirations of consumers to learn something new. In view of the fact that 48.3% of respondents were employed and 21.3% were students, it is possible to conclude that the 'learning element' is revealed in the consumption of culture in these groups of respondents. Table 11.8 illustrates the structure of respondents according to the criteria resident/non-resident and their interest in visiting cultural attractions in their leisure time.

Table 11.8 indicates that cultural attractions are visited by both tourists and residents. This means that the leisure product should be flexible in order to meet the needs and expectations of these groups of visitors. This finding must be taken into account in leisure management processes aimed at differentiating the intangible elements of the product, in order to provide information specific to the needs of a given group of visitors. By using marketing it is also possible to identify differences between students' and employed persons' preferences and 'adapt' the product to their needs. Growing competition in the leisure market necessitates the development

**Table 11.7.** Reasons for visiting the attraction.

| Reason | Respondents who fully agreed with reason given (%) |
|---|---|
| To experience new things | 34.2 |
| To accompany other people | 28.8 |
| Connection of visit with work | 15.4 |
| Holiday habits | 13.1 |
| To learn new things | 28.1 |
| To relax | 32.9 |
| Friends often visit this sort of attraction | 23.1 |

**Table 11.8.** Residents' and non-residents' interest in visiting attractions in leisure time.

| | Yes (%) | No (%) |
|---|---|---|
| Do you live in this area? | 64.8 | 35.2 |
| Are you on holiday at the moment? | 14.0 | 86.0 |
| Have you visited other cultural attractions? | 58.6 | 41.4 |
| Have you visited cultural attractions in your leisure time? | 63.7 | 36.3 |

of a leisure product that is acceptable to consumers. Among the whole range of potential strategies in the cultural tourism business, the quality of services is perceived to be an important tool in the attainment of this objective. Handszuh (1998, p. 14), writing about the challenge of preserving and enhancing the authenticity of tourism product, stresses:

> Tourism activities tend to ask for quality standards because tourism has become a commodity. However, standards-setting in tourism has limits which are required by the very nature of tourism, especially its components related to leisure and special interest motivations. . . . This concern brings to light the difference between 'hard' quality standards . . ., 'soft' service standards which can be achieved thanks to management and proper organisation of service, and 'product' standards. Hard standards should be common, service standards may vary according to different service cultures, and product standards, usually related to trade marks, should be open to innovation.

These words are of great importance for the cultural tourism product which usually emphasizes 'hard' elements such as safety, harmony and its non-reproducible components but is not so often differentiated according to the quality of service. This approach to the cultural tourism product can be seen as an important factor in the growth of consumption but wider research in this area is still necessary. Based on the current research findings we can draw the following conclusions:

- Cultural tourism in Poland can be defined as a professional and well-educated market consisting mainly of employed persons and students. In spite of the fact that the attractions surveyed could be classified as 'popular culture', respondents visiting them had a high level of education. The proportion of visitors with a first degree or postgraduate studies was 32.3%, and another 23.1% had completed further education. This percentage is lower than that indentified within the whole ATLAS Cultural Tourism Survey but greater than the European Union average of 21% of adults with a higher education diploma (Richards, 1998, p. 13). Most of the respondents belong to the occupational groups: professional (27.1%), technical professions (16.7%) and clerical (17.6%). The normal occupation of the respondents interviewed is, in general, not connected with culture. Only 3.2% of visitors connected their profession with monuments or museums, 3.1% with the performing arts, and 6.9% with visual arts.
- More than two-thirds of the cultural visitors were residents of the city/town in which the survey took place. This indicates that 'popular culture' attractions may cater mainly for local people, but the attractions surveyed also attracted reasonable numbers of tourists.
- The high occupational standard of respondents does not relate to high levels of income. More than 50% of respondents belonged to the households in the lower bracket of gross annual income. This confirms Jung's (1994) contention that Polish cultural consumption is characterized by

individuals with high levels of cultural capital but low levels of economic capital.

- The cultural visitors interviewed in 1997 were young: 51.9% of them were between 16 and 29 years, and 22.6% between 30 and 39. The research was carried out during the academic year and many students were interviewed.
- An analysis of visitor motivations for cultural tourism gives a differentiated picture. Many people visit cultural tourism attractions to learn (about 60% indicating this as important), but for about 30% of the respondents relaxation is an important aspect of visiting cultural attractions. This illustrates the impossibility of separating recreational activities from cultural activities, particularly from elements of 'popular culture'. It is important to stress this because cultural tourism has not become habitual for Polish respondents – only 13.1% always visit a museum when they go on holiday. The influence of friends on cultural tourism participation is clear – about 30% visit cultural attractions to accompany other people. More than 15.0% of visitors indicated that they visit cultural attractions because they are connected with their work. This proportion confirms the results of earlier studies that people with cultural occupations are over-represented in cultural tourism in comparison with their proportion of total employed persons. Only 1% of the workforce is employed in culture, recreation and sport. However, in keeping with the general findings of the current Cultural Tourism Project, they were very often motivated by the 'learning element' of such activities. On the other hand it is also true 'that keeping up, in a system with rising expectations and norms, is a very important motivator of modern consumer behaviour' (Schor, 1998, p. 10). Based on these two motivators ('learning' and 'keeping up') we can see that functional aspects of tourism services play an important role in consumption. The cultural tourism product has become essential to the experience of many consumers throughout Europe.

# References

Bocock, R. (1993) *Consumption*. Routledge, London.

Devereux, C. (1998) More than 'have a nice day': cross cultural service competence and the tourist industry. In: Richards, G. (ed.) *Developments in the European Tourism Curriculum*. ATLAS, Tilburg, pp. 31–48.

Fladmark, J.M. (ed.) (1994) *Cultural Tourism*. Douhead, Wimbledon Publishing.

Hall, D.R. (1998) Tourism development and sustainability issues in Central and South-Eastern Europe. *Tourism Management* 19(5), 423–431.

Handszuh, H. (1998) Paper presented on the conference 'Strategia rozwoju turystyki poprzez podnoszenie jakości'. 8–10 pa dziernik 1998. Kraków.

Jung, B. (1990) The impact of the crisis on leisure patterns in Poland. *Leisure Studies* 9(2), 95–105.

Jung, B. (1994) For what leisure? The role of culture and recreation in post-communist Poland. *Leisure Studies* 13(4), 262–276.

Marciszewska, B. (1998) Participation in free-time sport recreation activities: comparison of Gdańsk Region, Poland and Guildford, United Kingdom. In: Scraton, S. (ed.) *Leisure, Time and Space: Meanings and Values in People's Lives.* LSA Publication No. 57, pp. 177–191.

Moulin, C.M. (1991) Cultural heritage and tourism development in Canada. *Tourism Recreation Research* 16(1), 50–55.

Page, S.J. (1994) Developing heritage tourism in Ireland in the 1990s. *Tourism Recreation Research* 19(2), 79–89.

Poon, A. (1993) *Tourism, Technology and Competitive Strategies.* CAB International, Wallingford, UK.

Richards, G. (ed.) (1996). *Cultural Tourism in Europe.* CAB International, Wallingford, UK.

Richards, G. (1998) Cultural tourism in Europe: recent developments. *ATLAS News* 17 June, 12–15.

*Rocznik Statystyczny* (1998) GUS, Warsaw.

Ryan, C. (1991) *Recreational Tourism. a Social Science Perspective.* Routledge, London and New York.

Schor, J. (1998) Beyond work and spend: time, leisure and consumption. In: Scraton, S. (ed.) *Leisure, Time and Space: Meanings and Values in People's Lives.* LSA Publication No. 57, pp. 7–12.

*Tourism Market Research in the Province of Gdańsk* (1994) Prosperitas Ltd. Economy and Strategy Consultants, Sopot.

Wanhill, S. (1993). Attractions. In: Cooper, C., Fletcher, J., Gilbert, D. and Wanhill, S. (eds) *Tourism Principles and Practice.* Pitman, London.

# Creative Industries as Milieux of Innovation: the Westergasfabriek, Amsterdam

## Caro Bonink[1] and Erik Hitters[2]

[1]Caro Consulting, Amsterdam, The Netherlands;
[2]Department of Arts and Cultural Studies, Erasmus
University Rotterdam, Rotterdam, The Netherlands

## Introduction: Creative Industries as Attractions

The distinction between the traditional high arts and popularized mass culture is deeply rooted in western thought. In this view the 'fragile' high arts on the one hand can only flourish autonomously under the protection of the patron-state, and the commercial cultural industry on the other hand is completely guided by market forces and popular demand. Furthermore, in the contemporary political and policy arena high arts and popular culture are very persistent categories. In practice, however, the distinction proves not to be very relevant, neither for the audiences, nor for the suppliers in the cultural field. The public prefers to listen to both Tom Jones and Gustav Mahler, decides between buying a painting or a designer suit, and sees *Titanic* on Thursday and *Faust* on Friday.

That both sectors have more similarities than differences is slowly being acknowledged by policy makers and administrators, encouraged by alliances with the private and the non-profit sector. Several innovative urban renewal projects provide opportunities for what we label as 'creative industries'. We wish to draw attention to the importance of these industries for the attractiveness of cities to cultural consumers, be they residents, visitors or tourists, as well as to businesses and private investors. By using the concept of creative industry, we avoid the reproduction of the persistent gap between the subsidized high arts and commercial popular culture. Instead, we emphasize their similarity. Consequently, the definition includes the 'classical' cultural industries and the 'traditional' arts. The creative industries, then, incorporate all branches of industry and trade that rely on imaginative creation and cultural innovation aimed at the production, distribution and consumption of symbolic goods. They include film, literature and publishing, theatre, recorded music, concerts and performance, fashion, design, architecture, old (broadcast) and new media, visual art, crafts, museums and galleries (O'Connor, 1999).

In our view, these creative industries are central assets of the contemporary urban economy and the city's social fabric. They operate through a specific spatial logic, by which they are strongly linked to the mutual dependency of culture and the city. Furthermore, they are highly dependent upon each other's proximity, as this provides them with competitive advantages through creative exchange and networking (Porter, 1998). Creative industries show a strong proclivity to clustering. This explains why specifically urban renewal areas in inner cities have provided the opportunities for such spatially concentrated industries to develop and for these new collaborations to emerge. Examples of initiatives that centre on this new concept of clustered creative industries are the Northern Quarter in Manchester, Rotterdam's Witte de Withstraat, the Veemarktkwartier in Tilburg and the Westergasfabriek in Amsterdam. The latter will be central to our concern in this chapter.

We will argue that creative industries are connected to an increasingly global network economy, an economic space that percolates symbolic value across the world using information technology and global communication networks. This then would suggest a diminished importance of location factors to these industries. However, not only does the evidence indicate that creative industries tend to cluster, they also derive much of their symbolic value from their local identity. The question we pose here, therefore, is what is the underlying logic of these clusters of creativity and to what extent do they provide an answer to the homogenizing consequences of globalization? We will try to show how, in these projects, seemingly fixed boundaries are transgressed, old points of reference are dropped, by replacing them with new forms of collaboration between creativity, commerce and community. Although questions of public policy intervention and governance go beyond the focus of this chapter, it is quite obvious that these projects and clusters have positive impacts on the quality of urban cultural facilities. However, they are usually not initiated or planned by the established cultural bureaucracy. Consequently, their scope goes far beyond traditional cultural policy values of accessibility and cultural democracy. But before we take this argument further, we want to elaborate on the process of globalization and its consequences for culture.

## Globalization and the Network Society

Although the study of globalization processes is firmly embedded in academic research, its focus is predominantly on the economic causes and consequences. Globalization primarily refers to the continuous scaling-up of markets and the increasing growth of transnational financial and economic networks (Sassen, 1994; Waters, 1995). But this process is equally characterized by the fading of national cultural identities, increasing geographical mobility, worldwide migration, ethnic hybridization and apparent cultural homogenization (Zukin, 1995). The other side of the process of globalization, and inevitably linked with it, is the revival of local autonomy. This is as apparent in the strengthening of local identities and ethnicities, as in the stronger urgency of administrative and political intervention on a local level. This duality in the process of globalization can be characterized by the term 'glocalization'.

This process is precipitated in the city. The contemporary metropolis is confronted with the concrete consequences of the process of economic and cultural globalization. The internationalization of markets has intensified inter-urban competition. As a result of the increased mobility of capital and the diminishing importance of purely physical location factors, cities attempt to distinguish themselves by their social, cultural and symbolic characteristics. But behind the façades polarization and fragmentation are very visible. On the one hand there is a polarization between *haves* and *have-nots*, who profit or suffer from the consequences of globalization. On the other hand there is a notable evanescence to existing patterns in style, taste and cultural preference (Peterson and Kern, 1996). The cultural sector not only experiences the consequences but is the centre of this development. After all, cultural diversity, in its broad sense, is essential to the attractiveness of a city.

The recent work of the Spanish sociologist Manuel Castells (1996) on the 'network society' provides a powerful analytical background to the processes of globalization, their causes and their consequences. The combination of an information society and a globally networked economy has introduced a new logic of economic space, which Castells defines as the 'space of flows'. He opposes the space of flows to the 'space of places', the localities that shape people's daily activities. Castells warns us that those two spaces become fundamentally separated from one another unless 'cultural and physical bridges are deliberately built between those two forms of space' (Castells, 1996, p. 428). What we will argue here, is that the creative industries can function as such a bridge. But before looking further into that matter we have to consider Castells' notions of the network society more closely.

Castells' theory of the network society involves two important transformations that are central to our concern. The first is the increased use of information and communication technologies, and the consequent convergence of these technologies to give rise to an 'information society' on a global scale. The second is the subsequent change in the nature of doing business in the network society.

According to Castells, the current technological revolution uses knowledge and information for knowledge generation and the processing of information through communication devices, 'in a cumulative feedback loop between innovation and the users of innovation' (Castells, 1996, p. 32). This convergence of information technology and communication is led by so-called 'milieux of innovation'. These are clusters of innovative companies, creating a synergetic and dynamic environment (e.g. Silicon Valley). Such milieux of innovation can generate synergy by virtue of their flexibility and their network structure. Such a network, then, can deal with increasing complexity of interaction '. . . networking logic is needed to structure the unstructured while preserving flexibility, since the unstructured is the driving force of innovation in human activity' (Castells, 1996, p. 61).

Furthermore, the global scale of the informational society gives rise to a new network economy (Shapiro and Varian, 1999). Economic activity has taken the shape of flows of capital, knowledge and information, which travel between the nodes on the global network. In this network economy, the central economic activities operate on a global scale. Globalization, subsequently, connects the core areas of economic activity through a tight network. Successful firms have to be able to compete in this network, which subsequently ties in their local markets into the global network. But it leaves out large parts of the world, containing the largest share of the world population that is not connected to the global economic flows and thus reduced to marginality.

The second major transformation is the shift to a new business logic in the global and informational economy. Castells (1996, p. 61) points out that businesses operate in networks. According to Kelly (1998) this network logic is driven by perpetual and inevitable innovation. It involves three interrelated organizational principles: flexible specialization, networking and competitive collaboration. Here, then, it becomes clear that the physical agglomeration of businesses can be advantageous. van Bon (1999) has found that especially small and medium sized businesses apply these new principles and thus oppose the global footloose economy with a renewed meaning and importance of locality. Likewise, Amin and Graham (1997, p. 415) have argued that

> . . . the advantages of proximity, associated with the exchange of information, goods and services, . . . face-to-face contact, . . . incremental innovation, learning and the exchange of tacit knowledge, are the assets of comparative advantage in a global context of increasingly ubiquitous forms of codified or scientific knowledge. Thus localisation is a source of dynamic learning that reinforces and is reinforced by the agglomeration of firms in the same industry.

Castells (1996) subsequently stresses the persistent importance of cities. The geographical implications of the networking of dominant economic interests are characterized by simultaneous concentration and dispersion. Metropolises remain important as nodes in the global network, while advanced services are decentralized to the periphery, but connected through new technologies (e.g. software programming in India). Thus, this new economic spatial logic is able to separate the milieux of innovation from technological production, giving way to a new global division of labour. As the milieux of innovation in western metropolises take a central position, mega-cities are central nodes in the global network economy, the space of flows. However, such urban innovative milieux, while globally connected, run the risk of remaining locally disconnected, disqualifying local populations as participants in the global economy. Thus, the space of flows is the new spatial form characteristic of social practices that dominate and shape the network society. All interactions between social agents in physically disconnected places, mediated by communication technologies, are located on the space of flows. It incorporates the spatial organization of the dominant managerial elites, their interactions that shape the global economy and the spaces that are associated with it, corporate office towers, hotels, airports' VIP lounges, exclusive restaurants (Castells, 1996, pp. 412–418).

But the roots of most people's experiences, culture and history lie not in the space of flows. Castells introduces the space of places, where the majority of the world population lives. A place is 'a locale whose form, function and meaning are self-contained within the boundaries of physical contiguity' (Castells, 1996, p. 423). Consequently, the space of flows is the spatial manifestation of globalization, whereas the space of places shapes the simultaneous process of localization. Castells expresses his fear that the two spatial realities will become increasingly separated, disconnecting the economy from the real lives of the vast majority of the population. While the space of flows extends its influence across the globe, places are estranging from each other, as they are less and less able to share cultural codes. The networks of the space of flows become superimposed on a landscape of fragmented and disconnected places. 'Unless cultural and physical bridges are built between these two forms of space, we may be heading toward life in parallel universes whose times cannot meet, because they are warped into different dimensions of a social cyberspace' (Castells, 1996, p. 428).

## The Westergasfabriek: Project Background

In the next section we will argue that the spatial logic of the creative industries is similar to that of the space of flows. They adapt to the logic of the new network economy and are connected to the global economic flows. However, they are also characterized by a necessary connection to place. Much of their quality is derived from a very localized identity that is strengthened by agglomeration advantages. Therefore, they have specific characteristics as milieux of innovation that can act as the bridges that are needed to reconnect the space of flows and the space of places[1]. The Westergasfabriek in Amsterdam can function as an example of such a milieu of innovation.

The Westergasfabriek (WGF) is located west of the inner city of Amsterdam[2]. It is a former gas factory, which was shut down in the 1960s when the discovery of natural gas resources in The Netherlands made the production of gas redundant. Many of the Westergasfabriek buildings were demolished, the remaining ones served as storage yards for years. During the last decade, however, there has been a growing interest in and appreciation of old industrial sites as historically valuable urban areas. The grounds of the Westergasfabriek cover 15,827 square metres and today 13 of the factory's 19 remaining buildings are state-protected monuments. The city council already started discussing possible new uses of the WGF complex in the late 1970s. Developing the site met with great difficulty, because of a lack of funds, the level of soil pollution and the lack of consensus among the various groups involved. In the meantime, in 1992, the buildings were put to temporary use, and leased for short periods to different cultural organizations. A motivation for that decision was the great need for 'cultural' spaces in Amsterdam at the time. Because of their different shapes and sizes the buildings proved to be good locations for all sorts of activities. Many of the buildings were very popular and for some a waiting list existed. The giant gas holder proved suitable for big events like house parties, pop concerts, operas and other manifestations. For a few big festivals (Drum Rhythm Festival, Holland Festival) the grounds as well as the buildings were used. A few times the grounds also provided the location for a fair. In 3 years over 300 exhibitions, performances and concerts were held at the WGF and since 1995 the area has attracted some 250,000 visitors annually.

## Management and administration

Since 1994, a project team, led by project manager Evert Verhagen, has managed the development and coordination of activities at the Westergasfabriek. The project team has been, and still is, a key element in the project's success. In 1996 the district council of Westerpark published a development plan for the WGF, prepared by the project team. The plan provided a structure for the WGF in three themes: 'park', 'culture' and 'cultural enterprise'. The new Westerpark will be an extension of the existing park that is situated east of the factory grounds. It will also include the Overbrakerpolders north of the site. The total area of the new park will be more than 50 ha. It can be built when the clean-up of polluted soil is in a far-advanced phase (Stadsdeel Westerpark, 1996, p. 26). In 1996 the central

---

[1]   Others have likewise argued that clusters of micro, small and medium cultural businesses can be seen as milieux of innovation (see Amin and Graham, 1997; Verwijnen, 1998; van Bon, 1999).

[2]   This section is based on material taken from the Westergasfabriek homepage; EPA (undated); Stadsdeel Westerpark, 1996; and Buwalda *et al.*, 1999.

city government approved the park/culture concept, and reserved almost 12 million guilders (€5.5 million) for its development. The district council chose a design by landscape architect Kathryn Gustafson. Final approval for the park budget was reached in early 1998 (EPA, undated, p. 6). Construction of the park will start in spring 2000. The grounds of the WGF will be used to combine a 'culture park' with a traditional park. Since the temporary use of the buildings for mostly cultural purposes proved to be a success, this policy will be continued. The existing cultural enterprises at the site (distribution, organization, catering, stage design, special effects, etc.) will remain there as well. These existing uses of the WGF will be extended by the transformation of the grounds into a park that will give the surrounding neighbourhoods the large green space they have always lacked. The cultural and the park destinations of the site are expected to go well together and stimulate each other (Stadsdeel Westerpark, 1996, p. 7).

The idea behind the future development of the park is that the buildings and their cultural activities will be integrated into the surrounding park, in order to preserve the unique character of the site. The project team and city council want the new Westerpark to be a park for the 21st century, a park that is as multifaceted as its users and whose multifunctionality answers the different needs of the local community and the entire city. They want it to be an egalitarian public space, available to everyone. However, they also want to create a unique character that is not especially democratic, but responding to the tastes and motives of the actors involved, and not the surrounding neighbourhoods. The park is meant to be open-ended, dynamic and evolving. The cultural site is meant to be sophisticated, unique and particular to the cultural geography of Amsterdam.

The future development of the WGF will take the shape of a public–private partnership. The need for private resources and management expertise to rehabilitate the buildings and operate the cultural venues was based on two premises. Firstly, it would increase the stability of the project. Were it to remain connected to the district council, it would be dependent on changeable politics with the risk of stagnation and disintegration. Secondly, the budget of the council was too small to invest in the WGF. At this moment the project requires an additional investment budget of 60 million guilders (€27 million).

The private developer that is involved is property developer MAB, which will become owner of the buildings on the site. MAB expects the WGF in its current form to be sustainable for 10 or 20 years, but to them only the profitability over the next 5 years is relevant. MAB will restore the buildings, and create 600 square metres of new building space that will account for 30% of the total site. The new buildings will be made complementary to the existing site. This investment will add value to the site, making its sale profitable after 5 years. MAB will not invest in the park, which remains the responsibility of the district council. The only risk for MAB is the possibility that they will not attract enough tenants – new occupants will have to pay and cultural organizations are notorious for being poor. Fuelled by market research and current negotiations with potential tenants, MAB is confident about the future of the WGF (Buwalda *et al.*, 1999, p. 48). At the beginning of 2000 the contracts between MAB and the district council were finalized.

MAB is not interested in the management of the site, which is not unusual for project developers. The project bureau will continue to be the operational unit for the Westerpark District. MAB will set up a new formal management corporation, which will become responsible for programming and management of the buildings. This corporation ('De West') will rent space from the owners and lease the spaces to tenants. Thus, the project bureau will hand over control of the buildings to MAB and De West. A point of discussion is to what extent it is possible to retain low rents for current tenants, within a commercial setting. And is it possible to allow differentiation between old and new tenants, or for instance between non-profit and commercial users? Overseeing the sustainability of the cultural function of the project will be an important task of the district council.

The district council, as owner, plays a key role in the privatization of the buildings. The council has fixed the cultural use of the buildings, the rent levels, and rules for temporary and permanent leasing in the deeds of sale. The district council will also stay involved in the project now the buildings have been sold. Even though MAB owns the buildings and management corporation De West, many formal and legal ties bind MAB to the Westerpark district. Firstly, as land owner the district can fix functions in a land use plan. Also, the district is responsible for construction of the park. Secondly, the buildings are designated as National Monuments, and therefore have restrictions placed on their redevelopment. Thirdly, an advisory board will oversee the future private development of the site. This board is made up of community representatives and it will have to approve of changes in the current planning (Daems *et al.*, 2000). The district council stresses the value of the site for the neighbourhood and it is expected that the council will foster the 'wholeness' of the site as a cultural park, including both green space and buildings. The question here, is to what extent the politics of culture can prevail over the politics of economy.

## Current Use of the Area

Because of the impending extensive restoration of the beautiful old buildings and the construction of the new park, most of the buildings are occupied by temporary tenants. Most of these are cultural or culturally-related organizations. They are, we would argue, typical of the creative industries. Between 1992 and 1997 400 contracts were given out for incidental rental. Half of these were for festivals, performances and exhibitions, the other half were for business events, fashion shows, movie and video recording and other non-public activities. Permanent tenants include the 'Toneelgroep

Amsterdam', operating a venue for performing arts in the Transformatorhuis, 'West Pacific', a dining and dancing café, 'Studio Wenck', a studio for video and movie productions, 'Orkater', a performing arts group and rehearsal studio, and 'Dasarts', a school for advanced education in performing arts.

The local government development plan (Stadsdeel Westerpark, 1996) gave clear criteria for redeveloping the area. These were used by the project bureau as guidelines for the selection of temporary and long-term tenants:

- A combination of visitor attractions and cultural activities
- A combination of cultural use and park use
- Cultural attractions should not be orientated to the mass market, but mixed cultural forms of subsidized and commercial activities
- Opportunities for starting organizations through differentiated rents
- Day and night activities to spread the number of visitors
- Flexible use of the buildings
- Use of a number of buildings by the inhabitants of the area (local organizations, cultural education)
- Intercultural character.

In order to establish the attractiveness of the WGF for cultural organizations, research was conducted among current and potential users of the site. Around 40 organizations were interviewed about their present activities, their future activities, the reasons for their interest and their expectations and requirements for working in the area.

The main reasons why organizations were interested in renting space in one of the buildings were:

- The mix of cultural organizations
- A large historical area which gives opportunities to set up and bundle cultural activities
- The cultural and creative image of the area
- The monumental industrial buildings give an extra impulse to creative work
- The area is well situated and can be easily reached by car
- The presence of other cultural and related organizations
- An atmosphere of creativity and new impulses.

The cultural organizations obviously recognize the advantages of clustering in a competitive–collaborative way. Their main interest in the area is being a part of a mixed cultural environment. The respondents clearly state that it is important to be surrounded by other cultural organizations and organizations indirectly involved with culture. They are attracted by experimental new developments. Creativity and new impulses should dominate the area. The small-scale innovative and alternative nature of the WGF is important here. The respondents do not want large commercial corporations, noisy discothèques, large mass-market suppliers or indeed any organizations with a non-cultural character.

Being in the same area as similar organizations gives the opportunity to cooperate in:

- Promotion and publicity
- Facilities, such as reception, ticketing and admission, studio facilities, parking (car and bicycle), security, childcare, café, mail services, maintenance, storage
- Activities for the people in the neighbourhood
- Other themed public activities.

## A Clustered Milieu of Innovation?

Returning to our initial question, how can we understand the spatial logic of this specific case and, to what extent can we characterize this area as a milieu of innovation? It is difficult to give a definitive answer to this question. We contend, however, that this analysis can give us valuable insights into the specific qualities of the creative industries and their importance for the attractiveness of cities. We wish to focus here on five distinctive features of the Westergasfabriek which are important in terms of the creative industries:

**1.** *Creative industries in the network economy.* Cultural businesses operate in an unpredictable market. Similar to information, taste is equally quickly outdated because of constant innovation. Thus, creative industries face additional uncertainties, as their products are judged according to aesthetic and symbolic criteria. The cultural products of the Westergasfabriek (art works, club nights, crafts, and performances) are valued through the lifestyle they are associated with. The atmosphere in this cluster of old industrial buildings is a source of value in this respect. The creative producers in this area create this value through their dynamic and innovative use of the area. In this way they can keep attracting the attention of consumers. At the WGF it is clear that clustering, flexible specialization and informal networking are tools that the creative industries use to maintain their dynamism.

**2.** *Mixed permanent and incidental use of public and non-public cultural activities.* The mixed use of the area leads to optimal use of the buildings and the area in general. It will be lively during both day and night, used by workers and visitors to the historical buildings, the park and the activities held there. Permanent users are needed for financial continuity of the Westergasfabriek. A few major users are needed to give the area financial stability and to provide an identity. Major users are the performing arts, cinema, film studios, new media, education, designers, artists, photographers, etc. Incidental users are needed for setting up lively events and exhibitions. These users also make more use of the area itself (instead of only the buildings). For visitors, the incidental public activities are the major attraction of the area. In addition, visitors who go to an event often come back later to visit other activities.

Furthermore, the mix of activities is very important for the organizations as well. It is essential in providing a network of innovative creativity.

**3.** *Attracting a broad and diverse range of visitors.* For the cultural producers in this area, it is important that the activities attract a diverse audience as opposed to a mass audience. In their view, it is easy to attract the mass. It is more difficult to attract a broad and diverse range of visitors who are interested in culture and specifically experimental culture. Therefore it is important to set up low threshold activities, that will provide easy access to such an audience. The park is obviously one of those easily accessible attractions of the area. The other is the fair that is held there twice a year. These will bring many people from the surrounding communities in touch with the Westergasfabriek and the cultural activities that take place there. It is therefore extremely important that further research is done into the visitors to the area, their demographics and their experiences.

**4.** *Experimental character.* For most leaseholders, the experimental character of the area is its most important attraction. In this sense, the area is truly experienced as a milieu of innovation by those who work there. The mix of traditional and high culture, forged together in the creative industries concept, appears to be binding the activities together. Traditional dichotomies have lost their significance. The marginality and peripheral location of the area, outside of the city centre, strengthens this concept. The old buildings have huge empty spaces, that can be used flexibly and have low rents. It is vital to the area that the experimental character is not lost. It is therefore important to think of differentiated rents, subsidies from the local government, and sponsors.

**5.** *Mixing public and private investment.* The mixed investment in the area, public funds for the park and the project bureau, and commercial investors to develop rental space is not unique. It is, however, unique that the area has a cultural function. What is more, the private investors have agreed to maintain the mixed cultural use of the area, to differentiate rent levels for different users and to maintain the specific industrial heritage of the buildings. Obviously, political intervention is vital here, to ensure that this public–private partnership has a sustainable future.

## Conclusion

Finally, the question remains whether the Westergasfabriek can, in the Castellian sense, bridge the gap between the space of flows and the space of places. In order to answer that, we have to examine the bond to place at the two central characteristics of the network society: its informational and global character and its business network logic (flexible specialization, networking and competitive collaboration).

Firstly, let us focus on the informational and global character. We contend that the creative industries operate in very similar ways to the industries in information and communication technologies. In a network economy, where information generation and perpetual innovation are important, the central position of a 'milieu of innovation' is similar for both technological and creative industries. It is made up out of a cluster of companies, innovative through local informal networks, while globally connected with other centres of innovation and core economic or symbolic activity. In the creative industries, perpetual innovation is crucial in order to keep up with the shifting tastes of consumers. Here, innovation is finding new ways to manipulate signs and symbols, in order to generate new meanings.

In order to be innovative, creative industries have to be integrated in local economies. After all, their own networks, in which they exchange experiences, ideas and facilities, are locally embedded within a cluster. Being close to similar industries gives the opportunity for face-to-face interactions in a shared building, complex or quarter. Scott (1997) rightly argues that elements of identity and lifestyle are important in this context. A place has a cultural identity that is the product of its communities. This provides a place with culture and meaning, shaping the lives and tastes of the people that live and work there. Furthermore, in a cluster of industries the employees and visitors share a lifestyle, which they consume and produce simultaneously. Cultural producers are influenced by global trends, but their products also gain their specific quality from their local context. van Bon (1999, p. 47) suggests that identity is rooted not just in the history of social relations and the morphology of that specific place, but also in the new meanings it has gained related to the lifestyle characteristics produced and consumed within its borders. Thus, the physical environment is crucial. The industrial history of the Westergasfabriek (and the characteristics and atmosphere it created) is greatly appreciated by the cultural producers in the area, as it inspires and stimulates their work.

Secondly, looking at the business network logic, flexible specialization, competitive collaboration and networking are obvious characteristics of the creative industries we have studied at the Westergasfabriek. The fact that they are clustered is crucial here. The small businesses at the WGF have highly specialized products and services for a very specialized market. Based on changing information and taste they constantly have to adapt their output (Shapiro and Varian, 1999). Flexibility and collaboration are agglomeration effects. Within clusters, creative businesses are not isolated, but are part of the larger network. Synergetic effects occur as the result of the sharing of ideas, talents, skills, information and facilities. The local network, with its face-to-face interactions offers the opportunities for this exchange to occur. This enables cultural producers to think outside the constraints of their own specific business. Here, the traditional boundaries between high and popular culture prove to be obsolete. Furthermore, the loss of relevance of these distinctions can overcome the universalistic nature of high culture and the commercialized localism of popular culture (Blau, 1989). In that sense, the innovative nature of the creative industries can also bridge the traditional difference in the separated networks of high and popular culture.

In conclusion, the creative industries in the Westergasfabriek seem to be able to merge the networks of the global economy and the experience of ordinary people's daily life. The findings of the research show how the connection to the global network and its subsequent business logic are dependent on local experiences and the abilities of cultural producers to translate the cultural meanings of places into global flows of signs and symbols. Their presence in both the space of flows and the space of places suggests that they can build the bridges Castells (1996) thinks are necessary to prevent these two spatial realities from becoming completely separated. On the other hand, they also have to provide the concrete public space for local people to participate. At the Westergasfabriek, the park offers good possibilities for this. But it remains to be seen to what extent the users of the park also cross the physical and cultural bridge that has been opened for them.

# References

Amin, A. and Graham, S. (1997) The ordinary city. *Transactions of the Institute of British Geographers* 22(4), 411–429.

Blau, J. (1989) *The Shape of Culture: a Study of Contemporary Cultural Patterns in the United States.* Cambridge University Press, New York.

BRO adviseurs in ruimtelijke ordening, economie en milieu (1997) *Marktonderzoek functiemix Westergasfabriek, Amsterdam.* BRO, Vught.

Buwalda, D., Delalex, G., Sluiter, F., Valentin, C. and van Bon, S. (1999) *Westergasfabriek. The Culture Factory.* POLIS Group Report 1998/99, Tilburg University, Tilburg, The Netherlands.

Castells, M. (1996) *The Information Age: Economy, Society and Culture. Volume I: The Rise of the Network Society.* Blackwell, Oxford.

Deams, G., James, K., Kerchmar, C. and Andreen, I. (2000) *The Westergasfabriek.* POLIS Group Report 1999/2000, Tilburg University, Tilburg, The Netherlands.

EPA (undated) *Westergasfabriek: Collaboration of Local Government and Community, Amsterdam, the Netherlands. An International Brownfields Case Study.* http://www.epa.gov/swerosps/bf/html-doc/westrgas.htm

Kelly, K. (1998) *New Rules for the New Economy: 10 Radical Strategies for a Connected World.* Penguin, New York.

O'Connor, J. (1998) The definition of cultural industries. Unpublished paper. Manchester Metropolitan University, Manchester.

Peterson, R.A. and Kern, R. (1996) Changing highbrow taste: from snob to omnivore. *American Sociological Review* 61(5), 900–907.

Porter, M. (1998) *On Competition.* HBS Press, Boston.

Sassen, S. (1994) *Cities in a World Economy.* Pine Forge Press, Thousand Oaks, California.

Scott, A.J. (1997) The cultural economy of cities. *International Journal of Urban and Regional Research* 21(2), 323–339.

Shapiro, C. and Varian, H.R. (1999) *Information Rules: a Strategic Guide to the Network Economy*. Harvard Business School Press, Boston, Massachusetts.

Stadsdeel Westerpark (1996) *Ontwikkelingsplan voor de Westergasfabriek*. Amsterdam.

van Bon, S. (1999) The cultural industries: fostering the local in the network economy. A case study of the Northern Quarter in Manchester. POLIS MA thesis. Tilburg University, Tilburg, The Netherlands.

Verwijnen, J. (1998) The creative city as field condition. Can urban innovation and creativity overcome bureaucracy and technocracy? *Built Environment* 24(2/3), 142–154.

Waters, M. (1995) *Globalization*. Routledge, London.

Westergasfabriek Homepage. http://www.westergasfabriek.nl

Zukin, S. (1995) *The Cultures of Cities*. Blackwell, Cambridge, Massachusetts.

# European Cultural Attractions: Trends and Prospects

## Greg Richards

*Tilburg University, Department of Lesiure Studies, Tilburg, The Netherlands*

Our analysis of the European cultural attraction market indicates that attraction managers live in interesting times, as the Chinese curse would have it. The stable environment in which cultural attractions found themselves after the Second World War, with growing visitor interest matched by unquestioning state support, has been replaced by a volatile landscape dominated by change and uncertainty. This has created new challenges for attraction managers in terms of balancing the often conflicting demands of conservation and presentation, as Wil Munsters has suggested in Chapter 5. This chapter examines some of the major trends that have emerged from the analyses presented in the preceding chapters, and identifies some of the major challenges cultural attractions are likely to face in the future.

## The Management of Cultural Attractions

As Green (Chapter 9) argues, the future of cultural attractions, not just in Europe but also in other world regions, will increasingly be dominated by the forces of globalization and localization. The emergence of global cultural markets has created global cultural 'brands', such as the Guggenheim, which can use their global image to attract tourists from all corners of the globe. The larger attractions will be forced to compete against these global icons for attention, either by securing big 'names', or as the example of the Bonnefanten Museum (Chapter 5) suggests, by creating new and unusual products. Smaller attractions, on the other hand, will benefit from the dialectic between globalization and localization, particularly if they are seen to offer meaningful alternatives to cultural 'McDonaldization'.

A further consequence of globalization is the de-differentiation of culture, tourism and leisure. This will create new opportunities and challenges for cultural attractions, but will also increase the extent to which they must compete with other attractions in the leisure field. As competition for visitors increases, the legitimacy implied by the cultural basis of an attraction will be an important factor. As leisure also has an important role in learning and the development of consumption skills and cultural capital, so a claim to cultural values will be attractive for many visitors, particularly families with children. The value of the cultural label is already evident in attempts by museums to protect the word 'museum' and to restrict the type of attractions this is applied to. However, this value has already been recognized by theme parks and other 'leisure' attractions, which are only too glad to use cultural themes to gain a foothold in the educational market.

Being able to attract a broader public is essential for many attractions these days, not just because this generates more revenue directly, but also because this adds legitimacy to the claims of cultural institutions for public support. A broader public usually means new visitor groups, many of whom are not used to visiting cultural attractions, and who may not be socialized into the expectations of the institution. This raises a number of issues to do with visitor management, as the Clonmacnoise and Maastricht case studies illustrate. In particular, the European Association for Tourism and Leisure Education (ATLAS) research has consistently emphasized that many visitors come not for cultural reasons, but to be entertained or to relax, or simply because they are accompanying someone else. There is already some evidence to suggest that cultural attractions are beginning to take this on board, with a growing number of attractions adding entertainment elements to their product range and shifting towards quadrants 3 and 4 of the attraction typology presented in Chapter 1 (Fig. 1.1).

Such a shift in emphasis will tend to heighten the tensions already present within cultural institutions, as Wil Munster's model in Chapter 5 (Fig. 5.4) suggests. Just as museums are currently faced with the task of reconciling the roles of curation and tour operation, so other cultural attractions will have to find their own balance between commercial and cultural concerns. In many cases resolving this tension will require more attention being paid to visitor management and the management of the visitor experience. Provision of differing levels of information and inter-pretation, modes of display and visitor flows through the attraction can all play an important role. In this respect cultural attractions can probably learn a lot from theme parks and other major leisure attractions, which have had to become more professional in visitor management as visitor numbers have increased over the years.

Another area in which many cultural attractions can learn from their commercial counterparts is in the area of funding. As David Leslie suggests in Chapter 6, this is probably the biggest management issue facing museums and other cultural attractions today. Public sector funding can no longer be taken for granted, particularly as the number of cultural institutions competing for these funds increases. This has meant that attractions have had to increase the proportion of funding they derive directly from visitors through admission charges and merchandising, and from other sources such as sponsorship. In this respect European attractions are still lagging behind their American counterparts, although as Berry and Shephard point out (Chapter 8), many heritage attractions are becoming more professional in their approach to fundraising.

Many cultural attractions also need to become more professional in terms of marketing. Although most cultural attractions now have a person or department responsible for marketing, this is far from making the institution itself market orientated. Most cultural attractions remain geared to the needs of their product and not to the needs of the visitor. Market research is also limited, so it is difficult for many attractions to know exactly what their visitors want. By making marketing more central to the concerns of the organization, however, cultural attractions can learn more from their audiences and their competitors, and increase the quality of the experience they offer to visitors. As McGettigan and Burns suggest in Chapter 7, de-marketing can also play an important role in matching the expectations of those that do visit to the capabilities of the attraction, and thereby reduce potential disappointment.

A further strategy, now being adopted by some smaller cultural institutions, is to opt out of the visitor rat race altogether and make themselves less rather than more accessible. This increases the cachet associated with visiting them, and ensures an elite (and elitist) clientele, but it is also debatable if these institutions can then be considered as visitor attractions.

## Growing Competition

The oversupply of cultural attractions noted by Berry and Shephard in Chapter 8 is evident in many different areas of Europe. The market is becoming saturated not just by the growth in cultural supply, but from attractions in other sectors of the leisure market. The de-differentiation of the leisure sector means that cultural attractions are no longer a distinct sector, but increasingly overlap and therefore compete with theme parks, cinemas and leisure shopping.

Growing competition is stimulated not just by the attractions themselves, but is encouraged by local and regional authorities eager to develop their cultural provision. As Green explains in Chapter 9, Europe is entering an era of 'New Medievalism', in which the emerging 'city states' compete with one another to expand their sphere of influence. Culture has become a major element in this competitive struggle:

> Today this is one of the main points of criticism of this practice of turning
> cultural policy into an urban festival. Both the arrangement of the city centres
> orientated on tourism as much as the production of cultural events with a great
> degree of predictability are characterized by the paradox of mobility. The
> cultural mobility is low, the physical mobility tends to the maximum.
>
> (Rásky, 1998, p. 79)

People are travelling further to visit cultural events, but the cultural content
of those events is becoming steadily more homogenized, as event organizers
seek to cater for the widest possible audience. Europe now has hundreds
of arts festivals, mainly concentrated in the peak summer season. Many
of these events function as showcases for the same performers, who tour
different cities performing similar shows. The cultural tourist may be able to
change his or her location, but will not necessarily experience anything new
in terms of the cultural product.

This is one reason why different elements of the living culture, such as
gastronomy, language and ethnicity, have become such an important part of
the cultural tourism product in recent years. As other elements of the cultural
offer become more homogenized, there is a greater need to emphasize the
cultural distinctiveness of each destination, in order to convince the tourist
that their travelling is worth while. This distinctiveness will increasingly
need to come from a combination of factors, including the cultural products
and living culture of the destination itself and the links that the destination
can create bridges with global cultural flows, as Bonink and Hitters stress in
Chapter 12.

Growing competition for cultural visitors and the need to innovate the
product will force cultural attractions to deal with the realities of the
network society. In particular, links and alliances will need to be struck with
organizations outside the cultural sector. At present, however, there is a lack
of collaborative marketing and management initiatives within the cultural
sector, let alone cross-sectoral initiatives. Not only do cultural attractions
often fail to make optimal use of the tourism industry as a partner, but
individual attractions also tend to see each other as competitors rather than
potential collaborators.

The forces of globalization, which have done much to increase competitive pressures in the cultural tourism market, may eventually also lead to
greater collaboration between attractions. Globalization stimulates the
polarization of cultural tourism markets, with an increasing gap between
international 'mega-attractions' and local and regional institutions. Major
international attractions will increasingly need to attract larger audiences in
order to support a level of cultural provision attractive to a global audience.
Achieving this will often require working together with other attractions
and the tourism industry. Smaller attractions, on the other hand, will need
to work together in order to achieve the economies of scale and scope
necessary to survive in a competitive market.

# Distribution of the Cultural Product

One development that may change the relationship between the tourism industry and the cultural sector is the development of new distribution channels. In particular Internet and other new technologies offer the possibility of reaching the fragmented cultural audience far more effectively.

Internet has opened up new opportunities for cultural attractions to market themselves to a relatively thinly scattered group of specific cultural tourists, particularly in foreign markets. Traditional 'push' media, such as brochures, are often difficult to distribute to cultural tourists before they make their decision which destination to visit. Cultural attractions must often rely on the city they are located in to act as a generating market to stimulate tourists to visit (Leiper, 1990), as few cultural attractions will act as generating markers in their own right. This means that alliances with other elements of the destination product must be formed in order to attract tourists to the destination, after which they can be persuaded to visit specific cultural attractions.

There are already indications that the Internet is beginning to have a significant impact in the cultural tourism market. A study in The Netherlands in 1998 indicated that only 2.3% of heritage visitors gathered information via Internet (De Jong and Paulissen, 1998). Research carried out by ATLAS in 1999 indicated that Internet was being used by 20% of cultural visitors to gather information about the attraction they were visiting (Richards, 2000b). This figure is likely to grow significantly as the number of Internet subscribers increases. As a 'push' medium Internet has the advantage that consumers search for products based on their own motivations. The use of Internet is therefore more likely to produce a good match between the needs of cultural tourists and the products of cultural attractions, providing cultural attractions learn to use the medium effectively.

In the future the use of new technology will also have far-reaching implications not just for marketing attractions, but also for managing the visitor experience. Timed ticketing is already being used to avoid crowding at popular exhibitions, and in future consumers will be able to order and print their own tickets via their mobile communication devices. This will solve many of the problems currently associated with gaining access to cultural events, particularly if translation programmes make information available in several languages. Personal communication devices will also enable visitors to access information about the attractions they visit as they view them, and give them the opportunity to ask questions of intelligent databases. Given the fact that learning is one of the key elements of cultural tourism, this is bound to increase the quality of the visitor experience.

One example of potential future developments is the ARCHEOGUIDE project, which aims to develop a system to enhance the visitor experience of archaeological sites through an 'augmented reality' reconstruction of archaeological remains. Virtual representations of the original state of the ruins can be overlaid on the physical environment via a head-mounted display, allowing the visitor to experience the site in its original state. The visitor will also be able to access information about the different elements of the site from an interactive database, which will be able to respond to questions in a similar fashion to a human guide (Papageorgiou *et al.*, 2000). Such technology also offers the opportunity to present differing interpretations of cultural attractions, and to let the multiple voices of 'dissonant heritage' be heard.

New technology also appears to offer a solution to one of the biggest challenges for cultural attractions – how to preserve their cultural products while increasing visitor access. Cultural objects will increasingly be available through virtual systems, which will allow visitors to examine them without touching the physical objects themselves. Although some museums may be worried that making their collections available through virtual reality may discourage visitation – this seems unlikely to happen. Just as the wide availability of reprints of famous artworks has not dented the cultural tourism market for art museums, so the widespread production of virtual copies of cultural objects is likely to add to the value of the original. Paradoxically, therefore, the development of virtual exhibitions may simply lead to some cultural attractions having more visitors than ever.

The attractions featured in this volume indicate that many cultural attractions still have to come to terms with the far-reaching implications of technological change. Few attractions have the technological expertise necessary to develop their own web sites, for example (Evans *et al.*, 2000). Most cultural attractions will remain dependent on destination marketing organizations or collective marketing initiatives in the short term. In the longer term cultural attractions will probably have to undertake a far more proactive information management and distribution role than at present.

## The Changing Nature of the Visitor Experience

Reaching the visitor is one thing, but ensuring the visitor experience meets the increasingly demanding standards of the modern consumer is another. Consumer tastes tend to change rapidly, while the decision-making process in most cultural institutions is still relatively slow.

As cultural attractions have shifted their role in recent decades from being temples of culture to becoming cathedrals of consumption they are being forced to realize that the consumption process is increasingly central to their operation. As part of the means of consumption (Ritzer, 1999), cultural attractions must provide not just information or interpretation, but complete experiences. As Pine and Gilmore (1999) have suggested, attractions must combine absorption and immersion, passive and active participation in order to create complete, satisfying experiences.

Existing attractions can adjust to the demands of the experience economy by adding new elements to their existing products in order to provide a balance between the different elements of the visitor experience. This trend is already evident in cultural attractions, as many add interactive elements in order to create more active participation, or posing questions of the visitor in order to increase the degree of immersion. Disparate elements of an attraction can also be linked through themeing, which helps to create a narrative that is understandable for the visitor. Such themes can also provide a means of linking different cultural attractions in a destination region together, as Rooijakkers (1999) has demonstrated in The Netherlands.

Such product developments are becoming necessary because of the changing demands of the consumer. The modern cultural tourist is an eclectic consumer, with the varied holiday patterns characteristic of the postmodern tourist. As Chapter 4 has shown, the traditional products emphasizing high culture are no longer sufficient. Tour operators are developing their products to suit these new markets by widening the range of cultural forms included in their packages. Combinations that were previously considered unthinkable, such as theme park and museum, or football and opera, are becoming more plausible.

New attractions are also being produced by new forms of consumption. The tendency of consumers towards cultural grazing, or skimming the surface of many different cultural forms, has led to the development of new types of attractions, such as the heritage centre and the museum shop. The power of consumption is underlined by the fact that some visitors consider a visit to the shop a worthy substitute for a visit to the attraction itself.

These forms of consumption are indicative of the emerging economy of signs, in which the cultural object can be replaced by its representation. In this process, the signs of the attraction become detached from the attraction itself, and become free floating cultural markers. Museum shops become outposts of the museum, as in the case of the SoHo Guggenheim in New York. The name of the museum itself also becomes a brand image, capable of being applied to products far beyond the original scope of the physical cultural attraction itself. The global development of the Guggenheim 'brand' is a good example of this.

In order to counteract the footloose markers of global culture, it is important to develop cultural attractions that are embedded in local culture. The Budapest Spring Festival (Chapter 10) has attempted to do this by using Hungarian artists to headline the festival. Ironically, many of these artists are exiles, illustrating the footloose nature of many cultural forms. More concrete anchoring often requires starting at grass roots level. An example of this is the 'Crossing Brussels' initiative staged as part of the City of Culture 2000 festival in the Belgian capital (Corijn and de Lannoy, 2000). Taking a transect across the multicultural landscape of Brussels, researchers from the Vrije Universiteit Brussel are exploring the relationships between different communities in one of Europe's richest regions, which also has 40% of its population living in deprived neighbourhoods. In doing so, they are using a mobile culture centre to cross the city, showing the community to itself, through images, words and performance. The reactions of the locals to this confrontation will be incorporated into *De Kwaliteit van het Verschil* (The Quality of Difference) 'a book in the making' (Corijn and de Lannoy, 2000). The resulting product will at the same time be profoundly local, but will link the culture of Brussels as the 'Mediterranean Capital of Europe' into the cultural undercurrents of European migration and cultural hybridization and creolization. Such initiatives offer a model for the development of creative modes of display that can reclaim and ground the experience of local communities and present these in innovative ways to local residents and tourists alike.

## Challenges for Cultural Policy

In the face of globalization and the apparent rise of cultural imperialism, what role is there for cultural policy in a unified Europe? Green points out in Chapter 9 that there is still too much disparity between different levels of policy making in Europe to generate an integrated and effective approach to cultural policy in the European Union (EU) as a whole. As Rásky has noted, EU programmes also tend to focus on relatively narrow areas related to high culture, leaving significant areas underdeveloped at the European level.

The policies of the EU and the Council of Europe seem almost fossilized into an era of universal values, while the postmodern agenda forges ahead into increasing division and uncertainty. Whereas in the past cultural attractions were firmly embedded in their local or national contexts, this is no longer certain. Artworks become more mobile, just as artists always have been. Is Picasso French or Spanish? Does Mondriaan belong to Amsterdam or New York? The growing mobility of individuals and social groups problematizes the very concept of 'Europe', let alone the concept of 'European culture'.

European cultural policy, most clearly expressed in the Maastricht Treaty, is directed towards supporting the national cultures of the Member States, while developing narrow areas of transnational action. The three major objectives for community action in the cultural field are:

- To contribute to the flowering of the cultures of the Member States, while respecting their national and regional diversity and at the same time bringing the common cultural heritage to the fore.
- To encourage contemporary cultural creation.
- To foster cooperation between the Member States and with third countries and the competent international organizations.

Looking at the activities of the EU in the cultural field, however, most activities still seem to be orientated towards cultural heritage and cultural products rather to 'encourage contemporary cultural creation'. Apart from specific programmes related to the performing and literary arts, such as Kaleidoscope and Ariane, the bulk of measures undertaken by the EU concern the material heritage. A further problem of heritage development, as the Clonmacnoise case study suggests, is that the 'past' in itself is often not enough to interest (potential) visitors. If cultural attractions are to compete with the growing number of leisure attractions and increase the quality of visitor experience, they must find ways of involving their visitors in the cultural process.

The development of cultural heritage programmes, although stimulated by an admirable desire to preserve the material culture for all Europeans, is to some extent adding to the existing problems of the cultural attraction market in Europe. As in the case of tourism policy, most funding for cultural projects actually comes through the structural funds to support regional development, rather than through cultural budget lines. This places the emphasis squarely on regional and economic development, rather than culture per se. The bulk of EU funded projects in the field of culture are therefore aimed at attracting tourists in order to generate revenue to support culture. In doing so, many of these projects simply add to the number of attractions competing for the attention of cultural tourists in different regions of Europe. This is not problematic as long as the attractions being developed are distinctive and do not divert visitors from existing attractions. One suspects this is seldom the case, however.

Existing cultural policies are still based on a product-orientated logic, which dictates that cultural facilities are in themselves 'good' for the local population. This is fine, as long as the public sector continues to subsidize these facilities, and/or the local population is able to pay for them. As soon as the existence of cultural attractions is dependent on visitors, however, the logic of the market begins to exert itself. If these attractions are not interesting or exciting enough to attract visitors, they can become a financial burden rather than an asset.

The dilemma for many cultural attractions will be balancing the demands of the eclectic postmodern consumer with the increasingly diverse cultural needs of the citizen. There is always a danger that in assuming their new role in the experience economy, some cultural institutions may lose sight of their civic function:

> How do the new art museums, with their single-minded emphasis on the art experience, fit into a society obsessed with the accountability of institutions to a public with a variety of expectations? Do they educate or instruct, address the pluralism of our heritage, revise cultural history? Are they sending messages that are 'politically correct', or any messages at all?
>
> (Huxtable, 1999)

# Future Trends

In a recent review, Richards (2000a) identified a number of trends which should also become increasingly important in the cultural tourism market in the future. These include:

- Continued growth in cultural tourism demand, stimulated by higher levels of education and a thirst for knowledge.
- An explosion of supply of cultural attractions, which is rapidly outpacing the growth in demand.
- A blurring of the distinction between 'high' and 'popular' culture, and between culture and economy, which have been fuelling the growing supply of attractions and events.
- An extension of the cultural tourism market towards mass tourism through the opening of new popularized cultural attractions.
- Divergence between large- and small-scale attractions.
- Increasing globalization and localization of cultural tourism demand and supply.
- A growing commercialization of cultural tourism, through the creation of commercial cultural tourism products and the provision, distribution and sale of information on cultural products.
- The emergence of a group of 'new producers' from the cultural field who have discovered tourism as a means of capitalizing their knowledge of culture to create new forms of employment.

Many of these trends have already been dealt with in some detail in the previous chapters. However, one can identify three basic shifts that characterize the major changes taking place in the cultural tourism arena: market growth, market fragmentation and the development of new forms of distribution (Richards, 2000b).

The cultural tourism market will continue to grow in future, if only because tourism as a whole is growing. Cultural attractions are a vital part of the destination product, and will continue to meet visitor needs for education and entertainment in the future. Much of the current growth in the market, however, is derived from a growth in general cultural tourism, which is not directly related to cultural motivations. The much smaller specific cultural tourism market is unlikely to grow in terms of number of participants, but probably will grow in terms of numbers of trips as people take more frequent, shorter holidays. Cultural attractions will need to pay close attention to the needs of these different segments if they are to hold or increase their share of the cultural tourism market.

Alongside growth there is a significant fragmentation of the cultural tourism market. As the range of cultural phenomena covered by 'cultural tourism' continue to increase, particularly with the de-differentiation of high and popular culture, it becomes debatable if the term is a useful container. The cultural tourism field is splintering into a number of niche markets, such as arts tourism, heritage tourism, ethnic tourism, architectural tourism, opera tourism, gastronomy tourism, and so on. In view of the fact that the cultural tourism field is already so fragmented on the production side, the only thing that seems to unite these disparate products is the nature of demand, which is still dominated by highly educated, high income professionals. These consumers use their tourism experiences to develop their cultural capital, and just like the acquisition of cultural capital through education, this process is becoming increasingly specialized.

One potential solution to the problems of servicing a market which is at the same time expanding and fragmenting is the application of new technology to the distribution process. As market segments become more difficult to identify through traditional marketing channels, the 'pull' medium of the Internet offers the opportunity for cultural attractions to offer their products to a highly motivated but thinly spread worldwide audience. Reaching that audience is only the first step in the battle for the hearts and minds of the cultural tourist, however. People must be given a reason for choosing your attraction above the growing host of competing attractions both inside and outside the cultural sector. This means defining very clearly what the benefits provided by the attraction are, and how these match the needs, wants and desires of potential visitors.

The ability of producers to meet the increasingly diverse needs of consumers will also depend on their ability to develop a bridge between the space of flows and the space of places, as Bonink and Hitters point out in Chapter 12. In the new spatial logic of the network society, the dialectic between the global and the local will become stronger, forcing attractions not only to ground their product more firmly in the local context, but also to search more actively for links with the global tourist culture.

One means of doing this will be to pay more attention to the mobility of cultures and the growing importance of ethnic and cultural minorities in Europe. These groups are adept at cultural cross-fertilization, but the products of their cultural mixing are often ignored by the traditional cultural institutions. Stimulating ethnic minority attendance at cultural events is often a policy priority, but the products on offer are usually related either to the host culture or to the minority culture – less attention is paid to the new cultures forming at the intersection between the two. Paying more attention to other cultures is also important from the point of view of new segments in the cultural tourism market. In the past, there has been a fairly comfortable assumption that European or 'western' culture is universal, and that visitors would have the cultural competence necessary to understand the cultural attractions they visited. The number of cultural tourists coming to Europe from Asia, for example, is at present relatively low, but is likely to increase substantially in the future, particuarly as major markets such as China begin to open up. As the number of tourists visiting Europe from other world regions and other cultural backgrounds increases, new links will have to be forged between European and other cultures in order to enable them to understand and enjoy what is being presented.

Just as we need to stimulate creative thinking about the global flows of culture, so we need to analyse critically the effect of globalization on local spaces. The 'space of places' of the network society is increasingly becoming cluttered with monuments to the past and modern cathedrals of consumption: 'Not only are we building more museums than ever, we are raising things from the dead – restoring and reconstructing fantasies and simulacra of a real or imaginary past' (Huxtable, 1999).

This proliferation of culture and heritage is creating problems not only for the conservationists, but it also increases the competition for existing cultural attractions. One potential solution to the problems of the gathering burden of the past and the need to increase visitor involvement is to concentrate more effort on the development of contemporary creative potential. Creativity has rarely been linked directly to the development of tourism, but as Richards and Raymond (2000) suggest, there are a number of advantages linked to the development of creative tourism which make it a potentially fruitful area for future development (see Chapter 3).

Creative tourism concerns not just the creative capacity of the tourist, but also the creativity of the cultural producers. Many of the cultural tourism products now being developed are not truly innovative, but represent a re-packaging of existing products. The approach to product development is still very much product-led – 'we have culture, come and see it'. The major products of the 'Field of Dreams' culture are still museums, monuments, cultural itineraries and increasingly cultural festivals. Too often the attraction of such products is based on their being 'unique'. It's about time that some policy makers and marketeers realized that there is nothing unique about uniqueness any more.

In terms of experience development, however, cultural tourism products also tend to be rather limited. Most of the products on offer can provide strong educational and aesthetic elements, but they are lacking those other important elements of experience – entertainment and escapism. Perhaps there is still a feeling that 'fun' and culture don't mix.

But in the experience economy of the future, the way in which the experience is presented will become increasingly important. It is not enough to offer the bare product, because what people actually want to buy is the story, or experience behind the product. Success in cultural tourism will increasingly depend on who can deliver the best cultural experiences, and who can create the most imaginative stories around their products. The element of creativity will be important for developing the product and will be increasingly important for the consumer as well. Just as consumers have demanded more interactivity from static museum displays in recent years, so they will demand more freedom to be creative themselves in the cultural arena in the future. Each consumer is actually capable of developing their own story on the basis of the experiences cultural attractions provide. No two experiences are ever the same. Perhaps we should stop thinking about cultural attractions, and start thinking about 'creative attractions' instead.

# References

Corijn, E. and de Lannoy, W. (2000) *De Kwaliteit van het Verschil.* VUB Press, Brussels.

De Jong, J. and Paulissen, H. (1998) *Onderzoek naar de Haalbaarheid van de Toeristisch Ontsluiting van het Cultureel Erfgoed in de Provincie Limburg met behulp van Moderne Communicatiemiddelen.* University of Maastricht, Maastricht.

Evans, G., Peacock, M. and Richards, G. (2000) Small is beautiful? ICT and tourism SMEs: a comparative European survey. In: Fesenmaier, D., Klein, S. and Buhalis, D. (eds) *Information and Communication Technologies in Tourism 2000.* Springer-Verlag, Vienna, pp. 497–508.

Huxtable, A.L. (1999) Museums: making it new. *New York Review of Books* 22 April.

Leiper, N. (1990) Tourist attraction systems. *Annals of Tourism Research* 17, 367–384.

Papageorgiou, D., Ioannides, N., Cristou, I., Papathomas, M. and Diorinos, M. (2000) ARCHEOGUIDE: an augmented reality based system for personalized tours in cultural heritage sites. *Cultivate Interactive* 1. http://www.cultivate-int. org/issue1/

Pine, B.J. and Gilmore, J.H. (1999) *The Experience Economy.* Harvard University Press, Harvard.

Rásky, B. (1998) Cultural policy/policies in Europe. In: Ellmeier, A. and Rásky, B. (eds) *Cultural Policy in Europe – European Cultural Policy?* Österreichische Kulturdokumentation, Internationals Archiv für Kulturanalysen, Vienna, pp. 5–85.

Richards, G. (2000a) Cultural tourism: challenges for management and marketing. In: Gartner, W.C. and Lime, D.W. (eds) *Trends in Outdoor Recreation, Leisure and Tourism.* CAB International, Wallingford, pp. 187–195.

Richards, G. (2000b) Development and evolution of cultural tourism in Europe. Paper delivered at the Cultural Tourism Expert Meeting, Barcelona, April 2000.

Richards, G. and Raymond, C. (2000) Creative tourism. *ATLAS News* No. 23.

Ritzer, G. (1999) *Enchanting a Disenchanted World: Revolutionizing the Means of Consumption.* Pine Forge Press, Thousand Oaks, California.

Rooijakkers, G. (1999) Identity factory southeast: towards a flexible cultural leisure infrastructure. In: Dodd, D. and van Hemel, A.-M. (eds) *Planning European Cultural Tourism.* Boekman Foundation, Amsterdam, pp. 101–111.

# Index

Page numbers in *italics* refer to figures and tables.

accommodation 49
age 40, 44
Amsterdam 34, 60, 66, 72, 81,
    231–239
Antieke Wereld 73
Art Cities in Europe 72
ArtBase 72
arts
    funding 114
    tourism 113
    tourist 33
Asian tourists 251
ATLAS Cultural Tourism Research
    Project 35–51, 74, 93, 118,
    145, 166, 220
atmosphere 48, 85
attraction
    attendance 9, 113
    development 116, 140–141,
        184–187, 200–201, 204
    distribution 162
    market 31–51

origin of the term 14
typologies 22–24, 137–138,
    162–163, 220
authenticity 12, 78, 181, 224

Bali 20
Barcelona 78
Benetton 101–102
Bilbao 62–63, 178, 183
Bonnefanten Museum 14, 93–110
Boorstin, Daniel 14
Bord Failte 12, 136
Bourdieu, Pierre 74–75
bourgeoisie 74
branding 241
British Tourist Authority 56, 72
Brussels 247–248
Budapest 199–213
    Spring Festival 199–213
Burrell Collection 123–131
business plan 103–104

Camiño de Santiago 5
capacity 162
Castells, Manuel 229
Catalonia 21
Central and Eastern Europe 49–51,
    199–226, 217–225
Centre Georges Pompidou 97
cities 11, 47–49, 60, 81–82, 85–88,
    181–194, 229
city marketing 58
Clonmacnoise 135–156
clustering 228, 235, 238
commodification 13, 190
community 152
competition 243
conferences 117
conservation 5
consumption
    cathedrals of 17, 58, 246
    cultural 64, 66, 215–216
    new means of 17, 58, 247
contracts 234
Council of Europe 5, 248
creative
    industries 12, 227–239
    tourism 64–67
creativity 64, 66–67, 252
cultural
    activities 79
    capital 57, 62, 75, 81
    destinations 47–49, 80–82
    diversity 193, 229
    economy 57
    enterprise 232
    flows 176
    intermediaries 74
    mobility 251
    participation 99
    production system 71
    supply of attractions 6, 11–13
    tourism
        definition of 37, 118, 137–139,
            216–217
        doctrine of 20
        growth of 8, 19–22,
            163–164
        in the UK 113–114
    visitors 33, 51
    visits 8, 147

culture
    definition of 6–7
    interest in 7–11
    popular 108–109
    tourist 4
culturization 19

Debord, Guy 16
de-industrializing 191
demand 124
Department of Tourism and Trade
    (Ireland) 136
destination
    cultural 47–49
    fashionable 87
    marketing organization 71–72
developers 233–234
development plan 235
differentiation 175
Disney 65
distinction 75
distribution 71–88, 245–246
Dúchas 142, 150
Dumazedier, J. 64

Eastern Europe 49–51, 199–226
ecomuseums 6
economic restructuring 177–179, 183,
    190
Edinburgh 60–61
education 40, 153
elite art 108
employment 114, 123
enclavic space 18, 56
enchantment 58
English Heritage 6
enterprise, cultural 105–106
ethnic minorities 188, 193
EuroBarometer 34
Europe of the Regions 180
European
    Commission 3
    Cultural Capital 58, 61–62,
        115–116
    Inventory of Cultural Resources
        47–48
    Tourism Monitor 34

Union 5, 22, 150, 180, 248
events 42, 43, 106–108, 199–213, 244
expectations 100
experience
    cultural 55
    economy 55–57, 252
    factories 62–64
    industry 55–67
    sector 57–59
    society 59

festivalization 12, 60
festivals 35, 106, 199–213
Field of Dreams 13
field of tension, cultural 104–105
Finland 35
Florence 85
Fordism 73, 178
France 6
funding 114, 127–130, 242–243, 249

Gaeltacht 143
galleries 111–131
Gallery of Modern Art (Glasgow) 121
gaze, tourist 67, 83
Gdañsk 218–219
gender 40
Germany 9, 33, 62
Glasgow 111–131
globalization 173–194, 228, 241, 244
    concept of 174–175

heritage 137, 189, 219
    attractions 144
    built 137
    Council 143
    industrial 191
    industry 6
    preservation 6
    sites 159–170
    tourism *65*, 113, 173–194
    typology 138
heritagization 181
heterogeneous space 18, 56
high arts 227

history 140–141, 160, 164
holiday 43, 82–83, 99
    characteristics 49
    destination 77
homogenization 175
Hungary 199–213

identity 186, 188, 193
image 115, 192, 204
impact 122–123
income 41
industrial heritage 191
innovation 230, 238
intellectual property 57
inviolate belt 154
Ireland 135–156
Italy 35, 85

Kelvingrove Art Gallery 120–121

Lapland 13
Leicester 183–184
Leiper, Neil 16
leisure time 43, 79, 82–83, 208, 216
lending 125–127
Limburg 98, 101
lifestyle 78–80
local
    actors 190
    authority 187–191, 234–235
    people 168
localization 173–194
London 18
lottery 128

MacCannell, Dean 14–15
management 126–127, 141–143, 202–203, 232–234, 241–243
markers 4, 15
market
    cultural attractions 31–51
    cultural tourism 143–145
    growth 102–103
    segments 204
    tourism 164–166

marketing
de-marketing 152
issues 150, 243
policy 101–104, 150–153
mass culture 227
McLellan Galleries 121
methodology 38
mixed use 236
modernity 14
modernization 3
monuments 135–156
motivation 9, 34, 45–47, 55, 144, 207,
223, 225, 242
museum
visitors 98
museums 62–64, 66, 93–110, 192
definition of 112–113
Guggenheim 62–63
musterbation 4
must-see sights 4, 14

narratives 18
nation state 177, 179–181
National Trust 6, 163, 167
The Netherlands 8, 9, 10, 13, 62, 83,
95, 182–183
network economy 228, 230, 236, 244
new medievalism 180, 243
new producers 75–83
new technology 245–246, 251
Nike 56
non-visitors 33
nostalgia 6
nucleus 154

occupation 40
open air museums 5

Paris 97
partnership 152, 233, 237
performance, tourism as 18
planning 168
product
orientation 249
tourist 94–95
Poland 215–225

policy 189
cultural 21, 248–249
European 5
experience production 59–62
popular culture 108–109
Portugal 12
positioning 93
post-Fordism 178
postmodern tourism 75
post-tourist 18
Prague 50, 86–87, 210–213
preservation 6
product/market grid *103*
production
cultural 64
programming 203
pseudo events 14

questionnaire 38

regions 63, 160–163, 180
repeat visits 42
research
ATLAS Research 35–51
cultural tourism 32–35
methodology 38–39
visitor 156, 169, 205
Ritzer, George 17
Rome 80
Rossi, Aldo 96
rural areas 12

Schulze, Gerhard 59
seaside resorts 160
seasonality 149
service quality 220
sight sacrilization 15
signs, attractions as 15
skilled consumption 35, 64, 242
South-East England 159–170
Spain 3, 62–63, 86, 183
spas 160
spectacle, society of the 16
status 40
strategy 187
Studiosus 73, 74

surveys 32, 36, 39
sustainable tourism 21

Textile Museum 192
Thomas Cook 73
Tilburg 182–183
Toscani, Oliviero 101
tour operators 73–88, 83–85
    brochures 87
    mass-market 73, 83–85
    specialist 74, 83–85
tourism
    demand 117–118
    'good' 19
    product 218
    postmodern 75
    region 160–162
    strategy 115, 130
    sustainable 21
tourist
    boards 187, 189
    gaze 67
transport 161
travel arrangements 49
Treaty of Maastricht 5
trends 241–253
Turespaña 72
typology
    attractions 22–24
    cultural tourist *109*

UK 9, 10, 13, 33, 63, 112–114, 159,
    183–184
UNESCO 5, 19

urban
    heritage tourism 173–194
    regeneration 112
    tourism 112
USA 34

Venice 4
Verzetsmuseum 66
Vienna 210–213
visitor
    centre 142
    characteristics *120*
    control 149
    expectations 100
    experience 246–248
    numbers 93, 98, 144, 167–168
    origin 4, 100
    profiles 39–44, 100–101,
        118–119, 125, 148–149, 166,
        205–206, 221–222, 237
    satisfaction 102, 139
    surveys 36, 99, 118–119, 145–148
visitors
    cultural 33
    repeat 42, 100, 102, 168

Wales 34
Westergasfabriek 231–239
work 76–78, 82–83
World Decade for Cultural
    Development 5, 18

zone of closure 155